Psalms I

John F. Brug

Publishing House
St. Louis

The interior illustrations were originally executed by James Tissot
(1836-1902). The drawings of the musical instruments are by NPH artist
Duane Weaver.

Commentary and pictures are reprinted from PSALMS: VOLUME 1
(The People's Bible Series), copyright © 1989 by Northwestern
Publishing House. Used by permission.

Scripture is taken from The Holy Bible: NEW INTERNATIONAL
VERSION, © 1973, 1978, 1984 by the International Bible Society.
Used by permission of Zondervan Bible Publishers.

Copyright © 1992 Concordia Publishing House
3558 S. Jefferson Avenue, St. Louis, MO 63118-3968
Manufactured in the United States of America

1 2 3 4 5 6 7 8 9 10   01 00 99 98 97 96 95 94 93 92

CONTENTS

Editor's Preface   v

Author's Preface   vii

Introduction   1

BOOK I: Psalms 1-41   39

BOOK II: Psalms 42-72   175

ILLUSTRATIONS

The Musical Instruments of the Psalms   34

The Death of Absalom   51

Solomon Dedicates the Temple at Jerusalem   131

God Is Near the Afflicted   146

As the Deer Pants for Streams of Water   178

Nathan Reproaches David   216

Praying in the Temple   256

MAP

Israel and Neighboring Nations   242

PREFACE

The People's Bible Commentary is just what the name implies—a Bible and commentary for the people. It includes the complete text of the Holy Scriptures in the popular New International Version. The commentary following the Scripture sections contains personal applications as well as historical background and explanations of the text.

The authors of *The People's Bible Commentary* are men of scholarship and practical insight gained from years of experience in the teaching and preaching ministries. They have tried to avoid the technical jargon which limits so many commentary series to professional Bible scholars.

The most important feature of these books is that they are Christ-centered. Speaking of the Old Testament Scriptures, Jesus himself declared, "These are the Scriptures that testify about me" (John 5:39). Each volume of *The People's Bible Commentary* directs our attention to Jesus Christ. He is the center of the entire Bible. He is our only Savior.

We dedicate these volumes to the glory of God and to the good of his people.

The Publishers

PREFACE

The study of the book of Psalms is complicated by the special poetic character of the book and by the length of the book. This commentary aims to help the reader overcome these two obstacles by setting two goals for our study of Psalms.

First, it is hoped that the introduction, which is somewhat more lengthy and technical than the introductions of other volumes of *The People's Bible*, will introduce the reader to the special features and problems of Hebrew poetry. This introduction will serve as the introduction to both volumes of this commentary on Psalms.

The second goal of this commentary is to help the Bible student read through the whole book of Psalms as a connected, well-organized collection of hymns. Although we will take a more in-depth look at a few of the most important psalms, in general we will have to limit our aim to gaining an overview of the book as a whole. Even so, the length of Psalms will make it necessary to divide this commentary into two volumes. Volume I will cover the introduction and Psalms 1-72. Psalms 73-150 will be covered in Volume II.

INTRODUCTION

Sing praises to God, sing praises;
sing praises to our King, sing praises.
For God is the King of all the earth;
sing to him a psalm of praise. (Psalm 47:6,7)

God invites us to praise him. God's goodness motivates us to praise him. For these reasons God's people love to praise him with songs. Since the beginning of creation God's angels have been singing his praises in heaven (Job 38:7). Throughout history God's people have been singing his praises on earth.

Moses and all the people of Israel sang a song of victory on the shores of the Red Sea after the Lord had delivered them from Pharaoh's army (Exodus 15). Deborah and Barak sang a song of victory after God had delivered the Canaanites into their hands (Judges 5). Hannah celebrated the gift of a son with a song (1 Samuel 2). David wrote songs for almost every occasion of life — happy songs to celebrate God's blessings to him (Psalm 18) and sad songs to lament his sins (Psalm 38). Jesus and his disciples sang hymns in their last hours together before his death (Matthew 26:30). Paul and Silas sang hymns to God in the jail of Philippi (Acts 16:25). Throughout eternity God's people will sing, "Great and marvelous are your deeds, Lord God Almighty. Just and true are your ways" (Revelation 15:3).

Music is a precious gift of God to his people. Luther said, "Music is an endowment and gift of God. It drives away the devil and makes people cheerful. I place music next to theology and give it the highest praise." Partly because of Luther's love for music Lutherans have made music a very important part of their worship. The Lutheran church has become known as "the singing church."

Christians regularly join in hymns to express their love for their Savior. Hymns are our joyful response to the Lord's invitation to sing his praises. Many of us have a hymnal which we received on our confirmation day, which we cherish as one of the most important books we own. Because the love of Christ rules in our hearts, we are eager to practice the admonition of Scripture, "Let the word of Christ dwell in you richly as you teach and admonish one another with all wisdom, and as you sing psalms, hymns and spiritual songs with gratitude in your hearts to God" (Colossians 3:16).

Our love for Christian music, expressed in the preceding paragraphs, is one of the reasons that a study of the book of Psalms is important for us. The book of Psalms is the hymnbook of the Bible, a hymnbook given by inspiration of God. More than any other book, Psalms teaches us how to sing with gratitude in our hearts to God. Luther said, "Every Christian ought to know the psalms as well as he knows his five fingers."

In the book of Psalms the Holy Spirit himself teaches us words and thoughts for our prayers. In the psalms we find many passages we can use without change as our own prayers. The psalms also give us many beautiful models to imitate in creating our own prayers. The book of Psalms expresses the whole range of emotions which God's people experience in this life. Nowhere will you find words expressing greater joy than in the psalms of praise and thanksgiving. Nowhere will you find words expressing deeper sorrow than in the psalms of repentance. Nowhere will you find a more fervent expression of both the sorrows and the joys which life brings. The book of Psalms is a book for every occasion and for every season of life.

Psalms, which has far more chapters than any other book of the Bible, is a rich source of biblical doctrine. It teaches us about such varied topics as sin, repentance and forgiveness (Psalm 51), God's attributes (Psalm 139), and God's work of creation and providence (Psalm 104). The most important topic in the psalms is the portrait of Christ our Savior presented in the many Messianic prophecies found in the psalms. The book of Psalms had more influence on the New Testament than did any other book. It is quoted approximately 80 times in the New Testament. About 120 of the 150 psalms are reflected in some way in the New Testament. It is obvious that a study of Psalms will help us gain a better understanding of the New Testament.

Many of our hymns and much of our liturgy are based on the psalms. For example, the offertory, "Create in me a clean heart, O God," which we sing each Sunday, is taken from Psalm 51. Many other responses in our liturgy come from the psalms. These will be noted at appropriate places in the commentary. The traditional New Year's hymn, "Our God, Our Help in Ages Past," and many other familiar hymns are simply rhymed versions of the psalms. A fuller understanding of our way of worship will be a secondary benefit of our study of Psalms.

Every Christian who meditates on the words and teachings of the psalms will be blessed with spiritual growth. Like all Scripture, the psalms have been written for our learning. They are useful for teaching, rebuking, correcting and training in righteousness (2 Timothy 3:16). Let us pray that the Lord will bless our study of the book of Psalms so that it will yield rich blessings to us.

THE BOOK OF PSALMS

The book of Psalms is a collection of 150 hymns. The Hebrew title of this book is not "Psalms" but "Songs of Praise" (*tehillim* in Hebrew). Although Psalm 145 is the only psalm which is called a song of praise in its heading, "Songs of Praise" is, nevertheless, a very fitting title for the book as a whole. The book is filled with praise and thanksgiving. The last five psalms, which emphasize the theme of the whole book, all begin and end with the exclamation, "Praise the Lord" (*hallelujah* in Hebrew).

The English title "Psalms" was adopted from the title this book received in the Greek translation of the Old Testament known as the Septuagint, which became the standard Bible of the early Christian church. The Greek word *psalmos* means the music of a stringed instrument, or a song sung to the accompaniment of a stringed instrument. *Psalmos* was used as the Greek translation of the Hebrew word *mizmor*, which also means "a song" or "a song accompanied by a stringed instrument." This Hebrew word *mizmor* is used in the headings of 57 of the hymns in the book of Psalms. For examples, see Psalms 3-6 and 82-85. It is this word *mizmor* which is translated "psalm" in the NIV Bible. Some commentators suggest that this word *mizmor* is derived from a Hebrew word that means "to trim" and that a *mizmor* or "psalm" is a song with carefully "trimmed" or measured lines. However, it is more likely that the word simply means "a song sung to the accompaniment of a stringed instrument."

Since the title "psalm" is assigned to so many of the hymns collected in this book, "Psalms" certainly is a suitable title for the book as a whole, even though it is not the original Hebrew title of the book. In this commentary we will follow the traditional practice of calling all of the hymns in the book of Psalms "psalms," even though, strictly speaking, almost two-thirds of them are some other type of song.

TYPES OF PSALMS

It has been noted that only 57 of the 150 hymns in the book of Psalms are specifically classified as "psalms" in the technical sense. Some of the hymns in the book of Psalms are assigned to some other musical category. About 30 of these hymns are called "songs" (Hebrew *shir*). (For example , see Psalms 18 and 96.) The precise technical meaning of this title is uncertain. This title "song" sometimes occurs together with the title "a psalm." (For examples, see Psalms 65-68).

Some of the hymns are called "prayers" (Psalms 17, 86, 90, 102, 142). A plea to God to protect the writer's life is a prominent element in most of the psalms with this title. In Psalm 72:20 the title "prayers" is also assigned to the larger collection of hymns which makes up Part II of Psalms.

The meaning of several of the hymn titles used in Psalms is so uncertain that they are left untranslated by the NIV. Several of the psalms are called *miktam* (Psalms 16, 56-60). Some commentators, including Luther, have suggested that *miktam* means "a choice piece," "a gem" or "a jewel." Other suggestions are that the title *miktam* refers to a song inscribed on a tablet or to a poem of memorable thoughts.

Thirteen psalms are called *maskil*. (For examples, see Psalms 42-45.) This title is usually understood to refer to a psalm for teaching or meditation. Another suggestion is that *maskil* means "a skillful psalm."

Some additional titles which are applied to only one psalm or to a compact group of psalms will be discussed at the appropriate places in the commentary. In general, it can be said that we do not know the precise difference between these various kinds of hymns, largely because we no longer know what kind of music accompanied them.

In addition to these classifications which are based on the original headings of the psalms, ancient and modern commentators have suggested several additional categories based on their own analysis of the style and subject matter of the psalms. The most ancient example of such a classification is that of the seven Penitential Psalms, which have been treated as a group since at least A.D. 250 (Psalms 6, 32, 38, 51, 102, 130, 143).

Luther suggested that the psalms could be divided into five main types: 1) Messianic psalms which speak of Christ (for example, Psalms 2, 22, 110); 2) teaching psalms which emphasize doctrine (Psalms 1, 139); 3) comfort psalms (Psalms 4, 37, 91); 4) psalms of prayer and petition (Psalms 3, 137, 143); and 5) thanksgiving psalms (Psalms 103, 104, 136).

Luther's five categories are useful for analyzing the main point of each psalm, but many of the psalms fit more than one category. As a result, the specific classification of many of the psalms is debatable, and some of the classifications of specific psalms used in this commentary are different from Luther's. Nevertheless, the idea of classifying psalms is useful. In fact, there are two classifications of psalms which deserve special discussion. These are the Messianic psalms and the imprecatory psalms.

Messianic Psalms

Messianic psalms foretell important facts about the person, work and kingdom of Christ. The Old Testament contains three types of prophecies concerning the coming Christ.

Direct prophecies are those prophecies in which the prophet is writing only about Christ. An example of a direct prophecy is Isaiah 7:14, "The virgin will be with child and will give birth to a son." This is a unique event which finds fulfillment only in the life of Christ. An example of a direct prophecy in the psalms is Psalm 16:10, "You will not abandon me to the grave, nor will you let your Holy One see decay." Here David was not talking about himself, since he died, was buried, and remains in the grave to this day. He was foretelling Christ's resurrection.

A second type of Messianic prophecy is *typical prophecy*. A *type* is a real person, thing or event in the Old Testament which points ahead to a similar person or event in the New Testament. In a typical prophecy the prophet writes about something in his own life which points ahead to a similar happening in the life of Christ. Occasionally a prophet may use a type which is not part of his own experience, as Hosea did when he used the Exodus from Egypt as a type of Christ's exodus from Egypt (Hosea 11:1). However, in Psalms the types are usually from the psalmist's life.

David was a type of the Messiah. In one Old Testament prophecy the Messiah is even called "David" (Ezekiel 34:23,24). Therefore, there are many events in David's life which point to similar events in Christ's life. For example, David was betrayed by a friend named Ahithophel, who then committed suicide. When David wrote about this event in Psalm 41:9, he was writing both about himself and about the similar betrayal suffered by Christ (John 13:18).

The third type of Messianic prophecy is *prophecy with an intermediate fulfillment*. In such prophecies the prophet writes about at least two future events: one, a partial, incomplete fulfillment of the prophecy; the second, the complete fulfillment accomplished by Christ. For example, in 2 Samuel 7:1-16 God tells David that he will have a son who will rule after him and who will build God's house. This is fulfilled in a partial, intermediate way by Solomon, who built the temple in Jerusalem. However, the prophecy receives its complete fulfillment only in Christ, who builds God's house, the church, and who rules forever.

It is important to emphasize that all three types of Messianic prophecy are real prophecy given by God. In the typical prophecies the prophets were not simply writing statements about Old Testament events or people which New Testament writers later borrowed and applied to Christ. God guided both the lives and the words of the prophets so that certain Old Testament events and the words which the prophets wrote about those events would serve as true prophecies of Christ.

In identifying Messianic prophecies in the psalms we must distinguish between two groups of prophecies. One group consists of Messianic prophecies which can be identified with certainty because they are quoted in the New Testament as Messianic. Since the Holy Spirit is the source of all Scripture, all of these passages must be recognized as Messianic prophecies even if the Messianic interpretation is not obvious to us from a superficial reading of the Old Testament. The second group consists of Messianic prophecies which have not been identified as Messianic by the New Testament. Commentators have nevertheless classified these passages as Messianic prophecies because they noticed a correspondence between events described in specific Old Testament passages and events in Christ's life.

How can we recognize Messianic prophecies which are not identified by Scripture? If a psalm speaks of a person whose characteristics and deeds are beyond human power, this is an indication that it is a Messianic prophecy. For example, the achievements of the king in Psalm 72 are too great to be accomplished by any human king of Israel. Another indication of a possible Messianic psalm is the occurrence of a title of the Messiah, such as "the Anointed." However, some of these titles are not limited to Christ alone, so these titles are not a sure indicator of Messianic psalms.

The classification of these Messianic prophecies which commentators identify by their own deductions is less certain than that of those which are identified by the New Testament, so we should allow for some differences of interpretation in such cases. At times there may also be a difference of opinion about whether a given prophecy is direct or typical. We should, however, be on guard against a tendency even among recent conservative Lutheran commentators to overemphasize typical prophecy to the near elimination of direct prophecy.

The reality of Messianic prophecy is being emphasized in this introduction because many contemporary commentators deny the existence of Messianic prophecy in the Old Testament. Since many of these critics deny the very possibility of prophecy, they interpret the Messianic prophecies as exaggerated descriptions of the kings of Israel which were later applied to a hoped-for Messiah by both Jews and Christians. When such critics treat Messianic psalms as "royal psalms" which refer only to the kings of Israel, they are directly contradicting the testimony of Christ who said, "Everything must be fulfilled that is written about me in the Law of Moses, the Prophets and the Psalms" (Luke 24:44). Speaking of the Old Testament, Jesus said, "These are the Scriptures that testify about me" (John 5:39).

The Messianic psalms have great value as a testimony to Christ. Only the four Gospels and perhaps Isaiah surpass the psalms as sources of information about the feelings, words and deeds of Christ while he was on earth completing his work as our Savior. The Messianic psalms were a source of strength and encouragement for Old Testament believers, and they remain the same for us today. In our treatment of the individual Messianic psalms, we will be studying what the psalms say about Christ, but because of the special importance of this subject we will offer a summary of the most important facts here.

Christ in the Psalms

Before the psalms were written, Old Testament believers apparently had been provided with few details about the work of the coming Savior. Adam and Eve had learned that a descendant of the woman would come to crush Satan's head (Genesis 3:15). Later prophecies successively narrowed the line of the Savior to the descendants of Shem, Abraham and Judah (Genesis 9:26, 12:3, 49:8-10). Moses prophesied that God would raise up a special prophet like him for Israel (Deuteronomy 18:15). Balaam spoke of the ruler who would rise like a star out of Jacob to defeat Israel's enemies (Numbers 24:17). Believers knew of and believed in the Messiah before the writing of the psalms, but they knew few details about him.

The writing of the psalms was a major step forward in the unfolding of Messianic prophecy. The prophet Nathan had revealed to David that the Messianic king would be his descendant (2 Samuel 7). In the psalms David was privileged to reveal many things about his great descendant. The Messiah, though he was David's descendant, would also be true God (Psalms 2:7, 45:6, 110:1). His rule would be eternal and it would include the whole world (Psalm 72, 2, 89). As true man he would obtain the complete dominion over the earth which Adam had lost through sin (Psalm 8).

However, the Messiah would also come to suffer for sin. This suffering is most fully described in Psalms 22 and 69. He would be rejected by the leaders of Israel (Psalm 118:22) and mocked during his suffering (Psalm 22:8). The Messiah would be betrayed by a friend (Psalm 41:9). His hands and feet would be pierced during his suffering (Psalm 22:16). He would be given vinegar to drink (Psalm 69:21). His clothing would be divided by lot (Psalm 22:18). Though he suffered the anguish of being forsaken by God, he would also be exalted (Psalm 22). He would rise from the dead (Psalm 16:10), and he will reign forever as priest and king (Psalm 110).

This summary of the teaching of the psalms concerning Christ demonstrates the importance of the book of Psalms in the unfolding of Messianic prophecy. The fuller development of this important teaching will be one of the main goals of our study of Psalms.

The Imprecatory Psalms

We use the term "imprecatory psalms" to describe those psalms that contain curses or prayers for the punishment of the psalmist's enemies. We will study each of these curses in our commentary on the psalms in which they occur, but here we would like to summarize some of the general principles which apply to all of them.

People are often shocked by some of the prayers in the psalms. One of the harshest is the prayer against the Babylonians in Psalm 137: "O Daughter of Babylon, doomed to destruction, happy is he who repays you for what you have done to us — who seizes your infants and dashes them against the rocks." Similar prayers are contained in Psalms 55, 56, 58, 69, 109 and other psalms.

Many commentators dismiss these prayers as remnants of a less developed stage of religion, which we have now outgrown. They claim that such prayers are no longer valid in New Testament times, since we are now told to love our enemies and not to take revenge (Matthew 5:38-44). Such claims, however, are not supported by a careful study of these psalms or of the rest of Scripture. These prayers, harsh as they sound, were proper prayers when they were first uttered, and they are still proper today.

These curses are part of God's inspired word. It is true that Scripture sometimes reports improper statements made by believers in moments of distress. For example, not all of the statements made by Job and his friends in the book of Job were proper. However, the curses in the psalms do not fall into this category, because Scripture itself shows that they were proper prayers. Several of these curses occur in Messianic psalms as the words of Christ himself. For example, one of the strongest curses is recorded in Psalm 69, a Messianic psalm quoted in the New Testament: "May they be blotted out of the book of life and not be listed with the righteous" (Psalm 69:28). Curses found in Psalms 69 and 109 are quoted by Peter in Acts 1:20 as finding their fulfillment in God's judgment on Judas.

These curses can hardly be explained away as due to a bloodthirsty, vengeful spirit on the part of David. On the contrary, David was an example of patience, who on more than one occasion refused to avenge himself on his persecutor Saul (1 Samuel 24 and 26). If David had a weakness in this regard, it was being too lenient with such offenders as Shimei, who cursed him (2 Samuel 16), and his son Absalom, who rebelled against him (2 Samuel 18, 19). David refused to seek personal vengeance on his enemies, but he could hardly pray that Saul should win or that God's promise to David, which included the promise of the Savior, should be overthrown by Saul or Absalom. He very properly opposed their schemes with prayer.

Luther once commented that we cannot pray the Lord's Prayer without cursing. Every time we pray, "Hallowed be thy name, thy kingdom come, thy will be done," we are praying that the plans of Satan and all who serve him will fail and that they will receive the judgment which they deserve. We should indeed pray that God will lead our enemies to repentance and forgiveness as Christ and Stephen did, but we must also pray that all who continue to defy God will receive the justice they deserve.

God is a God of absolute holiness. It is in harmony with God's character and his attributes revealed in Scripture when the psalmist prays, "If only you would slay the wicked, O God! . . . Do I not hate those who hate you, O LORD, and abhor those who rise up against you?" (Psalm 139:19-21) When the psalmist uttered such prayers, his concern was for God's glory and for the success of God's plans.

The psalmist (or in some cases the Messiah, who was speaking through him) was being persecuted "without cause," since the attacks on him were not because of anything he had done, but because of his role in God's plans (Psalms 69:4,7,9; 35:19; 109:3). Even when the psalmist prayed such prayers, he still hoped that God's judgments would serve as a warning that would lead at least some of the wicked to repentance. "Cover their faces with shame so that men will seek your name, O LORD" (Psalm 83:16).

Similar prayers for God to display his justice occur in the New Testament. Paul prayed for God's judgment against those who opposed his preaching of the gospel (Galatians 1:8, 2 Timothy 4:14). Even the saints in heaven pray, "How long, Sovereign Lord, holy and true, until you judge the inhabitants of the earth and avenge our blood?" (Revelation 6:10).

Scripture delivers strong warnings against taking personal vengeance on our enemies, but it also promises us that the just God will repay the wicked. "Do not take revenge, my friends, but leave room for God's wrath, for it is written, 'It is mine to avenge; I will repay,' says the Lord" (Romans

12:19). To punish the ungodly with force is the duty of God and of government as the servant of God, but we should oppose the enemies of God with prayer.

THE HEADINGS OF THE PSALMS

Headings or superscriptions are attached to 116 of the psalms. Among the types of information provided by these headings are the name of the author of the psalm, the historical circumstances which led to its writing, the intended liturgical use of the psalm, and musical directions for its use. There is no set format for these headings — some provide one kind of information about the psalm in question, others a different sort of information.

The content of these headings will be discussed in other sections of this introduction and in the commentary on specific psalms. Our only purpose here is to discuss their authenticity. Many commentators claim that these headings are late additions to the text of Psalms and that the information contained in them is unreliable. The translators of the *New English Bible* arbitrarily omitted them from their translation. The *Good News Bible* relegated them to footnotes. There is no evidence to justify such omission or rejection of these headings. On the contrary, there are a number of indications of their antiquity and reliability.

There is nothing unusual about finding such notations attached to ancient hymns. Similar notations are found with ancient Sumerian and Egyptian hymns and with poetic compositions found in other books of the Bible. Examples of such headings from other books of the Bible are the Song of Deborah (Judges 5:1), the Psalm of Habakkuk (Habakkuk 3:1), and a psalm of David which appears both in 2 Samuel 22 and in the book of Psalms as Psalm 18.

These headings do not have the characteristics we would expect to find in late, artificial inventions. They are not provided for all of the psalms. They have no set pattern or format. In several cases the historical setting attributed to the psalm by the heading could not be readily deduced from the content of the psalm. Some headings refer to events in David's life which are not recorded in the historical books. For example, the heading of Psalm 7 refers to "Cush, a Benjamite," a name which does not occur in the scriptural narrative of David's life. It is not likely that a late inventor of headings would compose such headings with no obvious basis in the text of the psalm or in the historical books.

The standard Hebrew text of Psalms, the psalms found among the Dead Sea manuscripts, and the Septuagint translation of the psalms into Greek all include the headings. (The Septuagint and Dead Sea psalms manuscripts also have some additional headings.) The inability of the Septuagint translators to understand some of the terms in the headings suggests that these terms were already ancient when the Septuagint was translated about 200 B.C.

Important evidence for the antiquity of the psalm headings is the spelling of David's name in these headings. In the Hebrew text of the headings David's name is consistently rendered with the short spelling which appears regularly in the more ancient preexilic books of the Old Testament such as Samuel and Kings and the text of the psalms themselves (*dvd*). The headings do not use the longer spelling of David's name which is standard in the late, postexilic books like Chronicles, Ezra and Nehemiah (*dvyd*).

We conclude that in most cases the heading was attached to the psalm by the authors or by the person to whom the author delivered the psalm. It is possible that some headings were added by the person who collected the psalms into a book, but in either case we are confident that they provide reliable information about the origin and purpose of the psalm and that they are part of God's inspired word.

Many of the 34 psalms without headings, which are called "orphan psalms," are grouped together in the last two sections of the book of Psalms.

THE WRITING OF THE PSALMS

The headings name the authors of 100 of the 150 psalms. Seventy-three psalms are credited to David. These Davidic psalms are spread throughout the book of Psalms, but they are especially prominent in the first two sections of the book. It is likely that quite a few of the anonymous psalms were also written by David. The book of Chronicles ascribes at least portions of Psalms 96, 105 and 106 to David, even though they are anonymous in the book of Psalms. Psalms 2 and 95, which are not credited to David in the Old Testament, are attributed to him in the New Testament (Acts 4:25,26; Hebrews 4:7). The attribution of most of the psalms to David fits perfectly with David's reputation as "Israel's singer of songs" (2 Samuel 23:1).

Twenty-four or twenty-five psalms are attributed to the Levites to whom David had assigned responsibility for music in the temple. The composers of these psalms are Asaph, Heman the Ezrahite, Ethan the Ezrahite, and a group called the sons of Korah. Since these psalms are grouped together in two collections, Psalms 42-50 and 73-89 (Psalm 86 is attributed to David), the authors and dating of these psalms will be discussed more fully in those sections of the commentary. It is likely that most of these psalms are contemporary with the psalms of David.

Two psalms are credited to David's son Solomon (Psalms 72, 127). Some commentators have suggested that the heading of these psalms should be translated "for Solomon" rather than "by Solomon," but we will maintain the traditional interpretation of Solomonic authorship. In view of the fact that 1 Kings 4:32 credits Solomon with writing

1005 songs, it is remarkable that only two of them were inspired sacred songs which were included in the book of Psalms.

Psalm 90 is attributed to Moses. This makes it the oldest psalm in the collection. The poems of Moses recorded in Exodus 15 and Deuteronomy 32 and 33 are further evidence of his work as a poet.

THE DATING OF PSALMS

The scriptural headings credit a majority of the psalms to David and his contemporaries, who lived about 1000 B.C. A single psalm is credited to Moses, who lived about 400 years before David. A few of the psalms of Asaph, such as 74, 79, 83, and some of the anonymous psalms, such as 126 and 137, may have been written at the time of the destruction of the temple and the Babylonian Captivity in 586 B.C. We will discuss the dating of these psalms and a few of the psalms of the sons of Korah, which may be post-Davidic, at the appropriate points of the commentary.

On the basis of the Old Testament evidence it is clear that anyone who takes the authority of Scripture seriously must assign the majority of the psalms to the time of David. The New Testament also confirms the Davidic authorship of certain psalms. It is clear that the Davidic authorship of psalms can be rejected only by contradicting the clear statements of Scripture which point to David as the author.

In spite of this, many critics of the Old Testament reject the Davidic authorship of most of the psalms. Not long ago it was fashionable to place the writing of most of the psalms after Israel's return from the Babylonian Captivity in 539 B.C. Today most critics admit that many of the psalms were written before the exile to Babylon, but they still question or deny Davidic authorship.

For people who accept the inerrancy of Scripture, the testimony of the New Testament by itself is enough to rebut these rejections of Davidic authorship. The best response to critics of Davidic authorship is the testimony of numerous New Testament passages which uphold it (Matthew 22:43, Luke 20:42, Acts 1:16; 2:25; 4:25; 13:36). In Matthew 22:41-46 Jesus' assertion of the Davidic authorship of Psalm 110 is not a side comment, but is essential to the point he is making. However, since it is useful for those who have a high view of Scripture to be able to counter critical attacks on Scripture, we will briefly list the most common objections to Davidic authorship and respond to them.

Objections to Davidic Authorship

OBJECTION 1) The expression "of David" in the headings of the psalms does not denote authorship, but means "dedicated to David's memory" or "belonging to the Davidic hymnbook" or "in the style of David."

RESPONSE: It is grammatically possible for the expression "of David" to mean something other than authorship, but the context does not permit such an interpretation here. The headings frequently give information about the situation in David's life which led him to write a certain psalm. Psalm 18 is quoted in 2 Samuel 22 as a psalm of David. The interpretation of Psalm 110 in Matthew 22:43 also makes it clear that the expression "of David" in the heading of Psalm 110 is to be interpreted as a reference to authorship. All the evidence indicates that "of David" is intended to be a statement of authorship.

Furthermore, it is difficult to imagine why later writers would be so eager to attribute or dedicate their psalms to David unless he was indeed the writer of many psalms just as Scripture declares.

OBJECTION 2) David cannot be the author, since some of the psalms attributed to David refer to him in the third person as "David," rather than in the first person as "I" or "me."

RESPONSE: Such third person references to David are rare. David refers to himself in the first person in the great majority of the psalms attributed to him. Such exceptions as Psalm 18:50, "[The LORD] shows unfailing kindness to his anointed, to David and his descendants forever," are solemn restatements of the promise God had made to David in 2 Samuel 7. Furthermore, even if there were more than a handful of such third person references, they would not be evidence against Davidic authorship, since it is not unusual in formal writing for an author to refer to himself in the third person. Biblical examples of such usage are Matthew 9:9, where Matthew refers to himself in the third person, and Jesus' frequent references to himself as the Son of Man in solemn proclamations such as Matthew 16:27.

OBJECTION 3) Some psalms attributed to David, such as Psalm 20:9, pray for the king in the third person and, therefore, could not be the prayers of David.

RESPONSE: Such prayers are intended for public worship, and these references are no more unusual than a present-day pastor praying "for this congregation and its pastor" in a public prayer.

OBJECTION 4) Some of the psalms attributed to David which refer to "the temple," "the sanctuary," "the house of God," and so on must have been written after the building of the temple. Since this did not occur until after David's death, he could not have written these psalms.

RESPONSE: All of these terms can refer to the tabernacle, the temporary sanctuary in which the ark of the covenant was housed. This is very clear from Psalm 27 where "house of the LORD," "temple" and "tabernacle" are used as synonymous terms. Some of David's psalms may also have been written in anticipation of the building of the temple.

OBJECTION 5) The language of the psalms includes words and expressions which belong to late Hebrew, not the Hebrew of the time of David.

RESPONSE: Recent discoveries of ancient inscriptions in Hebrew and other related dialects have demonstrated that many of the words which critics once considered to be late, postexilic influences from Aramaic were, in fact, in use in the dialects of Syria and Palestine long before Aramaic influence became dominant. Actually the linguistic argument is just as strong for early authorship, since the psalms contain many grammatical and linguistic usages that were outdated by the postexilic era into which many critics place the psalms. Reference was made earlier to the ancient spelling of David's name as one such usage.

There is no good reason for departing from the traditional belief that David was the author of most of the psalms. On the contrary, there are many good reasons to maintain it.

THE COLLECTION OF THE PSALMS

Although most of the psalms were written during the lifetime of David, the final collection and arrangement of the book of Psalms was apparently done much later. The presence of a few exilic or postexilic psalms in the book of Psalms suggests that the final collection was assembled after the return from Babylon, perhaps by Ezra in about 440 B.C. This should not be surprising, since Ezra is traditionally believed to be the person who gathered the books of the Old Testament into a collection.

Ezra, or whoever assembled the book of Psalms, apparently used earlier collections of psalms as the basis for organizing the book into its present form. Our book of Psalms appears to be a "collection of collections." The first collections of psalms were probably prepared by David or his musicians. The heading "For the director of music," which occurs frequently in the first parts of the book of Psalms, apparently designates psalms intended for inclusion in such collections.

In 2 Chronicles 29:30 we learn that the psalms of David and Asaph were being used in public worship at the time of Hezekiah (about 700 B.C.). According to Proverbs 25:1 the biblical scholars of Hezekiah's time played a role in collecting the proverbs of Solomon. Perhaps they also had a role in the gathering of individual psalms into a collection. Additional work on the collection and publishing of psalms may have been done about 620 B.C. during the religious reforms of King Josiah.

It should be emphasized that the collection of David's psalms into hymnbooks which may have been assembled three or four hundred years after his death does not detract from the Davidic authorship of those psalms any more than the collection of Luther's hymns into modern hymnbooks diminishes Luther's authorship. The only difference is that Ezra, who was probably the final collector of David's psalms, was an inspired writer of Scripture, but the editors of modern hymnals are not. In principle, there is no difference between the collection of individual inspired psalms into the book we call Psalms and the collection of individual inspired books into the book we call the Bible.

THE ARRANGEMENT OF THE PSALMS

The biblical book of Psalms is divided into five parts which are traditionally called "books." This five-fold division may be patterned after the five-fold division of the writings of Moses. The five divisions of the book of

Psalms are Book I (Psalms 1-41), Book II (Psalms 42-72), Book III (Psalms 73-89), Book IV (Psalms 90-106), and Book V (Psalms 107-150). A doxology marks the end of each of these books. Within these five "books" groups of psalms are arranged on the basis of such criteria as authorship, psalm type, and subject matter. We will consider the details of this arrangement at the appropriate places in the commentary. At this point we will merely note a few of the basic principles of arrangement.

BOOK I   The basic criterion for inclusion in this book is Davidic authorship. Since many of these psalms were submitted to the director of music, it appears that this book originated as a collection of David's psalms intended for use in the tabernacle and temple.

A striking characteristic of this book is a strong preference for the use of the divine name "LORD" rather than "God."

BOOK II   Book II ends with the words, "This concludes the prayers of David son of Jesse." In addition to Davidic psalms this book includes psalms by the sons of Korah, a single psalm by Asaph, and a closing psalm by Solomon. Perhaps this book was a collection of the psalms of David and his musicians, motivated by the building of Solomon's temple. It appears that Books I and II were the basic kernel from which the book of Psalms was developed.

There is no one principle which governs the arrangement of Book II. This book contains several groups of psalms arranged on the basis of psalm types, for example, a group of *maskil* (Psalm 52-55), a group of *miktam* (Psalm 56-60), and a group of songs (Psalm 66-68). An example of arrangement by subject matter is the emphasis on events of David's flight from Saul in Psalms 52-59.

A peculiar, unexplained trait of Book II is a strong preference for the name "God," rather than the name "LORD."

BOOK III   The main criterion of Book III is authorship by Asaph or the sons of Korah. Only one Davidic psalm appears (Psalm 86). In this book the name "God" predominates in the Asaph group (Psalms 73-83), but the name "LORD" dominates in the sons of Korah group (Psalms 84-89). This collection of psalms shows a special concern for the welfare of Israel, Jerusalem and the temple.

BOOK IV Only two psalms of this book are directly attributed to David (Psalms 101, 103), but others are probably his as well. This group of psalms uses the divine name LORD exclusively. The main principle of arrangement for the last two books of the Psalter seems to be groups of psalms arranged around the themes of praise and thanksgiving. Notable groups in Book IV are Psalms 94-100, which emphasize the Lord's rule, and Psalms 103-106, which emphasize his work as creator and preserver.

BOOK V   Book V includes two blocks of Davidic psalms and a scattering of other Davidic psalms, but the basic principles of arrangement seems to be groups of psalms arranged around the themes of thanksgiving and praise, rather than authorship. Again there is a strong preference for the name "LORD." Notable groups are the "Praise Psalms" (Psalms 111-118 and Psalms 145-150) and the "Songs of Ascents" (Psalms 120-134).

An interesting feature which tends to support the independent origin of the five books of the Psalter is the presence of several "doublets," that is, psalms or psalm portions which occur in more than one book. Psalm 53 parallels Psalm 14; Psalm 70 parallels Psalm 40:13-17; Psalm 108:1-5 parallels Psalm 57:7-11; Psalm 108:6-13 parallels Psalm 60:5-12. The reasons for this repetition are unclear, but suggestions will be discussed in the commentary on the respective psalms.

Although there is a clear pattern of organization present in the book of Psalms, it is not possible to explain the position of every psalm in the Psalter. Nevertheless, the commentary will suggest a reason for the position of each psalm within the structure of the book whenever this seems possible.

THE POETRY OF PSALMS

Parallelism

The distinctive features of most English poetry are rhyme and meter. Hebrew poetry is quite different. Its most important feature is *parallelism*. Instead of rhyming words at the ends of successive lines, parallelism matches corresponding thoughts in successive lines. Poetry which uses parallelism as its main technique is therefore primarily a poetry of thoughts, rather than a poetry of sounds.

Hebrew poetry uses three main kinds of parallelism.

1) In *synonymous parallelism* the second segment of the parallelism repeats the same thought as the first portion in almost identical words. The opening verse of Psalm 19 is an excellent example of balanced synonymous parallelism.

> The heavens declare the glory of God;
> the skies proclaim the work of his hands.

Many examples of synonymous parallelism occur in Psalm 2.

> Why do the nations conspire/
> and the peoples plot in vain?
> The kings of the earth take their stand/
> and the rulers gather together. . . .
> "Let us break their chains," they say,/
> "and throw off their fetters."

Even when parallelism is synonymous, the second member is not mere repetition. The repetition intensifies the emotion and focuses the reader's attention on the thoughts and feelings being expressed.

Sometimes parallelism is incomplete, that is, not every item in the first segment is matched in the second segment. An example is Psalm 24:1.

> The earth is the LORD's, and everything in it,
> the world,   and all who live in it.

2) In *antithetic parallelism* the second segment is the opposite of the first. This type of parallelism is especially common in Proverbs. An example is found in Psalm 1:6.

> For the LORD watches over the way of the righteous,/
> but the way of the wicked will perish.

In this example notice that the corresponding items are not in the same order in both segments. "The way of the righteous" is last in the first segment, but its matching phrase, "the way of the wicked," is first in the second segment. This reversal of order is a deliberate stylistic feature known as *chiasm*.

3) In *synthetic parallelism* the second portion advances the thought of the first. Consider these examples from Psalm 1.

> Blessed is the man who does not
>   *walk* in the counsel of the wicked or
>   *stand* in the way of sinners or
>   *sit*   in the seat of mockers.

> But his delight is in the law of the LORD,
> and on his law he meditates *day and night*.

These examples are basically synonymous, but in both cases the emphasized words show how each new segment intensifies the thought. However, in many examples of synthetic parallelism there is much less parallelism between the two

25

segments of the verse than there is in the previous examples. Psalm 4:6-8 illustrates some of the many possible types of synthetic parallelism.

Parallelism may set forth a question and answer.

> Many are asking, "Who can show us any good?"
> Let the light of your face shine upon us, O LORD.
> (Psalm 4:6)

The second member may simply give an illustration or comparison.

> You have filled my heart with greater joy
> than when their grain and new wine abound.
> (Psalm 4:7)

The second member may give a reason for the first statement.

> I will lie down and sleep in peace,
> for you alone, O LORD, make me dwell in safety.
> (Psalm 4:8)

Sometimes the second member merely gives a further description of the first member of the parallelism.

> Praise be to the LORD,
> who has not let us be torn by their teeth.
> (Psalm 124:6)

There are even some verses which cannot be easily divided into two members.

> Be strong and take heart,
> All you who hope in the LORD. (Psalm 31:24)

The use of parallelism is often irregular. Sometimes there are lines which have no parallel. Parallelism often does not follow a set pattern within a poem. Nevertheless, parallelism is the main poetic feature of every Hebrew poem. Some guidance in following the poetic structure of the psalms will be provided by the way the psalms are printed in the text of this commentary. All the main statements of the parallelisms of a psalm are aligned with a *straight left margin* as they are in the examples above. You should be able to match each line with its corresponding line on the basis of meaning. Very often the verse numbers of the English Bible also indicate which lines belong together. In this commentary lines which are *indented* are subordinate thoughts which explain the preceding lines. Sometimes indentation indicates that the line in question is not the beginning of a new parallel thought, but merely the continuation of the preceding line, which had to be divided to fit the width of the page.

Parallelism of thought can, of course, be translated into other languages much more easily than rhyme or meter can. It is interesting that the inspired poetry of Scripture was written in the poetic technique which is most easily translated into other languages.

As you read the psalms, remember that observing the parallelism is often an aid in understanding the meaning of the poem. Turn to Psalms 1 and 2 and see if you can pick out the parallelisms.

Other Poetic Features

Although Hebrew poetry does not have regular rhyme and meter as most English poetry does, some scholars have attempted to find some rhythmic pattern or meter in Hebrew poetry. There is a great deal of controversy about this subject. It does not seem possible to discover any consistent metrical system in Hebrew poetry. Since this question can be discussed only on the basis of the Hebrew text, we will not concern ourselves further with it.

Usually Hebrew poetry does not have regular stanzas or verses as our English hymns do. Sometimes it is possible to divide psalms into stanzas of grouped lines, but these are seldom regular. Occasionally Hebrew poems are divided into sections by a refrain (for example, in Psalms 42,43 and 107), but this is rare.

One type of systematic arrangement in Hebrew poetry is called *acrostic*. In this form each line of the poem starts with the next letter of the Hebrew alphabet. This could be done in English by beginning the first line of a poem with the letter *A*, the second with *B*, the third with *C*, and so on throughout the alphabet. In extended acrostics each line of Stanza One may start with *A*, each line of Stanza Two with *B*, and so on. This is the pattern of Psalm 119, which is the most elaborate acrostic and the most structured psalm in the book of Psalms. Each stanza of Psalm 119 has eight lines, each of which begins with the same letter of the alphabet.

Other acrostic psalms are 9,10, 25, 34, 37, 111, 112 and 145. Acrostic poems also occur in the book of Lamentations. In some cases the acrostic style may have been intended as an aid to memorization, but it is much more likely that it was intended to convey the idea of completeness ("from A to Z"). Acrostics occasionally omit or rearrange the letters of the alphabet, but when this happens there are stylistic reasons for such irregularities. The acrostic feature is not reproduced in the English translation of these poems.

Like most poetry, Hebrew poetry uses old-fashioned words and unusual expressions more frequently than prose does. This practice is similar to the continued use of archaic words like "thee" and "thou" in hymns and prayers long after they had passed out of use in daily speech. Since this feature is not apparent in the NIV translation, we will not discuss it further.

Hebrew poetry sometimes creates special effects by placing together words which begin with the same sound (alliteration) or by using puns and word-plays. These features are usually lost in translation, but they will be noted in the commentary if they are significant.

Like most poetry, Hebrew poetry makes extensive use of figures of speech. Among the common figures are

Simile: a comparison indicated by "like" or "as."

>The righteous man is *like a tree*
>>*planted by streams of water.*
>The ungodly are *like chaff that*
>>*the wind blows away.* (Psalm 1:3,4)

Metaphor: a comparison made without a comparative word such as "like."

>*Many bulls* surround me.
>*Dogs* have surrounded me. (Psalm 22:12,16)
>("Bulls" and "dogs" refer to vicious men.)

Synecdoche: the name of a part of something stands for the whole thing.

>Let the *bones* you have crushed rejoice.
>(Means "Let *me* rejoice.") (Psalm 51:8)

Personification: characteristics of living beings are ascribed to inanimate things.

>Love and faithfulness meet together;
>righteousness and peace kiss each other. (Psalm 85:10)

We read the psalms not simply to enjoy great literature, but to be edified by the word of God. The most important aspect of the psalms is their meaning, not their poetic beauty. Nevertheless, as you read them, watch for the literary and poetic features which will enhance your enjoyment of them.

THE MUSIC OF THE PSALMS

The exhortations to sing to the LORD contained in the psalms, the presence of musical terms in the psalm headings, the descriptions of the liturgical use of the psalms recorded in the historical books, and the traditional use of the psalms in the synagogue and church all make it obvious that the psalms are hymns which were written to be sung to the accompaniment of musical instruments.

Unfortunately, we have no way of knowing how the music of the psalms originally sounded. Many scholars believe that the style of chanting used in Jewish synagogues or the Gregorian chants used with the psalms in the Christian church have preserved some of the style of the original music of the psalms. Others believe that the original music of the psalms was more like present-day Middle Eastern folk music. There is no way of knowing for certain.

In the presentation of the psalms in the temple the vocal music was considered to be more important than the instrumental accompaniment, because the message conveyed by the words was the most important thing. David appointed certain Levitical families for the musical work in the tabernacle when the ark of the covenant was first brought to Jerusalem (1 Chronicles 15:15-22). A Levite named Kenaniah was the first leader of vocal music in the temple service (1 Chronicles 15:22). According to rabbinic tradition the minimum temple choir consisted of twelve adult males from the tribe of Levi. Some commentators suggest that young sons of the priests were used for the higher voices, but there is no support in Scripture for this idea.

According to rabbinic tradition the temple singing was done antiphonally or responsively. There were three main forms of responsive singing in the temple: 1) The first choir sang a line of the psalm, and the second choir responded with a refrain which was repeated throughout the psalm. Psalm 136 is an example of this style. 2) The first choir sang a line, and the second choir echoed it. 3) The two choirs sang alternate lines of the psalm. This is the way we usually do the responsive reading of the psalms today. The two choirs appointed by Nehemiah for the dedication of the walls of Jerusalem may have been arranged for antiphonal singing when they met in the temple after their procession around the walls of Jerusalem (Nehemiah 12:31).

It is clear from recent archeological finds that the art of music was highly developed at a much earlier date than people have often supposed. The recent decipherment of cuneiform tablets from the city of Ugarit in Syria has revealed that musical notation and the use of harmony in singing were known 400 years before the time of David. The song from Ugarit, which is apparently a hymn to the moon goddess, was written in a scale like our modern major scale. If this decipherment is correct, it appears that the people of the ancient Near East used a seven-note scale which closely resembles the do-re-mi scale we were taught as children.

The seven scales used in the tuning of ancient stringed instruments were similar to the seven scales which could be played on a piano with no black notes. Each scale would begin on one of the seven notes (C, D, E, F, G, A, B). Each scale would be different because, without the black notes, the half steps would come in different places within each scale. We do not know how many of these basic principles of musical theory were understood and used by David and his musicians, but they were known in their time.

It is interesting to note that the hymn from Ugarit discussed in the preceding paragraph had a notation which listed the composer, the copyist, and the scale to be used. This parallels the type of information provided in the psalm readings.

Musical Directions in the Psalms

Fifty-five psalms carry the heading "For the director of music." This title appears to designate psalms which were handed over to the chief of the tabernacle or to the temple musicians for use in the public service. An example of this practice appears in 1 Chronicles 16:7, "That day David first committed to Asaph and his associates this psalm of thanks to the LORD." This heading is most prominent in the first three books of Psalms.

A number of psalm headings appear to designate the name of the tune to be used, just as the headings in our hymnbook do. "Do not destroy" (Psalms 57-59, and 75), "A Dove on Distant Oaks" (Psalm 56), "Lilies" (Psalms 45 and 69), "The Lily [Lilies] of the Covenant" (Psalms 60 and 80), "The Death of the Son" (Psalm 9) and "The Doe of the Morning" (Psalm 22) all appear to be titles of melodies. Since none of these titles is distinctly sacred, it has been suggested that folk melodies were sometimes adopted as hymn melodies, just as they were at the time of the Reformation.

The brackets around the words "the tune of" in the NIV translation of these psalm headings indicate that these three words do not occur in the Hebrew text, but are the interpretation of the translator. Therefore, although the interpretation of these phrases as melody titles is probable, it is not certain. Some commentators have offered other interpretations of some of these phrases.

There are several additional titles which could be melodies but which more likely are musical directions of some other sort. The words "According to *mahalath*" (Psalm 53) and "According to *mahalath leannoth*" (Psalm 88) refer to sickness or suffering. This may be a reference to the mournful type of melody to be used with these psalms, but the phrase is admittedly obscure.

"According to *gittith*" (Psalms 8, 81, and 84) is another difficult phrase. It may refer to an instrument or melody brought from the Philistine city of Gath or the Levitical city of Gath Rimmon or to a melody associated with the grape harvest (*gath* means winepress).

"According to *alamoth*" (Psalm 46) appears to be derived from the word for "virgin." For this reason it is often understood as a reference to a high-pitched voice or instrument, perhaps some sort of double flute. It may refer to the tenor voice or to falsetto singing. In 1 Chronicles 15:20 this term refers to the manner of playing or tuning a harplike stringed instrument called the *nebel*. The meaning of *alamoth* remains obscure.

"According to *sheminith*" (Psalms 6 and 12) seems to be derived from the Hebrew word for "eight." This may refer to an eight-stringed instrument or perhaps the lower octave or bass voice. In 1 Chronicles 15:21 this terms refers to the manner of playing or tuning a stringed instrument called the *kinnor*. Again, the meaning remains obscure.

Jeduthun was one of the musicians of David (1 Chronicles 16:41). He may be the same as Ethan. "For Jeduthun" (Psalm 39) seems to refer to a song handed over to him for performance. "For Jeduthun" (Psalms 62 and 77) or better "according to Jeduthun" apparently means to be performed according to the melody or in the style of Jeduthun.

"Selah" occurs 71 times in 39 different psalms, mostly in the first three books. It occurs within psalms as a marker of some sort of interlude. Sometimes it occurs where there is a sharp break in the thought, but at other times it appears in the middle of a thought. In rare cases it appears at the end of a psalm. Apparently it is a musical notation, but its meaning remains obscure. It is believed to be derived from a Hebrew word meaning to "lift up" or from one meaning to "be quiet." Suggested interpretations include 1) an instrumental interlude between vocal sections of the psalm, 2) a pause, 3) an increase in the loudness of the music, 4) a sign to divide the hymn into sections, 5) an emphatic interjection like

Lyres

Lyre

Lyre of Ma'adanah the daughter of the King Jerusalem 7th century

Israelite
Lyre Player

Lachish 700 B.C.

Canaanite
Lyre Player

Megiddo 1200 B.C.

Trumpets

Metal
Trumpet

Ram's
Horn

Percussion

Rattles

Cymbals

Tof

The Musical Instruments of the Psalms

34

"amen," or 6) a repeat sign like *da capo*. The first suggestion seems most likely.

The Musical Instruments of the Psalms

In the public worship in the temple the singing of the psalms was accompanied by what we would call a full orchestra. When the ark was brought to Jerusalem, David's orchestra included 3 cymbal players and 14 players of stringed instruments. (1 Chronicles 15:19-21) The total number of David's temple musicians was 4000 (1 Chronicles 23:5). In New Testament times the minimum orchestra was 12 instruments. This regulation is apparently based on David's appointment of twenty-four groups of 12 musicians each in 1 Chronicles 25.

At the dedication of Solomon's temple 120 trumpets were used (2 Chronicles 5:12), so we would expect a proportionate number of other instruments. This was, of course, a very special occasion for which an especially large number of musicians was used.

The exact composition of the orchestra may have varied, depending on the occasion and the period of history, but it appears that lyres, harps and cymbals were the main instruments of the temple orchestra, with trumpets used mainly for fanfares between the singing (1 Chronicles 15:16; 2 Chronicles 5:12,13). The average orchestra probably consisted of 12 to 36 instruments. Apparently other types of instruments were used mainly outside of the temple worship, primarily for festival processions.

Our knowledge of the instruments used to accompany the psalms is limited. Very few examples of the instruments themselves have survived, but some ancient pictures and descriptions have come down to us. We often find contradictory descriptions of the various instruments, probably because the instruments changed through time. In most cases these instruments do not correspond exactly to any modern instrument. For this reason any English translation is somewhat misleading. An additional difficulty is that the NIV does not consistently translate the Hebrew name of an instrument with the same English word. Therefore, in our description of each instrument we will use the Hebrew name along with the translations adopted by the NIV.

The most important instruments were the stringed instruments. Several psalm headings contain the instructions "with stringed instruments" (Psalms 4, 6, 54, 55, 61, 67, 76). The stringed instrument played by David was the *kinnor*. This has traditionally been translated "harp," but the translation "lyre" adopted by the NIV in Psalm 150:3 is more accurate. The *kinnor* or lyre was smaller than our modern harp, but was similar to it in some respects. Like our harp it had an angular shape and a sound box at the bottom. The number of strings on a lyre varied from three to twenty-two, but seven and twelve were the most common numbers.

The *kinnor* could be played either with the fingers or with a plectrum or pick. 1 Samuel 19:9 refers to David playing the lyre "by hand" (this expression is in the Hebrew, but not in the NIV translation). The Greek translation of *kinnor* is *kitara*, from which our word "guitar" is derived. Although the guitar has undergone some major changes from the *kinnor*, among the instruments in common use today the guitar most closely resembles David's *kinnor* in form and function.

Fortunately we have a number of pictures of Israelite lyres. The lyre pictured in Figure 1 belonged to Ma'adanah, a daughter of one of the kings of Judah. The lyre player in Figure 2 is an Israelite player captured by the Assyrian king Sennacherib. Both of these pictures are from about 300 years after the time of David.

The *nebel* was probably a larger version of the *kinnor*. The NIV appropriately translates *nebel* as "harp" in Psalm 150:3 and several other passages. A 10-stringed *nebel* is mentioned in Psalms 33:2; 92:3; 144:9. (Unfortunately the NIV has translated *nebel* as "lyre" and *kinnor* as "harp" in these three passages, the exact opposite of its better translations in Psalm 150:3. Thus the NIV fails to distinguish these two instruments consistently.)

The *shophar* is sometimes translated "trumpet" by the NIV (Psalm 150:3), but at other times it is more correctly translated "ram's horn" (1 Chronicles 15:28, Psalm 98:6). The *shophar* apparently was used only for making "trumpet blasts," since melodies could not be played on it.

The *hatsotserah* was a straight metal trumpet. It was probably high pitched. In Psalm 98:6 the NIV translates *hatsotserah* "trumpet." The use of the trumpet to herald special festivals was already commanded by God in Numbers 10:9.

The *halil* was a flute or pipe of some sort. For sacred use it was more often made of wood than of metal. It apparently was thought of as a more secular instrument, and therefore it did not have a prominent role in the temple worship. However, it could be used on sacred festivals (Isaiah 30:29).

The *ugav* is a mystery. Suggestions range from a flute or pipes of some sort to an instrument similar to a bagpipe. The NIV has "flute" in Psalm 150:4. Some older versions translate *ugav* as "organ." Apparently it did not have an important role in temple worship.

The *tof* is a frame drum, similar to a tambourine, but without the metal rattlers. It was apparently used for processions and festive dance outside the temple (1 Chronicles 13:8) rather than for choral music in the temple. It is mentioned three times in the psalms (Psalms 81:2; 149:3; 150:4).

Other types of rattles or noisemakers were apparently used along with the tambourine. In 2 Samuel 6:5 the term "sistrum" refers to such a rattle or noisemaker.

Various types of cymbals were an important part of the temple orchestra. In fact, all three of the most famous Levitical musicians, Asaph, Heman and Ethan, were cymbal players (1 Chronicles 15:19). Perhaps the cymbals played a role in laying down the tempo or beat, much as the drums often do in a modern band.

Dance is mentioned twice as a form of praise (Psalms 149:3; 150:4.) David danced before the ark of the Lord when it was brought to Jerusalem (2 Samuel 6:14-16). However, we have no evidence that dance was used in the temple service itself. It may have been used mainly in festival processions to the temple.

For the people of Israel the psalms were one of the high points of their worship life. For those who were not priests and who, therefore, could not enter the sanctuary of the temple, the music of the festivals must have been the most exciting part of their worship. The music enriched their appreciation of the message, but the message remained the most important aspect of the psalms. In the psalms we have both God's message of sin and forgiveness and the human response to that message. As we now turn to our study of the psalms, let us take its message to heart and make the response of the psalmists our own.

BOOK I
PSALMS 1-41

The first "book" or subdivision of the larger book of Psalms is a collection of psalms of David, intended for use in the temple services. This collection may well have been assembled during David's lifetime. All of the psalms in this book, except for Psalms 1, 2, 10 and 33, are attributed to David by their headings. Even the four for which no author is given may be Davidic. Almost half of these psalms are addressed to the director of music, a clear indication that they had been submitted for use in the temple worship. A striking but unexplained characteristic of this book is a preference for the divine name "LORD," rather than "God."

Psalms 1 and 2 form an introduction to the whole book of Psalms. Together they deal with two of the most important themes of Psalms: the believer's attitude toward God's word and the believer's attitude toward God's Messiah. Psalm 1 begins with a blessing on the person who obeys God's word. Psalm 2 ends with a blessing on the person who trusts God's Messiah. These two benedictions neatly enclose these two psalms as a unit which is introductory to the whole book of Psalms.

We have no information about the writing of these two psalms. Psalm 1 may be a Davidic psalm which was later selected to serve as the introduction to the book of Psalms, or it may have been written especially for this purpose by someone else. However, since Acts 4:25 attributes Psalm 2 to David, it is most probable that Psalm 1, which is paired with it, is also David's.

PSALM 1

Two Responses to God's Word

The Way of the Godly Leads to Blessing

1 **Blessed is the man**
   who does not walk in the counsel of the wicked
   or stand in the way of sinners
   or sit in the seat of mockers.
2But his delight is in the law of the LORD,
 and on his law he meditates day and night.
3He is like a tree
   planted by streams of water,
   which yields its fruit in season
   and whose leaf does not wither.
Whatever he does prospers.

These verses set forth three characteristics of the godly: they resist sin, they love God's word, and they produce the fruits of faith.

Because the godly are guided by God's word, they do not govern their lives by the false values of the unbelieving world. In Romans 12:2 Paul admonishes us, "Do not conform any longer to the pattern of this world, but be transformed by the renewing of your mind. Then you will be able to test and approve what God's will is — his good, pleasing and perfect will." Psalm 1 implies the same warning. Christians must not derive their values and goals from the sinful standards of the world. Whatever shapes our thinking will soon shape our actions.

The three verbs, "walk," "stand," and "sit," warn Christians against letting ungodly influences gradually penetrate into their lives. Don't *walk* according to the advice of the wicked, that is, don't begin to accept their values. Don't *stand* in the way of sinners, that is, don't hang around with them and join in their sinful actions. Don't *sit* with the mockers, that is, don't make yourself at home with them. Don't join them in their impenitent way of life and their bold defiance of God. Don't become one of them.

When we see the prevalence of ungodly attitudes in the world around us — covetousness and materialism, sexual immorality and disregard for the family, violence and war, we realize that we must resist these influences before they gain a foothold in our lives. If we let them walk into our lives, they will soon stand firmly planted there. Finally, they will sit down and make themselves at home. We will soon grow comfortable with ideas and actions which once would have horrified us. When this happens, we will be no different from the world around us.

Christians cannot expect to resist the values of the unbelieving world if they devote one hour of the week to meditating on God's word and the other 167 hours to providing for the needs of their bodies and enjoying worldly entertainment. If we wish to have our whole life shaped by God's word, we need more than our Sunday worship hour. We need regular Bible study with fellow Christians. We need to recognize the importance of regular family devotions and personal Bible study. We need to cultivate the habit of remembering and applying the truths of God's word when we are confronted with temptations or faced with decisions in daily life. God's children will find their greatest joy and satisfaction in studying his word and thinking about it day and night.

We often use the word "law" to refer to God's command-ments, in which he tells us what to do. But in this psalm and in many other passages of the Bible the "law of the LORD" refers to the whole word of God, both law and gospel. "Law" is here the translation of a Hebrew word meaning "teaching" or "instruction." Christians finds their greatest joy in the gospel, which tells them of God's forgiveness of their sins. But when Christians are motivated by the new spirit of faith which the Holy Spirit has created within them, they also delight in God's law as it is summarized in the Ten Com-mandments and other passages of Scripture. Because they love their Savior, they want to obey his commands and do the things that will please God. They delight in all of God's word from beginning to end.

When believers are motivated by the gospel and guided by God's law, they will produce the fruits of faith, that is, works pleasing to God. The good works Christians produce in their lives are often called "fruits" because of the similarities between a Christian and a branch of a fruit tree. A branch of a tree can produce fruit only if it remains attached to the main trunk of the tree. A Christian can produce good works only if he is connected to Christ by a living faith. A tree can produce fruit only if it is well watered. A Christian can produce good works only if his faith is "watered" by God's word. A tree is a living organism which produces fruit according to the nature God has given it. It is the nature of a healthy apple tree to produce apples, of a grape vine to produce grapes. It is the new nature of a believer in Christ to produce Christ-like works.

Although verse one contains an implied warning against ungodly values, strictly speaking, this verse is a promise, not a warning. Those who guide their lives by God's word so that they avoid the way of the ungodly and produce the fruits of faith will be truly blessed. To be blessed means to enjoy the happy and rewarding life which comes from God alone. Real happiness is the peace which comes through the forgiveness of sins. Real happiness is receiving the freedom to live according to God's word. Real happiness is enjoying the glory of living with God throughout eternity. This is the blessing that awaits all those who delight in God's word.

The Way of the Ungodly Leads to Destruction

4Not so the wicked!
They are like chaff that the wind blows away.
5Therefore the wicked will not stand in the judgment,
nor sinners in the assembly of the righteous.

Conclusion

6For the LORD watches over the way of the righteous,
but the way of the wicked will perish.

This section is shorter than the description of the godly because nothing positive can be said about the way of the ungodly. They don't heed God's word. They produce no fruit. They will receive no blessing. To God their achievements are as worthless as the chaff which is blown away when the farmer threshes his grain.

On Judgment Day God will gather believers into their heavenly home just as a farmer gathers the good grain into his barn, but the ungodly will be blown away from God's presence like chaff. The ungodly will not pass God's judgment. They will not join the assembly of his saints in heaven. On Judgment Day the Lord will announce that he approves of the way of all those who are his children through faith in Christ, but the rebellion of the wicked against God will come to an end, and they will be excluded from his presence forever.

There are only two roads people can travel: the road of obedience to God, which leads to life, and the road of rebellion, which leads to hell. There are no other alternatives. Nothing in life is more important than being sure you are traveling the right road.

PSALM 2

The Nations Conspire, but God's King Rules Securely

Psalm 2 is one of the most important Messianic psalms. In this psalm David describes the futile resistance of the rulers of this world to the kingdom of the Messiah.

The Futile Conspiracy of the Nations

1 Why do the nations conspire
and the peoples plot in vain?
²The kings of the earth take their stand
and the rulers gather together
against the LORD
and against his Anointed One.
³"Let us break their chains," they say,
"and throw off their fetters."

⁴The One enthroned in heaven laughs;
the Lord scoffs at them.
⁵Then he rebukes them in his anger
and terrifies them in his wrath, saying,
⁶"I have installed my King on Zion, my holy hill."

The psalmist is amazed that this world's rulers dare to plot against God's anointed king. What could be more foolish? What could be more hopeless? Nevertheless, the rulers of this evil world, who disagree about so many things, find themselves united on one point — their opposition to God's rule. Acts 4:27 tells us that the conspiracy against Jesus which led to his death was the chief example of such plotting against God's king. Pilate and Herod hated each other, but they cooperated in Jesus' trial. The Pharisees and Sadducees were bitter enemies, but they agreed on one thing — Jesus had to die.

Such futile efforts to overthrow God's royal reign have continued throughout history. The Roman Empire tried to crush Christianity. The papacy suppressed the truth in the church. Communist governments are working to destroy the church in their lands. All these efforts have failed. In spite of them, the gospel marches on, gathering God's elect from every nation.

Sometimes the rebellion against God's king is less violent than the bloody persecutions mentioned above. Today people try to "break God's chains" whenever they despise the moral principles of God's laws and adopt lifestyles which defy God's will. Leaders of the church "throw off God's fetters" whenever they refuse to let their teachings be governed by God's word. Self-righteous moralists who imagine they can satisfy God by their own efforts reject the rule of the Messiah-king, the only Savior who can lead them to eternal life.

The great tragedy of all these efforts to escape God's rule is that the obedience to God's word which these people regard as slavery is really the greatest freedom. Even more tragic for these rebels is the certainty that all such rebellion is doomed to failure. Those who refuse to be ruled by God's grace will be ruled by his wrath when he comes in judgment.

The English word "Anointed," the Hebrew word "Messiah," and the Greek word "Christ" all mean the same thing. They all refer to the anointing with oil by which an Israelite priest or king appointed by God was installed into his office. The title, "The Anointed," could be applied to any of the Old Testament high priests or kings. However, in this psalm the Lord's Anointed is Jesus Christ, the Son of God. This is made clear in the next section of the psalm. In these verses the Messiah himself announces the decree God the Father made to him.

The Secure Reign of God's King

> **⁷I will proclaim the decree of the LORD:**
> **He said to me,**
> > **"You are my Son;**
> > **today I have become your Father.**
> > **⁸Ask of me,**
> > **and I will make the nations your inheritance,**
> > **the ends of the earth your possession.**
> > **⁹You will rule them with an iron scepter;**
> > **you will dash them to pieces like pottery."**

In 2 Samuel 7 the Lord had promised David that he would have a son who would rule after him and build God's house. God promised that he himself would be a father to this king. David's successor Solomon partly fulfilled this prophecy. God was his spiritual father. Solomon ruled on David's throne. He built the temple as God's house. But Solomon died. His kingdom was divided. The temple he built was destroyed.

No earthly king could fulfill this prophecy. This promise was completely fulfilled only by Christ. Through the worldwide preaching of the gospel he is building God's house, the church. Only Christ, the Son of David, has established a kingdom that will last forever.

Like other believers, Solomon was God's son only by adoption into God's family through faith. Christ is God's Son by his very nature. He is God equal to the Father in every way. In the Nicene Creed we confess that Jesus is the only-begotten Son of God. "Beget" and "begotten" are simply old-fashioned terms that mean "to become someone's father" and "to be fathered by someone."

But when we use the term "begotten" to describe the relationship between God the Father and God the Son, we mean something quite different from the relationship between a human father and his son. Because Christ is the eternal second person of the Trinity, his being "begotten by the Father" is not an event which takes place at a specific point of time, as our conception and birth did. God the Father did not become Christ's father by an act of generation or conception that took place at a point in time. Christ's being "begotten by the Father" refers to an eternal, unchanging relationship which exists between the first and second persons of the Trinity.

This eternal Son of God entered into the world and took on a human nature when Jesus was conceived by the Virgin Mary and born in Bethlehem. But Christ did not become the Son of God when he was born in Bethlehem or at any other time. He always was the Son of God, and he always will be.

We would not know that this man, Jesus of Nazareth, is really the eternal Son of God unless God had revealed this to us. Jesus is the Son of God from eternity, but this is revealed to us only by the testimony God the Father gave to the ministry Jesus performed for us on this earth. Gabriel announced this truth to Mary before Jesus was born (Luke 1:35). God the Father announced this truth with a voice from heaven at Jesus' baptism (Luke 3:22), at his transfiguration (Luke 9:35), and again during Holy Week (John 12:28). But the outstanding testimony to Jesus' divine sonship was his resurrection from the dead. Jesus "was declared with power to be the Son of God by his resurrection from the dead" (Romans 1:4).

Three New Testament passages quote Psalm 2:7 as a Messianic prophecy which establishes that Jesus is the Son of God. In Acts 13:33 this declaration of sonship is closely associated with Jesus' resurrection. In Hebrews 1:5 this verse is cited to demonstrate Jesus's superiority to the angels, who are "sons of God" only by creation, not by eternal equality. In Hebrews 5:5 this psalm is quoted to show that Jesus did not usurp the position of being our High Priest and Savior, but that this office was assigned to him by the Father.

Jesus is now establishing his gracious rule throughout the world through the preaching of the gospel. In this kingdom of his grace people become children and heirs of God through faith in Christ and through the forgiveness of sins which he has won. Those who despise this grace will nevertheless be ruled by Christ's power when he returns on Judgment Day. Psalm 2:9 is cited in Revelation 2:27, 12:5 and 19:15 as a prophecy of Christ's authority to judge the world. He will share this authority with his people when he comes. The lesson to be learned from this royal power of Christ is evident, but the psalmist points it out so clearly that no reader can possibly overlook it.

The Lesson to Be Learned

> [10]Therefore, you kings, be wise;
>   be warned, you rulers of the earth.
> [11]Serve the LORD with fear
>   and rejoice with trembling.
> [12]Kiss the Son,
>   lest he be angry
>   and you be destroyed in your way,
>   for his wrath can flare up in a moment.
>   Blessed are all who take refuge in him.

If Christ will return to judge the world with almighty power, if every knee will bow to him, the lesson for the enemies of his kingdom is obvious. Bow to him in adoration, or you will kneel before him in fear. Repent and become reconciled to him.

The words "kiss the Son" in verse 12 have caused great difficulty for translators because the word translated "Son" is not the usual Hebrew word for "son." For this reason several translations interpret this verse quite differently than the NIV, but regardless of which translation is accepted, the basic sense of the verse is the same: Submit to Christ's rule while there still is time. Only those who trust in him will be blessed in time and in eternity.

PSALM 3

Psalms 3-6 are joined together by a number of common characteristics. All of them are morning or evening prayers. All of them are called "psalms" in their headings. They all refer to affliction or suffering at the hands of enemies. Perhaps David wrote all four of them during Absalom's rebellion, which is mentioned in the heading of Psalm 3. The events of this period of David's life are described in 2 Samuel 15-17. The following commentary will be limited to the distinctive features of each psalm.

How Many Are My Foes, but You Are My Shield

A psalm of David. When he fled from his son Absalom.

1 **O LORD, how many are my foes!**
   How many rise up against me!
²Many are saying of me,
   "God will not deliver him."   *Selah*

   ³But you are a shield around me, O LORD;
      you bestow glory on me and lift up my head.
   ⁴To the LORD I cry aloud,
      and he answers me from his holy hill.   *Selah*

The Death of Absalom

⁵I lie down and sleep;
  I wake again, because the LORD sustains me.
⁶I will not fear the tens of thousands
            drawn up against me on every side.

⁷Arise, O LORD! Deliver me, O my God!
  Strike all my enemies on the jaw;
  break the teeth of the wicked.

⁸From the LORD comes deliverance
  May your blessing be on your people.   *Selah*

In this psalm David contrasts the arrogant overconfidence of his enemies with the serenity he has because he trusts in the Lord. When Absalom rebelled, friends of David, like Ahithophel, deserted him because they thought Absalom would capture David's throne. Enemies of David, like Shimei, brought their secret hatred out into the open and kicked David when he was down. But because God was his shield, David could lie down and sleep in peace in spite of the foes arrayed against him. David appeals to God for help, and he rests his case with the Lord. With this confidence he can sleep peacefully in spite of the dangers that surround him.

When you are overwhelmed with troubles, turn to this psalm for a reminder of the security you have in the Lord. Cast all your cares on him. Try to put worry aside so that you can sleep peacefully. Awake refreshed, confident of his help in the troubles which still lie ahead of you.

PSALM 4

My Righteous God, Give Me Relief

For the director of music. With stringed instruments. A psalm of David.

A Prayer to God

1 Answer me when I call to you, O my righteous God.
Give me relief from my distress;
be merciful to me and hear my prayer.

A Rebuke to Enemies

²How long, O men, will you turn my glory into shame?
How long will you love delusions and seek false gods? *Selah*
³Know that the LORD has set apart the godly for himself;
the LORD will hear when I call to him.

Advice to Friends

⁴In your anger do not sin;
when you are on your beds,
search your hearts and be silent. *Selah*
⁵Offer right sacrifices
and trust in the LORD.

⁶Many are asking, "Who can show us any good?"
Let the light of your face shine upon us, O LORD.

Closing Prayer

⁷You have filled my heart with greater joy
than when their grain and new wine abound.
⁸I will lie down and sleep in peace,
for you alone, O LORD, make me dwell in safety.

The situation in this psalm is very similar to that in Psalm 3. Compare Psalm 3:1,2 with Psalm 4:2,3. In both cases David is taunted by enemies who are sure that he will get no help from God. The taunts of David's enemies remind us of the taunts of Jesus' enemies when he was on the cross.

In this brief psalm David speaks appropriate words about this situation to God, to his enemies, and to his friends. First David appeals to God for relief from his affliction. He then warns his enemies against the foolishness of opposing God's plans and attacking God's anointed king. He warns them that the victory of God's people is certain; therefore they should turn from their ways before it is too late. Then David admonishes his loyal followers not to become bitter or resentful against their enemies or against God because of the hardships they are suffering. If they remain patient and trust in the Lord, he will deliver them in his good time.

Finally, David encourages the faint-hearted among his followers. Their despairing question, "Who can show us any good?" suggests that even many of David's friends were losing heart and concluding that their cause was lost. But David says, "Don't give up! Don't despair! Your question has an answer. 'Who can show us any good?' The Lord will show us good. He will let the light of his face shine upon us. He will give us relief." David concludes with a simple prayer which expresses his confidence in the Lord and the peace of mind which flows from such confidence.

If you ever feel your situation is hopeless, if you ever ask yourself, "What's the use of being a Christian?", if you ever look at the world around you and say, "Who can show us any good?", remember this beautiful prayer of David. Even in the dark night of suffering, the light of God's face will shine upon us. He will show us the goodness of his grace and deliver us in due time.

PSALM 5

With You the Wicked Cannot Dwell

This psalm may also be from the time of Absalom's rebellion when David's enemies spread vicious lies to discredit him. The first half of the psalm declares that the godly have access to the Lord in prayer, but the wicked are excluded from his presence.

For the director of music. For flutes.
A psalm of David.

Access through Prayer

1 Give ear to my words, O LORD,
   consider my sighing.
2 Listen to my cry for help, my King and my God,
      for to you I pray.
3 In the morning, O LORD, you hear my voice;
   in the morning I lay my requests before you
      and wait in expectation.

No Access

4 You are not a God who takes pleasure in evil;
   with you the wicked cannot dwell.
5 The arrogant cannot stand in your presence;
   you hate all who do wrong.
6 You destroy those who tell lies;
   bloodthirsty and deceitful men the LORD abhors.

Access through Prayer

⁷But I, by your great mercy, will come into your house;
 in reverence will I bow down toward your holy temple.
⁸Lead me, O Lord, in your righteousness because of my enemies —
 make straight your way before me.

David uses the believer's privilege of coming before the Lord in prayer. Because we are God's children through faith in Christ Jesus, we can come before him with all boldness and confidence as dear children come to their loving father. But unbelievers and impenitent sinners have no access to God. God is a holy God. He hates sin. He can tolerate no sin in his presence. But God not only hates sin. "You hate all who do wrong," the psalmist emphasizes. God hates sinners and cannot tolerate having them in his presence. This is what God's law tells us.

But God's gospel tells us God loves sinners. Aren't these statements in hopeless contradiction? It seems so. God's law and God's gospel, God's holiness and God's love, God's hatred for sinners and God's love for sinners can be reconciled only at Calvary's cross. At Calvary we see the full extent of God's hatred for sin and sinners. There Jesus endured God's hatred against sin and sinners. There Jesus paid the full penalty which satisfied the demands of God's holy law. Not one sin was overlooked. Every sin was paid for.

At Calvary's cross we also see the full extent of God's love for sinners. God loved sinners so much that he gave his only Son into death for all of them. Because Christ has paid for every sin, you and I can appear before God with confidence. If it were not for Jesus' death, this verdict of the law would be true also of us: The wicked cannot dwell with God. We would be excluded from his presence forever. But thanks be to God! We, who were his enemies, have become his beloved children through Christ. We stand under the declaration of the gospel: We are all the children of God by faith in Christ Jesus.

The second half of Psalm 5 contrasts the lying tongues of the wicked with the praising tongues of God's people.

Lying Tongues

> 9Not a word from their mouth can be trusted;
> their heart is filled with destruction.
> Their throat is an open grave;
> with their tongue they speak deceit.
> 10Declare them guilty, O God!
> Let their intrigues be their downfall.
> Banish them for their many sins,
> for they have rebelled against you.

Praising Tongues

> 11But let all who take refuge in you be glad;
> let them ever sing for joy.
> Spread your protection over them.
> that those who love your name may rejoice in you.
> 12For surely, O LORD, you bless the righteous;
> you surround them with your favor as with a shield.

The wicked use their tongues to destroy their neighbors, but in the end they destroy themselves. God will not leave their sins unpunished if they do not repent. The godly use their tongues to sing to the Lord with joy. Though the godly are cursed by the wicked, they will be blessed by God.

PSALM 6

Do Not Rebuke Me in Your Anger

**For the director of music. With stringed instruments.
According to *sheminith*. A psalm of David.**

The word *sheminith* is related to the Hebrew word for
"eight." It may refer to an eight-stringed instrument or to a
method for tuning a stringed instrument. Perhaps it refers to
the bass voice. The meaning is uncertain.

This psalm is the first of the traditional seven penitential
psalms. The others are Psalms 32, 38, 51, 102, 130 and 143.

Like Psalms 4 and 5, this psalm may be from the time of
Absalom's rebellion. If not, it may be from the time of
Adonijah's conspiracy described in 1 Kings 1. During the
weakness of David's old age his son Adonijah and some of
David's most loyal followers plotted to thwart David's plans
to pass the throne on to Solomon, the successor chosen by
God. This strife in David's family was the result of David's
destruction of Uriah's family by his deeds of adultery and
murder. Although we are uncertain about the time when
Psalm 6 was composed, its threefold theme of personal
weakness, an awareness of sin, and the opposition of enemies seems to fit best with the circumstances surrounding
Adonijah's plot.

1 O LORD, do not rebuke me in your anger
　or discipline me in your wrath.
²Be merciful to me, LORD, for I am faint;
　O LORD, heal me, for my bones are in agony.

³My soul is in anguish.
How long, O LORD, how long?
⁴Turn, O LORD, and deliver me;
save me because of your unfailing love.

⁵No one remembers you when he is dead.
Who praises you from the grave?

⁶I am worn out from groaning;
all night long I flood my bed with weeping
and drench my couch with tears.
⁷My eyes grow weak with sorrow;
they fail because of all my foes.

⁸Away from me, all you who do evil,
for the LORD has heard my weeping.
⁹The LORD has heard my cry for mercy;
the LORD accepts my prayer.
¹⁰All my enemies will be ashamed and dismayed;
they will turn back in sudden disgrace.

David fervently pleads with the Lord to deliver him from anguish of body and soul and from the reproaches of his enemies. His burden is especially heavy because he feels he is being disciplined for his sins. Although David deserves judgment, he asks God to soften his discipline because of his mercy. David's most urgent need is to be at peace with God.

Even in his deepest anguish David bases his plea for forgiveness, healing and deliverance on God's unfailing love. At the time of Adonijah's plot all these blessings were granted to David — David was forgiven, the plot was thwarted, and David lived until the throne was passed on to Solomon.

Regardless of when Psalm 6 was first uttered, the failure of Adonijah's plot provides an example of how this prayer was answered in the life of David.

The statement of verse 5, "No one remembers you when he is dead," has caused problems for some interpreters.

Some critical commentators have argued that this statement proves that the ancient Israelites had not yet developed the belief that believers enter the presence of God in heaven when they die. However, there are numerous statements in the psalms, such as Psalm 16:11; 17:15; and 73:23-26, which reflect the Old Testament believer's confident hope of eternal life. Psalm 6:5 is not a denial of eternal life. It is simply a plea for a longer life so that David can finish his work of passing the throne to Solomon and preparing for the building of the temple.

PSALM 7

The Slandered Saint

Psalms 7-14 are a closely related group. In general they have the same theme as Psalms 3-6, David's affliction at the hands of his enemies.

A *shiggaion* of David, which he sang to the LORD concerning Cush, a Benjamite.

Shiggaion is a rare term that occurs only in this verse and in Habakkuk 3:1 in a different form. Its meaning is uncertain, but it may refer to a sad, emotional song, which is sung with deep feeling.

Although Psalm 7 is not a morning or evening prayer like the psalms which precede it, it is very similar to them in theme. Like the preceding psalms it is a plea for delivery from afflictions imposed by David's enemies.

The reference to Cush the Benjamite is puzzling, since no such person is mentioned in the accounts of David's life in the historical books. Two solutions have been suggested. Cush may be one of the unnamed slanderers mentioned in 1 Samuel 24:9. These men lied about David in order to encourage Saul's efforts to kill David.

Another possible setting for Psalm 7 is supplied by 2 Samuel 16. During Absalom's rebellion Shimei the Benjamite cursed David and falsely accused him of destroying the family of Saul. Cush may be another name for Shimei, or Cush may be a Benjamite who agreed with Shimei, but who is not mentioned in the historical accounts. In either case the basic theme of this psalm is David's indignation over the slanderous attacks of his enemies and a plea to God for justice.

David's Innocence

1 **O LORD my God, I take refuge in you;**
save and deliver me from all who pursue me,
²or they will tear me like a lion
and rip me to pieces with no one to rescue me.

³O LORD my God,
if I have done this and there is guilt on my hands —
⁴if I have done evil to him who is at peace with me
or without cause have robbed my foe —
⁵then let my enemy pursue and overtake me;
let him trample my life to the ground
and make me sleep in the dust. *Selah*

When David asks for God's help on the grounds that he is innocent and righteous, he is not declaring that he is without sin or that he has no guilt before God. He is simply defending himself against the false charges of the Benjamites. David has not harmed Saul's family. On the contrary, he has passed up more than one chance to kill Saul. He has praised the men who buried Saul and Jonathan. He has punished the murderers of Saul's son Ishbosheth. He has befriended Jonathan's son Mephibosheth. David certainly does not deserve the slanderous attacks of Saul's relatives, the Benjamites. Therefore he appeals to God's justice.

David's Appeal for Justice

⁶Arise, O LORD, in your anger;
rise up against the rage of my enemies.
Awake, my God; decree justice.
⁷Let the assembled peoples gather around you.
Rule over them from on high;
⁸let the LORD judge the peoples.
Judge me, O LORD, according to my righteousness,
according to my integrity, O Most High.
⁹O righteous God, who searches minds and hearts,
bring to an end the violence of the wicked
and make the righteous secure.

¹⁰My shield is God Most High,
who saves the upright in heart.
¹¹God is a righteous judge,
a God who expresses his wrath every day.
¹²If he does not relent,
he will sharpen his sword;
he will bend and string his bow.
¹³He has prepared his deadly weapons;
he makes ready his flaming arrows.

God's Judgment against the Wicked

¹⁴He who is pregnant with evil and conceives trouble
gives birth to disillusionment.
¹⁵He who digs a hole and scoops it out
falls into the pit he has made.
¹⁶The trouble he causes recoils on himself;
his violence comes down on his own head.

¹⁷I will give thanks to the LORD because of his righteousness
and will sing praise to the name of the LORD Most High.

David appeals to God's righteous anger against sin. We discussed this anger in connection with Psalm 5:5. Under the righteous rule of God "crime does not pay." Sin does pay it wages, but "the wages of sin is death" (Romans 6:23). The evildoer may seem to escape for a while, but his sins will catch up with him. His plots and lies will backfire on him. If he does not repent, he will not escape God's wrath. On Judgment Day God will repay the persecutors of his people for all the suffering they heaped on believers. Criminals will be repaid for the sufferings they caused their victims. God in heaven hears the cries of the oppressed. He will give them justice.

When we see persecution, violence and oppression in the world, we should pray with David, "Bring to an end the violence of the wicked and make the righteous secure."

PSALM 8

How Majestic Is Your Name

For the director of music. According to *gittith*. A psalm of David.

Gittith is derived from the Hebrew word *gath*, which means "winepress." Gath is also the name of several cities. As a psalm heading, the term *gittith* apparently refers to a musical style or a musical instrument developed in the Philistine city of Gath or to a type of music associated with the grape harvest.

Psalm 8 seems to be out of place in the book because it is so different from the psalms which precede and follow it. However, it forms a fitting contrast to them. It is a Messianic psalm which presents Christ as the second Adam, the perfect man, who is the exact opposite of the slanderers and the evil rulers of Psalms 7, 9, and 10. This psalm also contrasts the simple praise which God receives from children with the arrogant defiance of the wicked described in the surrounding psalms. When we compare Psalm 8 with the psalms which surround it, we see the sharp contrast between the glory for which God created mankind and the depths to which the human race has fallen. The glory the human race lost through the fall into sin can be regained for us only by Christ.

The Glory of God

1 **O LORD, our Lord, how majestic is your name in all the earth! You have set your glory above the heavens.**
2From the lips of children and infants you have ordained praise because of your enemies, to silence the foe and the avenger.

The Lord our God is praised by huge galaxies and by tiny babies. The sun, the moon and the stars testify to the majesty, power and wisdom of God (Psalm 19:1-5; Romans 1:19,20). But their testimony is a testimony without words, a testimony without love. More precious than the testimony of huge galaxies are the simple prayers and songs of a little child. Even infants, who cannot communicate with us, can praise God in ways we do not understand.

Jesus loved children and urged that they be brought to him. In Matthew 21:16 Jesus quotes this psalm as a testimony to the faith little children had in him. After Jesus' entry into Jerusalem on Palm Sunday, the little children continued to sing their hosannas to Jesus in the temple. The religious leaders of Israel were outraged and demanded that Jesus put a stop to these songs. But Jesus refused. When the leaders of Israel, who should have taken the lead in welcoming Jesus, refused to honor him, God gave Jesus the glory he deserved through the lips of children.

Today, when many of the leaders of government, religion and science refuse to give glory to God, God still receives praise from the lips of his children.

The Glory of the Son of Man

3When I consider your heavens, the work of your fingers, the moon and the stars, which you have set in place,

⁴what is man that you are mindful of him,
 the son of man that you care for him?

⁵You made him a little lower than the heavenly beings
 and crowned him with glory and honor.
⁶You made him ruler over the works of your hands;
 you put everything under his feet:
  ⁷all flocks and herds, and the beasts of the field,
  ⁸the birds of the air, and the fish of the sea,
  all that swim the paths of the seas.

⁹O LORD, our Lord, how majestic is your name in all the earth!

For God the work of creating huge galaxies was detailed finger-work, like fine needlepoint. We might think that the creation of mankind was even more trivial, since the whole human race is nothing but a microscopic speck compared to just one of God's stars. Yet God created Adam and Eve to have dominion over the universe. He created the sun, moon and stars to serve them. He created man and woman in his image so that they could be righteous and holy and live in happy fellowship with him. The hundreds of millions of people huddled on the earth are only an insignificant speck in the vast reaches of the universe, yet there is more understanding and comprehension of God in the mind of one child than in millions of stars.

But through the fall into sin mankind's fellowship with God was broken, and their dominion over the universe was diminished. We can still use the intelligence God has given us to gain a partial understanding and control over the world in which we live. But human beings no longer have an uncontested dominion over the earth. The peace which ruled in Eden is gone.

Now animals kill human beings. Human beings kill animals. Human beings slaughter other human beings. We live in

65

a hostile environment. In spite of modern medicine our control of diseases is imperfect. Even the tiniest viruses can kill us. We battle against weeds, pests and diseases, against floods and droughts in order to produce our food from the soil of the earth. We are killed by our own machines and poisoned by our own pollution. Thousands of people perish in earthquakes and other natural disasters. Inevitably the day comes when each of us must return to the ground from which we were created.

Through sin mankind lost the dominion over the earth which God had entrusted to his highest creatures, but God sent Christ as the second Adam, the Son of Man, in order to regain the dominion we had lost and to restore it to us. Psalm 8 is quoted twice in the New Testament as a Messianic prophecy which was fulfilled when Christ came and regained dominion over the world for us. As true God, Christ already had dominion over the whole universe. But when he was conceived by the Holy Ghost and born of the Virgin Mary, he took on a human nature like ours, though without sin. In this state he undertook the work of regaining our lost dominion for us.

During his state of humiliation God "made Jesus a little lower than the heavenly beings." This phrase could also be translated, "You made him a little lower than God," or "You made him lack apart from God for a while." There is a twofold difficulty in determining the proper translation of this phrase. The word which the NIV translates "heavenly beings" usually means "God," but occasionally it refers to the heavenly beings, the angels. The phrase "a little" may refer either to a short time or to a little difference. The quotation of Psalm 8:5 in Hebrews 2:5-9 follows the translation of the Greek version of the Old Testament, which reads, "You made him a little lower than the angels." This New Testament rendering supports the NIV translation of "heavenly beings" in Psalm 8:5.

Actually there is little difference in meaning among these various translations, since all of them point to the lowly appearance of Jesus during his humiliation. During his stay on earth Jesus did not look like God or even like an angel, but like an ordinary man. Psalm 8 was fulfilled throughout Jesus' ministry on earth when he assumed the form of a humble servant. Jesus was "made a little lower than the heavenly beings" when he was helped by angels at the time of his temptation and in Gethsemane (Matthew 4:11, Luke 22:43). Psalm 8 was fulfilled when Jesus' enemies refused to recognize him as God, but instead ridiculed him as a lowly carpenter, and when they mocked him on the cross. Psalm 8 was fulfilled at Calvary when Jesus cried, "My God, my God, why have you forsaken me?"

But Jesus did not stay in this humble condition. When he had finished his work of defeating sin, death and the devil, he ascended to heaven and was seated at the right hand of God. He now has all power in heaven and on earth. He is crowned with honor and glory. Psalm 8:6 is quoted in 1 Corinthians 15:27 as a statement of Christ's rule over all things.

Just as Adam brought death to all people, so Christ, the second Adam, won life for all people. Adam lost the dominion which had been entrusted to him, but Christ is now ruling the world for the benefit of his people. He will share this dominion with them in the new heavens and the new earth. There the peace of Eden will exist once again. Sin made the glorious view of mankind expressed in Psalm 8 untrue, but Christ, the Son of Man, has made it true once again. When we understand this truth, we can repeat the refrain of this psalm with greater appreciation: "O LORD, our Lord, how majestic is your name in all the earth!"

PSALM 9

Psalms 9 and 10 are treated as one psalm by the Septuagint, the Greek translation of the Old Testament. Psalm 10 is one of only two psalms in the collection of Psalms 3 through 41 which do not have a heading. This suggests that the heading of Psalm 9 may be intended to apply to Psalm 10 as well. Psalm 10 is also linked to Psalm 9 by a partial acrostic structure. (See comments in Introduction, p 28.) On the other hand, there is a change of thought at 10:1 which supports treating the two psalms as separate compositions. Psalm 9 is mainly thanksgiving for God's righteous judgment. Psalm 10 is a prayer against the wicked ruler.

We know of no specific occasion in David's life for these psalms. Perhaps they were written near the end of his life in thanks for his many victories over surrounding nations.

Praise for God's Righteous Judgment

For the director of music. To the tune of "The Death of the Son."
A psalm of David.

Opening Praise

1 **I will praise you, O LORD, with all my heart;**
I will tell of all your wonders.
²I will be glad and rejoice in you;
I will sing praise to your name, O Most High.

Judgment against David's Enemies

³My enemies turn back;
they stumble and perish before you.
⁴For you have upheld my right and my cause;
you have sat on your throne, judging righteously.
⁵You have rebuked the nations and destroyed the wicked;
you have blotted out their name for ever and ever.

⁶Endless ruin has overtaken the enemy,
  you have uprooted their cities;
  even the memory of them has perished.

Judgment against the Whole World

⁷The LORD reigns forever;
  he has established his throne for judgment.
⁸He will judge the world in righteousness;
  he will govern the peoples with justice.
⁹The LORD is a refuge for the oppressed,
  a stronghold in times of trouble.
¹⁰Those who know your name will trust in you,
      for you, LORD, have never forsaken those who seek you.

Closing Praise and Final Appeal

¹¹Sing praises to the LORD, enthroned in Zion;
  proclaim among the nations what he has done.
      ¹²For he who avenges blood remembers;
      he does not ignore the cry of the afflicted.

¹³O LORD, see how my enemies persecute me!
  Have mercy and lift me up from the gates of death,
      ¹⁴that I may declare your praises in the gates
      of the Daughter of Zion
      and there rejoice in your salvation.

David begins and ends this section with praise of God as
the just judge who punishes evil. The message of this psalm
is similar to the conclusion of Moses' song in Deuteronomy
32:39-43. Revenge and repayment for sin are not evil when
they are imposed by a just God. On the contrary, they are a
reflection of his holiness which cannot leave sin unpunished.
Even in the New Testament God is portrayed as the righteous judge who avenges his people (Revelation 19:2). " 'It is

mine to avenge; I will repay,' says the Lord" (Romans 12:19).

In verses 3-6 David thanks God for delivering him from the attempts of enemies like the Philistines, Arameans, and Ammonites to destroy Israel. Because temporal judgments such as these defeats of Israel's enemies are warnings and downpayments of the great judgment of the last day, David also praises God for his judgment of the whole world (v 7,8). In conclusion, David praises God for his faithful care of his people (v 10) and for giving his people freedom to worship him (v 14).

The Fate of the Wicked and a Final Appeal

> **15The nations have fallen into the pit they have dug;**
>   **their feet are caught in the net they have hidden.**
> **16The LORD is known by his justice;**
>   **the wicked are ensnared by the work of their hands.**
> *Higgaion. Selah*

> **17The wicked return to the grave,**
>   **all the nations that forget God.**
> **18But the needy will not always be forgotten,**
>   **nor the hope of the afflicted ever perish.**
> **19Arise, O LORD, let not man triumph**
>   **let the nations be judged in your presence.**
> **20Strike them with terror, O LORD;**
>   **let the nations know they are but men.**   *Selah*

The word *Higgaion* may indicate a pause for reflection or a musical interlude.

In this section David defends the fairness of God's judgment against the ungodly. They have brought God's punishment upon themselves by their rebellion against God and by their own treachery (v 15,16).

70

Verses 18 and 20 form a transition to the theme of Psalm 10. It sometimes seems that God has forgotten his people. When this happens, the oppressors grow arrogant. Psalm 10 is a rebuke of such arrogance of the oppressors and an appeal to God to bring it to an end.

PSALM 10

Break the Arm of the Wicked Man
An Opening Appeal for Action

1 Why, O LORD, do you stand far off?
Why do you hide yourself in times of trouble?

A Portrait of the Wicked Man

²In his arrogance the wicked man hunts down the weak,
who are caught in the schemes he devises.
³He boasts of the cravings of his heart;
he blesses the greedy and reviles the LORD.
⁴In his pride the wicked does not seek him;
in all his thoughts there is no room for God.
⁵His ways are always prosperous;
he is haughty and your laws are far from him;
he sneers at all his enemies.
⁶He says to himself, "Nothing will shake me;
I'll always be happy and never have trouble."
⁷His mouth is full of curses and lies and threats;
trouble and evil are under his tongue.
⁸He lies in wait near the villages;
from ambush he murders the innocent,
watching in secret for his victims.
⁹He lies in wait like a lion in cover;
he lies in wait to catch the helpless;
he catches the helpless
and drags them off in his net.

71

¹⁰His victims are crushed, they collapse;
   they fall under his strength.
¹¹He says to himself, "God has forgotten;
      he covers his face and never sees."

David gives a graphic description of the ruthless oppressor. The oppressor shows no mercy to his victims. He is ruthless and heartless (v 2, 8-10). He admires those who are as selfish as he is (v 3). He arrogantly defies God and thinks he can enjoy his unjust gains in security (v 4-6, 11). David therefore appeals to the Lord not to let such an arrogant and blasphemous oppressor escape unpunished.

An Appeal for Divine Justice

¹²Arise, LORD! Lift up your hand, O God.
   Do not forget the helpless.
¹³Why does the wicked man revile God?
   Why does he say to himself,
      "He won't call me to account"?
¹⁴But you, O God, do see trouble and grief;
   you consider it to take it in hand.
   The victim commits himself to you;
   you are the helper of the fatherless.
¹⁵Break the arm of the wicked and evil man;
   call him to account for his wickedness
      that would not be found out.

An Expression of Confidence in Divine Justice

¹⁶The LORD is King for ever and ever;
   the nations will perish from his land.
¹⁷You hear, O LORD, the desire of the afflicted;
   you encourage them,
   and you listen to their cry,
      ¹⁸defending the fatherless and the oppressed,
         in order that man, who is of the earth,
            may terrify no more.

Oppressors have their eyes so fixed on the earth and the treasure and power they are accumulating on earth that they cannot see the divine judgment hanging over their heads. David prays that God will "break the arm," that is, break the power, of the wicked, bring their cruelty to an end, and hold them accountable for all their deeds. Tyrants, dictators, and empire builders will answer to God for the misery they spread both among their own subjects and among the nations they attack. Criminals will not escape the justice of God, even if they escape earthly justice on a technicality. Wealthy oppressors who exploit their workers and underpay them will be paid back in full by God. Persecutors and false teachers who oppress the church will receive the punishment they have coming. David assures God's people, "The Lord is still on his throne. He watches over the weak. Though his righteous judgments delay for a while, they are sure to come. Be patient and you will see justice triumph in the end."

PSALM 11

Psalms 11-14 are similar in theme to Psalms 3 to 7. David again reminds the Lord of the wickedness of his enemies and and pleads for deliverance. He also encourages his own followers just as he did in Psalm 4.

Faith, Not Flight

For the director of music. Of David.

The Fear of the Fainthearted

1 **In the LORD I take refuge.**
How then can you say to me:
    "Flee like a bird to your mountain.
    ²For look, the wicked bend their bows;
    they set their arrows against the strings
            to shoot from the shadows at the upright in heart.

> ³**When the foundations are being destroyed,**
>   **what can the righteous do?"**

In this psalm David rebukes the faint-hearted among his followers. They are telling David, "Our enemies are too strong. We might as well give up and flee. Fly away like a bird and be safe." This psalm may be from the time of Saul's persecution of David or of Absalom's rebellion. To the fears of his friends David responds, "I take refuge in the Lord. How can you say that our enemies are too strong and that we should give up?" During Saul's persecutions and during Absalom's rebellion David did have to flee to preserve his life and the lives of his friends, but he did not despair or lose hope in the Lord. At times during his flight from Saul David's faith faltered, as it did when he allied himself with the Philistines, but he always regained his confidence in the Lord.

Today many people are repeating the despairing question of David's friends, "If the foundations of faith and morality are being destroyed, what can the righteous do?" Today we see the visible church abandoning even basic doctrines of God's word. We see the standards of morality and family life, which form the basis of society, crumbling. When the foundations are being destroyed, what can the righteous do? David answers this question in the remaining verses of this psalm.

David's Answer

> ⁴**The LORD is in his holy temple;**
>   **the LORD is on his heavenly throne.**
>   **He observes the sons of men;**
>   **his eyes examine them.**
> ⁵**The LORD examines the righteous,**
>   **but the wicked and those who love violence his soul hates.**

⁶ On the wicked he will rain fiery coals and burning sulfur;
   a scorching wind will be their lot.
⁷ For the LORD is righteous, he loves justice;
   upright men will see his face.

Although it may sometimes seem that the wicked are prospering in their wickedness, God is still ruling in the heavens. Nothing escapes his detection. He sees the deeds of the ungodly, and he will punish them fully in due time. The Lord hates evil and loves righteousness. When he comes in judgment, he will punish every sin of the unbeliever. But those who are righteous through Christ will dwell with God in eternal happiness.

Even when the foundations of society are being undermined, the assurance of Isaiah remains true, "[The Lord] will be the sure foundation for your times" (Isaiah 33:6). Even when wickedness and falsehood flourish, "God's solid foundation stands firm, sealed with this inscription: 'The Lord knows those who are his,' and 'Everyone who confesses the name of the Lord must turn away from wickedness" (2 Timothy 2:19).

PSALM 12

Proud Words vs. Pure Words

**For the director of music. According to sheminith.
A psalm of David.**

Sheminith is derived from the Hebrew word for "eight" and may refer to an eight-stringed instrument or to the scale used for tuning the instrument. It may refer to the bass voice. The heading of Psalm 6 has this same instruction.

In opening verses of this psalm David pleads with the Lord to punish the proud liars who are attacking God's word.

1 Help, LORD, for the godly are no more;
the faithful have vanished from among men.
[2] Everyone lies to his neighbor;
their flattering lips speak with deception.
[3] May the LORD cut off all flattering lips
[4] and every boastful tongue that says,
"We will triumph with our tongues;
we own our lips — who is our master?"

In the second section of this psalm the Lord responds to
David's plea with the assurance that he will indeed arise and
defend his people who stand for the truth. God's pure word
is the antidote to the poisonous words of false teachers and
promoters of immorality.

[5] "Because of the oppression of the weak
and the groaning of the needy,
I will now arise," says the LORD.
"I will protect them from those who malign them."
[6] And the words of the LORD are flawless,
like silver refined in a furnace of clay,
purified seven times.

Finally, David expresses his confidence that the Lord will
protect his people from the lies of the wicked with the truths
of his word, even though the wicked may strut about brag-
ging about their lies.

[7] O LORD, you will keep us safe
and protect us from such people forever.
[8] The wicked freely strut about
when what is vile is honored among men.

Psalm 12 may have been provoked by the lies directed
against David by the followers of Saul or Absalom. This
psalm was especially meaningful to Luther at the time of the

Reformation when he was battling the false teachings of Rome and the slanders Rome directed against him. This text was the basis for Luther's Reformation hymn, "O Lord, Look Down from Heaven, Behold."

This psalm, which strengthened David and Luther in their battles for the truth, can also give us courage to oppose the false teachings, the false philosophies, and the false moral values prevalent in the world.

PSALM 13

How Long, O LORD?
For the director of music. A psalm of David.

Anguished Questions

1 **How long, O LORD? Will you forget me forever?**
How long will you hide your face from me?
²How long must I wrestle with my thoughts
and every day have sorrow in my heart?
How long will my enemy triumph over me?
³Look on me and answer, O LORD my God.
Give light to my eyes,
or I will sleep in death;
⁴my enemy will say, "I have overcome him,"
and my foes will rejoice when I fall.

A Solid Answer

⁵But I trust in your unfailing love;
my heart rejoices in your salvation.
⁶I will sing to the LORD,
for he has been good to me.

Even God's saints sometimes grow impatient under suffering. They earnestly beseech God to deliver them. At times sinful weakness and dissatisfaction are part of their motivation for such pleas. It seems to them that God has forgotten them or is indifferent to their suffering.

David too was sometimes tempted with such feelings. But he did not let them overwhelm him. He remembered God's covenant, his solemn pledge of unfailing love and of salvation. He remembered God's past goodness. These memories renewed his confidence that God's promises would stand. In the end justice would prevail, and all things would work for the good of those who love God.

The cries of David and of all God's saints for deliverance are motivated, not only by self-interest, but also by love for truth and for God's honor. Even the saints in heaven, who rest securely, pray for the triumph of justice and the vindication of God's honor (Revelation 6:10).

When we observe the havoc sin has caused all around us, we should pray eagerly for Christ's return so that everything can be set right once again. With John we pray, "Come, Lord Jesus" (Revelation 22:20).

PSALM 14

The Fool

This condemnation of the folly of the wicked has many links with Psalms 10 through 12. Like them, it describes both the arrogance of the wicked and the ultimate triumph of God's justice.

For the director of music. Of David.

A Description of the Fool

1 The fool says in his heart, "There is no God."
They are corrupt,

> their deeds are vile;
> there is no one who does good.
>
> ²The LORD looks down from heaven on the sons of men
>   to see if there are any who understand,
>   any who seek God.
> ³All have turned aside,
>   they have together become corrupt;
>   there is no one who does good, not even one.

The Fate of the Fool

> ⁴Will evildoers never learn —
>   those who devour my people as men eat bread
>   and who do not call on the LORD?
> ⁵There they are, overwhelmed with dread,
>   for God is present in the company of the righteous.
> ⁶You evildoers frustrate the plans of the poor,
>   but the LORD is their refuge.

Closing Prayer

> ⁷Oh, that salvation for Israel would come out of Zion!
> When the LORD restores the fortunes of his people,
>   let Jacob rejoice and Israel be glad!

By nature we were all fools, no better than the fool described in this psalm. In Romans 3:10-12 Paul uses the words of this psalm as an indictment of the whole sinful human race. These verses prove that no one can ever become righteous in God's sight by observing the law, for all have sinned and come short of the glory of God. But God did not abandon us in our foolishness. By God's grace we have come to faith in Christ Jesus, "who has become for us wisdom from God — that is, our righteousness, holiness and redemption" (1 Corinthians 1:30).

But many still reject this wisdom of God in Christ as foolishness. They scorn God's word and live as if God did not exist. They live as if there were no law of God by which their conduct will be judged. Because they recognize no need for forgiveness, they live as if there were no gospel promises. An arrogant civilization once lived in defiance of God until the flood swept it away. A haughty people built the Tower of Babel in defiance of God until God scattered them. A foolish nation despised God's grace and turned to the Baals until God sent them into captivity in Assyria and Babylon.

But fools never learn. Today the unbelieving human race continues its headlong plunge to destruction, clinging to its folly and despising the wisdom of the gospel, which is its only hope. Ungodly people have learned nothing from the lessons of the past. They repeat the same errors which have brought misery to the human race for thousands of years. They increase their guilt by not only despising the grace of God, but also oppressing and devouring God's people. They hate God's people because the wisdom of God's people is a painful reminder to them of their own folly.

When Christ returns and appears in the midst of his saints, the ungodly will be overwhelmed with dread. But then it will be too late. What greater foolishness can there be than to throw away the eternal life Christ has won for all people? Let us reject such foolishness and cling to Christ, the wisdom of God. Then we will rejoice when salvation comes from God and the Lord restores the fortunes of his people.

Psalm 53 is a near duplicate of Psalm 14. We will discuss the relationship of these two psalms in the commentary on Psalm 53.

PSALM 15

Psalms 15-35 do not differ greatly from the preceding psalms, which dealt with the arrogance of the wicked and the suffering of God's servants, but there is a distinct shift of emphasis. Most of the following psalms place less emphasis on the misdeeds of the wicked and devote their attention primarily to the security and blessing of God's people.

Who May Dwell in Your Sanctuary

Psalm 15 contrasts the blameless saint who walks with God with the fool of Psalm 14. This psalm is a more elaborate version of Hebrews 12:14: "Make every effort . . . to be holy; without holiness no one will see the Lord." Jesus likewise said, "Unless your righteousness surpasses that of the Pharisees and the teachers of the law, you will certainly not enter the kingdom of heaven" (Matthew 5:20).

A psalm of David.

1 LORD, who may dwell in your sanctuary?
Who may live on your holy hill?

2He whose walk is blameless
and who does what is righteous,
who speaks the truth from his heart
3and has no slander on his tongue,
who does his neighbor no wrong
and casts no slur on his fellow man,
4who despises a vile man
but honors those who fear the LORD,
who keeps his oath even when it hurts,
5who lends his money without usury
and does not accept a bribe against the innocent.

He who does these things will never be shaken.

In this psalm David offers a partial description of the life of a child of God. Unlike the wicked who oppress others for their own advantage, God's children strive to love their neighbors as themselves. They do this by speaking well of their neighbors. They keep their promises even when it is to their own disadvantage to do so. They disapprove of evil and honor those who do good. They seek impartial justice. They lend to those in need. God's children want to follow the guidance of Psalm 15 and do good in every way possible. Those who do these things will never be shaken.

This emphasis on good works does not teach salvation by works any more than Christ, Paul, or James teach salvation by works when they stress the necessity of good works in the lives of God's children. In dozens of places Scripture emphasizes that we are saved by grace through faith and not by our own works. This message is especially prominent in Paul's epistles to the Romans and to the Galatians. But all of the writers of Scripture agree that a living faith expresses itself through good works. Our works motivated by Christian love demonstrate the reality of our faith. On Judgment Day Jesus will point to these works of love as evidence of our faith.

Lending money at interest has at times been a matter of controversy among Christians. It has been debated whether verse 5 of this psalm and similar verses in Scripture forbid all receiving of interest or only the receiving of usury, that is, excessive, oppressive interest. Literally, the Hebrew of verse 5 says, "Do not give out your money with a bite." This suggests that this passage is directed against the charging of oppressive interest. Israelites were not to receive any interest from poor neighbors who had to borrow for the necessities of life. Helping a fellow member of God's people was to be an act of charity, not a business deal. See such passages as Exodus 22:25-27 and Deuteronomy 23:19,20.

The same principle applies today. When people have suffered severe hardships or losses and cannot provide the food, shelter and medical care their families need, we should gladly lend or give them money without hope of financial gain. Jesus says, "If you lend to those from whom you expect repayment, what credit is that to you? Even 'sinners' lend to 'sinners,' expecting to be repaid in full. But love your enemies, do good to them, and lend to them without expecting to get anything back" (Luke 6:34,35).

Most loans today are used, not to obtain the necessities of life, but as capital for making profit or for raising one's standard of living. The Bible does not deal specifically with loans of this kind, but they are mentioned without disapproval in one of Jesus' parables (Matthew 25:27). Although we have an obligation to help those in need, we do not have an obligation to give or lend our family's money to other people so that they can use it to make a profit for themselves. In fact, Scripture warns against rash loans to others (Proverbs 6:1-5). On this basis, it is valid to recognize a difference between business loans and charitable loans when we are considering the propriety of receiving interest.

PSALM 16

You Will Not Abandon Me to the Grave

Psalm 16 elaborates on one of the key thoughts of Psalm 15, namely, dwelling with God. This psalm describes the security and eternal life of God's Holy One. This is a Messianic psalm which refers first of all to the resurrection of Christ, by which he conquered death for us. However, we can also use this psalm as our personal prayer, because Christ has won all the blessings of this psalm for us.

A *miktam* of David.

The meaning of *miktam* is uncertain. It may mean "a choice piece" or "an inscribed psalm."

The first verses of this psalm are the Messiah's plea for delivery and his expression of faith and loyalty to God.

1 Keep me safe, O God, for in you I take refuge.

²I said to the LORD, "You are my Lord;
  apart from you I have no good thing."
³As for the saints who are in the land,
    they are the glorious ones in whom is all my delight.
⁴The sorrows of those will increase who run after other gods.
    I will not pour out their libations of blood
    or take up their names on my lips.

In these verses the Messiah expresses his complete dedication to his Father's will and his love for all God's people. He also prays to God for delivery. These attitudes were reflected frequently throughout Jesus' ministry, especially in his prayer in Gethsemane. Though he prayed for deliverance from death, Christ put obedience to his Father's will and his love for God's people ahead of his own desires, and he willingly went to the cross for us.

The terms "running after other gods" and "pouring out their libations of blood" refer to participating in the worship of idols with the hope of receiving blessings from them. Christ rejected such idolatry when he refused Satan's offer of an easy way to glory if he would fall down and worship him.

In the second portion of this psalm Christ praises the Father for delivering him from death into eternal life.

⁵LORD, you have assigned me my portion and my cup;
  you have made my lot secure.
⁶The boundary lines have fallen for me in pleasant places;
  surely I have a delightful inheritance.

⁷I will praise the LORD, who counsels me;
    even at night my heart instructs me.
⁸I have set the LORD always before me.

Because he is at my right hand,
    I will not be shaken.
        ⁹Therefore my heart is glad
        and my tongue rejoices;
        my body also will rest secure,
          ¹⁰because you will not abandon me to the grave,
        nor will you let your Holy One see decay.
¹¹You have made known to me the path of life;
    you will fill me with joy in your presence,
    with eternal pleasures at your right hand.

Verses 7-10 express the confidence which sustained Christ as he approached his death and especially during his struggles on Maundy Thursday night. At the moment of his death Jesus commended his spirit into his Father's hands. His body rested safely in the grave for three days, but God did not abandon him in the grave. On the third day Jesus rose from the dead. He ascended to heaven. Now he rules at the right hand of God.

Because Christ humbled himself and drank the cup of suffering, he was exalted as Savior and Lord, and he now drinks the cup of eternal pleasure and joy. The portion and inheritance which Christ won is an eternal life of joy at the right hand of God in heaven. This heavenly glory of Jesus is described in verses 5, 6, and 11.

All the words of this psalm apply first of all to Christ. Acts 2:25-28 and Acts 13:35 indicate that this psalm could not be merely the prayer of David, because David died and remained in the grave. This psalm was fulfilled only by Christ, who did not remain in the grave, but rose and conquered death.

But because Christ fulfilled the words of this psalm, it became possible for David and for us to make this psalm our own prayer. All of us can apply all of the thoughts of this prayer to ourselves as we seek to follow in Christ's footsteps. We too have a delightful inheritance, because Christ has gone to prepare a place for us. Though we still must pass through physical death, Christ will keep our bodies safe at peaceful rest in the grave until he appears to call them to life again. Then we will enjoy eternal pleasures at his side forever. Because Christ has shown us the path of life, we have a secure inheritance in a pleasant place.

PSALM 17

My Righteous Plea

The final verses of both Psalms 16 and 17 express David's eager anticipation of eternal joy in the presence of God. In this psalm David emphasizes that his plea for help is righteous, since it is based on his faith in the goodness and mercy of the Lord. David gives three reasons for his confidence that the Lord will answer his prayer — God's love, David's faithfulness, and the ungodliness of his enemies.

A Prayer of David.

David's Righteousness

**1 Hear, O LORD, my righteous plea;
listen to my cry.
Give ear to my prayer —
it does not rise from deceitful lips.
²May my vindication come from you;
may your eyes see what is right.**

³Though you probe my heart
and examine me at night,
though you test me,
you will find nothing;
I have resolved that my mouth will not sin.
⁴As for the deeds of men —
by the word of your lips
I have kept myself from the ways of the violent.
⁵My steps have held to your paths;
my feet have not slipped.

In these verses David asks God to examine his plea. He maintains that his plea is just because he has not gone along with the ways of the wicked but has remained faithful to the ways of the Lord. Although David is not without sin, he is a believing child of God. As a member of God's family he can expect that God will defend him against the ruthlessness of the ungodly. Nevertheless, David does not base his hope primarily on his own uprightness, but upon the love and faithfulness of the Lord.

God's Love

⁶I call on you, O God,
for you will answer me;
give ear to me and hear my prayer.
⁷Show the wonder of your great love,
you who save by your right hand
those who take refuge in you from their foes.
⁸Keep me as the apple of your eye;
hide me in the shadow of your wings
⁹from the wicked who assail me,
from my mortal enemies who surround me.

God's very nature is the foundation of David's confidence. God's love for his children and his righteous zeal for his holy law compel him to come to the aid of his people when they are afflicted by their enemies. His love does not permit him to be indifferent to the cries of his people. His justice does not permit him to ignore the crimes of the wicked.

"The apple of the eye" is the pupil of the eye, which is essential to vision and must be carefully protected. God guards his people with the same care with which a person guards his own eyes. He shelters them with the same care with which a mother bird hovers over her babies and protects them.

The Enemies' Ruthlessness

> [10]They close up their callous hearts,
>   and their mouths speak with arrogance.
> [11]They have tracked me down,
>   they now surround me, with eyes alert,
>   to throw me to the ground.
> [12]They are like a lion hungry for prey,
>   like a great lion crouching in cover.
>
> [13]Rise up, O LORD, confront them,
>   bring them down;
>   rescue me from the wicked by your sword.
> [14]O LORD, by your hand save me from such men,
>   from men of this world whose reward is in this life.

Because the wicked show no mercy to others, they will receive no mercy from God. They pursue their victims as relentlessly as animals, who are driven by instinct. They show no compassion to their victims. Therefore God will cast them into eternal punishment. The way of the ruthless may seem rewarding while they are on earth dominating others. They may amass wealth, power and fame, but they will be stripped of it all. In eternity they will have nothing but pain and regret. The final outcome for the children of God is quite different. They will be blessed in time and in eternity.

Closing Confidence

> **You still the hunger of those you cherish;**
> **their sons have plenty,**
> **and they store up wealth for their children.**
> **¹⁵And I — in righteousness I will see your face;**
> **when I awake, I will be satisfied with seeing your likeness.**

God provides for the daily needs of his children. David discusses this provision for earthly needs more fully in Psalm 37. In the Sermon on the Mount Christ assures us, "Do not worry about your life, what you will eat or drink or about your body, what you will wear.... For the pagans run after all these things, and your heavenly Father knows that you need them. But seek first his kingdom and his righteousness, and all these things will be given to you as well" (Matthew 6:25,32,33).

But the greatest blessing God gives his children is the joy of spending eternity dwelling in the presence of God and seeing him as he is. Although the joys of eternity will be many, the presence of God alone would be enough to satisfy us throughout eternity. When we have been purified from sin, we will be able to stand in the presence of the holy God without fear. Though each of us must pass through death, like David we have the confidence that we will awake in God's presence and reign with him for ever and ever.

PSALM 18

Unfailing Kindness to David

For the director of music. Of David the servant of the Lord. He sang to the Lord the words of this song when the Lord delivered him from the hand of all his enemies and from the hand of Saul.

A slightly different version of this psalm appears in 2 Samuel 22, where it is placed immediately before the last words of David. This suggests that David wrote this psalm near the end of his life as a summary of God's acts of deliverance throughout his life. In the last verse of this psalm David expresses his confidence that God's blessings will continue upon his descendants even after he is dead. Because of the length of the psalm and its similarity to several previous psalms the commentary on this psalm will be limited to outlining the basic thoughts and calling attention to notable points and difficulties.

David's Opening Confession of Faith

He said:

1 I love you, O Lord, my strength.

2 The Lord is my rock, my fortress and my deliverer;
my God is my rock, in whom I take refuge.
He is my shield and the horn of my salvation,
my stronghold.
3 I call to the Lord, who is worthy of praise,
and I am saved from my enemies.

In this introduction David declares his love for the God of the covenant and praises the Lord for the great deliverance he has received. Because he is speaking about deliverance during war, David describes the Lord in military terms.

Deliverance from Death

> ⁴The cords of death entangled me;
>   the torrents of destruction overwhelmed me.
> ⁵The cords of the grave coiled around me;
>   the snares of death confronted me.
> ⁶In my distress I called to the LORD;
>   I cried to my God for help.
>   From his temple he heard my voice;
>   my cry came before him, into his ears.

David calls the many dangers he has faced "death traps." Recall how often David barely escaped death when he was being hunted by Saul. Absalom's rebellion nearly cost him his life. In his later years David had more close brushes with death. Read 2 Samuel 21:15-17 for a description of David's narrow escape from death in battle. This may have taken place shortly before he wrote this psalm.

The Greatness of the Deliverance

> ⁷The earth trembled and quaked,
>   and the foundations of the mountains shook;
>   they trembled because he was angry.
> ⁸Smoke rose from his nostrils;
>   consuming fire came from his mouth,
>   burning coals blazed out of it.
> ⁹He parted the heavens and came down;
>   dark clouds were under his feet.
> ¹⁰He mounted the cherubim and flew;
>   he soared on the wings of the wind.
> ¹¹He made darkness his covering,
>   his canopy around him —
>   the dark rain clouds of the sky.

¹²Out of the brightness of his presence clouds advanced,
  with hailstones and bolts of lightning.
¹³The LORD thundered from heaven;
  the voice of the Most High resounded.
¹⁴He shot his arrows and scattered the enemies,
  great bolts of lightning and routed them.
¹⁵The valleys of the sea were exposed
  and the foundations of the earth laid bare at your rebuke,
  O LORD, at the blast of breath from your nostrils.
¹⁶He reached down from on high and took hold of me;
  he drew me out of deep waters.
¹⁷He rescued me from my powerful enemy,
  from my foes, who were too strong for me.
¹⁸They confronted me in the day of my disaster,
  but the LORD was my support.
¹⁹He brought me out into a spacious place;
  he rescued me because he delighted in me.

The language of this section reminds us of two events, God's awesome appearance at Mount Sinai and his return on Judgment Day. Although God occasionally used storms as one of his instruments in defeating Israel's enemies (see Joshua 10:11 and 1 Samuel 7:10), it is likely that David is using figurative language to describe the greatness of God's victories. By using language borrowed from the last day David shows that God's present judgments on his enemies are foreshadowings of the great judgment to come.

David's Uprightness as a Basis for God's Judgment

²⁰The LORD has dealt with me according to my righteousness;
  according to the cleanness of my hands he has rewarded me.
²¹For I have kept the ways of the LORD;
  I have not done evil by turning from my God.
²²All his laws are before me;
  I have not turned away from his decrees.

²³I have been blameless before him
  and have kept myself from sin.
²⁴The LORD has rewarded me according to my righteousness,
  according to the cleanness of my hands in his sight.

²⁵To the faithful you show yourself faithful,
  to the blameless you show yourself blameless,
²⁶to the pure you show yourself pure,
  but to the crooked you show yourself shrewd.
²⁷You save the humble
  but bring low those whose eyes are haughty.

²⁸You, O LORD, keep my lamp burning;
  my God turns my darkness into light.
²⁹With your help I can advance against a troop;
  with my God I can scale a wall.

The opening verses of Psalms 7 and 17 contain claims of righteousness similar to the claim in verses 20 to 24. None of these are intended as arrogant boasts of sinless perfection. David knew his sinfulness and confessed it often. In all of these prayers, however, David is contrasting his faith and godliness with the defiant ungodliness of the enemies who are trying to destroy him and to thwart God's plans.

Verses 25 to 27 set forth the fairness and impartiality of God's judgment as a general principle. People reap what they sow. In verse 26 both of the Hebrew words translated "crooked" and "shrewd" mean "twisted," but the "twisted-ness" of God is quite different from the perversity of the ungodly. The point is that the ungodly cannot outsmart God no matter how clever they think they are.

Verses 28 and 29 apply the general principle of God's justice to David's particular case. Verse 28 is an especially beautiful picture of God's care for his children.

God Equips David for Victory

> [30]As for God, his way is perfect;
> the word of the LORD is flawless.
> He is a shield for all who take refuge in him.
>
> [31]For who is God besides the LORD?
> And who is the Rock except our God?
> [32]It is God who arms me with strength
> and makes my way perfect.
> [33]He makes my feet like the feet of a deer;
> he enables me to stand on the heights.
> [34]He trains my hands for battle;
> my arms can bend a bow of bronze.
> [35]You give me your shield of victory,
> and your right hand sustains me;
> you stoop down to make me great.
> [36]You broaden the path beneath me,
> so that my ankles do not turn.

David declares that God is the one who equips him for war. Today some Christians regard all waging of war as evil. War is indeed one of the greatest curses brought by sin, but at times the good must wage war against the evil to prevent them from accomplishing their evil plans. God equipped David to overcome such evil enemies as Goliath and Absalom in war. David's wars against such enemies were just.

David's Victories

> [37]I pursued my enemies and overtook them;
> I did not turn back till they were destroyed.
> [38]I crushed them so that they could not rise;
> they fell beneath my feet.
> [39]You armed me with strength for battle;
> you made my adversaries bow at my feet.

⁴⁰You made my enemies turn their backs in flight,
and I destroyed my foes.
⁴¹They cried for help, but there was no one to save them —
to the LORD, but he did not answer.
⁴²I beat them as fine as dust borne on the wind;
I poured them out like mud in the streets.
⁴³You have delivered me from the attacks of the people;
you have made me the head of nations;
people I did not know are subject to me.
⁴⁴As soon as they hear me, they obey me;
foreigners cringe before me.
⁴⁵They all lose heart;
they come trembling from their strongholds.

In these verses David describes his military victories in language which is more literal than that of verses 7 to 15.

Closing Words of Faith

⁴⁶The LORD lives!
Praise be to my Rock!
Exalted be God my Savior!
⁴⁷He is the God who avenges me,
who subdues nations under me,
⁴⁸who saves me from my enemies.
You exalted me above my foes;
from violent men you rescued me.
⁴⁹Therefore I will praise you among the nations, O LORD;
I will sing praises to your name.
⁵⁰He gives his king great victories;
he shows unfailing kindness to his anointed,
to David and his descendants forever.

David ends as he began, with confident words of faith. This time, however, he also looks to the future. He is confident that God will give the same victories to his successors on the throne. This confidence received its greatest fulfillment in the rule of Christ over the nations. The final verses of this psalm could also be the words of the exalted Savior, who rules forever as David's son and David's Lord.

PSALM 19

The Glory of God Is Revealed
For the director of music. A psalm of David.

Most of the psalms surrounding Psalm 19 are prayers for deliverance or thanksgiving for deliverance. Psalm 19 is an interlude of praise which momentarily sets aside David's concern with his enemies and directs our attention to the glory of God. The Lord deserves our praise, not only for delivering us from enemies, but simply because of the majesty and glory which are his by his very nature. This glory is revealed by creation, by God's word and by his power in the believer's life.

The Glory of God Revealed by Creation

**1 The heavens declare the glory of God;
the skies proclaim the work of his hands.
²Day after day they pour forth speech;
night after night they display knowledge.
³There is no speech or language
where their voice is not heard.
⁴Their voice goes out into all the earth,
their words to the ends of the world.**

**In the heavens he has pitched a tent for the sun,
⁵which is like a bridegroom coming forth from his pavilion.
like a champion rejoicing to run his course.
⁶It rises at one end of the heavens
and makes its circuit to the other;
nothing is hidden from its heat.**

The beautiful, orderly universe which the Lord created and still maintains gives silent testimony to the power and wisdom of its creator. The majesty and orderliness of the stars are a silent rebuke to all who deny the glory of their creator. The pagan who worships the stars instead of their creator, the astrologer who seeks wisdom from the stars instead of from their creator, and the atheistic evolutionist who worships the order of the cosmos instead of the creator who established that order are all condemned by the silent testimony of the universe and left without excuse (Romans 1:18-24). By night and by day, from one end of the world to the other, the stately procession of the heavenly bodies declares the power and wisdom of their creator. Everyone who has eyes should be able to read this testimony.

Although this testimony of the stars is silent, it reaches every person. Verse three may refer either to the silence or to the universality of this testimony. If we accept the main translation of the NIV given above, verse three declares the universality of the testimony of creation, and it is basically synonymous with the first part of verse four. If we accept the translation of the NIV footnote, "They have no speech; there are no words; no sound is heard from them," verse three testifies to the silence of this testimony and forms a striking contrast with verse four. Even though the stars give no audible sound, their testimony is heard throughout the world. Either translation is grammatically possible, and either makes good sense in the context.

Verses four and five strengthen the psalmist's assertion by emphasizing the most obvious example of the heavenly testimony. We all observe the brilliance and the dependable movement of the sun every day. The sky is called the sun's tent or pavilion, because to us it looks like a blue canopy over our heads. The sun is compared to a groom after his wedding night or to a racer crossing the finish line, in order to emphasize the happiness that attends the sun's life-sustaining reappearance.

As wonderful as the testimony of creation is, it nevertheless is limited. Creation can reveal God the creator, but it cannot reveal God the redeemer. "No eye has seen, no ear has heard, no mind has conceived what God has prepared for those who love him — but God has revealed it to us by his Spirit" (1 Corinthians 2:9,10). To learn the spiritual truths they need in order to be restored to a happy relationship with God, people need a better revelation of God's glory than we see in nature.

The Glory of God Revealed in His Word

⁷The law of the LORD is perfect, reviving the soul.
   The statutes of the LORD are trustworthy, making wise the simple.
 ⁸The precepts of the LORD are right, giving joy to the heart.
   The commands of the LORD are radiant, giving light to the eyes.
 ⁹The fear of the LORD is pure, enduring forever.
   The ordinances of the LORD are sure and altogether righteous.
¹⁰They are more precious than gold, than much pure gold;
   they are sweeter than honey, than honey from the comb.

In a series of balanced statements the psalmist lists six names of God's word, six attributes of that word, and six blessings that word gives to believers. The section concludes with a set of comparisons which illustrates the great value of God's word and the joy it brings.

The device of using a variety of names to praise the greatness of God's word is much more fully developed in Psalm 119 and will be more fully discussed in the commentary on that psalm. "The fear of the LORD" is an unusual name for the word of God since this term normally refers to an attitude the word produces in the believer. This name is apparently a figure of speech which uses the result the word produces as a name for the word itself. The terms "law," "statutes," "precepts," "commands," "fear" and "ordinances" make us think of God's law, in which he commands what we are to do and not to do. However, in the psalms such terms can refer to the whole word of God, even the gospel in which he announces salvation.

The attributes of the word, "perfect," "trustworthy," "right," "radiant," "pure" and "sure," correspond to the attributes of God himself, since he is the true author of his word even when it is delivered through human messengers. These attributes describe both God's law and his gospel, since his whole word is holy and perfect.

The six blessings from the word listed in these verses may come from both the law and the gospel insofar as the believer is concerned. Both the law and gospel are righteous. Both endure forever, although in eternity neither the law nor the gospel will operate in the same way as they do now. Both give light or guidance. Both give joy to the believer, since the believer delights in God's law, insofar as he has been renewed by the Holy Spirit. Both give wisdom to the simple (that is, those who have a childlike faith).

However, these terms apply primarily to the gospel, through which forgiveness and life are offered and delivered to the believer. This is especially true of the first blessing, "reviving the soul." Only the gospel can make a soul dead in sin alive again. Only the gospel can turn a soul headed for hell back to God again. The law can give life only to those who keep it perfectly. It can "turn the soul back to God" only when accepting its rebukes is the first step toward repentance. It also does this when those who are already motivated by the gospel accept its correction. This distinction of God's word as law and gospel will be discussed more fully in the commentary on Psalm 119.

The final verse of this section illustrates the value of the word by comparing it to gold and to honey. Gold can buy things which sustain and enrich earthly life. The word of God has the power to offer and deliver the gift of eternal life. The sweetness of honey gives pleasure, as those of us who have a "sweet tooth" know all too well. However, the pleasure it gives is nothing compared to the sweetness of forgiveness and peace with God.

The Glory of God Revealed in the Believer's Life

> [11]By them is your servant warned;
>   in keeping them there is great reward.
> [12]Who can discern his errors?
>   Forgive my hidden faults.
> [13]Keep your servant also from willful sins;
>   may they not rule over me.
>   Then will I be blameless,
>   innocent of great transgression.
>
> [14]May the words of my mouth
>   and the meditation of my heart
>   be pleasing in your sight,
>   O LORD, my Rock and my Redeemer.

Verse 11 is a transitional verse which could just as easily be placed in the previous section. It looks back to the blessings for the believer which were described in the preceding section, but it also points ahead to the impact of the word in the spiritual life of the believer, which is emphasized in this final section of the psalm. The words of God's law warn the believer against sin and its terrible consequences. The words of the gospel give the rewards which Christ has won to everyone who believes them. God's word also promises that the works of believers will be rewarded, even though these works deserve nothing.

So that he will not lose these blessings, David prays that the Lord will preserve him from sins of every sort. He recognizes that sin is so deeply ingrained in his nature that he often sins without realizing it. He asks God to forgive even those sins which he fails to confess because of his ignorance.

Because of our weakness we too sometimes sin even when we know better and even when we don't want to do it. For these sins too we need forgiveness. But David prays especially for God to preserve him from deliberate, malicious sins, which could destroy his faith and thus rob him of forgiveness. David was guilty of such sins when he committed adultery with Bathsheba and was responsible for the murder of Uriah. Even then the Lord graciously led David back to repentance and faith. We pray that the Lord will preserve us from such sin and that he will graciously restore us if we ever fall victim to them.

We would do well to memorize these words of David and make them our own prayer of confession as we battle against sin. For a deeper understanding of our struggle against sin read Psalms 32 and 51 and Paul's discussion of the topic in Romans 7.

David concludes with a prayer that God will not only forgive his sin, but will create a clean heart in him so that both the words that come out of his mouth and the thoughts that remain in his heart will be pure and pleasing to God. This verse too should be our daily prayer.

PSALM 20

Psalms 20 and 21 form a matched pair, since they are for use before and after battle. These prayers may have been intended especially for use by Israel's army, but they would also be appropriate for the whole nation. They may have been used in public services like the one Jehoshaphat held before his battle with Moab and Ammon recorded in 2 Chronicles 20.

A Prayer for Victory

For the director of music. A psalm of David.

The People's Prayer

1 **May the LORD answer you when you are in distress;**
may the name of the God of Jacob protect you.
²May he send you help from the sanctuary
and grant you support from Zion.
³May he remember all your sacrifices
and accept your burnt offerings. *Selah*
⁴May he give you the desire of your heart
and make all your plans succeed.
⁵We will shout for joy when you are victorious
and will lift up our banners in the name of our God.
May the LORD grant all your requests.

In these verses the people or the priests pray that God will grant victory to their king as he leads them into battle. In verse 3 they point to the king's piety and faithfulness in worship as a basis for their prayer. They promise that they will join the king in praising God when he returns victorious. Strictly speaking, these words are more of a benediction than a prayer, since they are spoken to the king rather than directly to God. However, the spirit and intent is that of prayer, since it is God alone who can provide the blessings promised here.

The King's Response

⁶Now I know that the LORD saves his anointed;
he answers him from his holy heaven
with the saving power of his right hand.

These words appear to be the king's response to the people's benediction. His confidence is bolstered by the support they are giving him through their prayers.

The People's Prayer

> **7Some trust in chariots and some in horses,**
> **but we trust in the name of the LORD our God.**
> **8They are brought to their knees and fall,**
> **but we rise up and stand firm.**
>
> **9O LORD, save the king! Answer us when we call!**

The people or the army reaffirm their faith in God as the army is about to depart for the battle. They conclude their preparation for battle with a final plea for the safety and the triumphant return of their king.

PSALM 21

Thanksgiving for Victory

For the director of music. A psalm of David.

The People Thank the Lord

> **1 O LORD, the king rejoices in your strength.**
> **How great is his joy in the victories you give!**
> **2You have granted him the desire of his heart**
> **and you have not withheld the request of his lips.** *Selah*
> **3You welcomed him with rich blessings**
> **and placed a crown of pure gold on his head.**
> **4He asked you for life, and you gave it to him —**
> **length of days, for ever and ever.**
> **5Through the victories you gave, his glory is great;**
> **you have bestowed on him splendor and majesty.**

⁶Surely you have granted him eternal blessings
and made him glad with the joy of your presence.

⁷For the king trusts in the LORD;
through the unfailing love of the Most High
he will not be shaken.

The people thank the Lord for the blessings he has given to their king. Notice how verse 2 of Psalm 21 echoes verse 4 of Psalm 20. This shows that God has granted the very blessing the people and the king had requested. The rich blessings and the crown of gold which the king receives may refer to booty captured in the battle. See 2 Samuel 12:30 for an example of David's receiving the crown of a conquered king. In verse 6 the people proclaim that the Lord has given the king more than he asked for. Not only has he saved his life in battle. He has assured him of eternal life through faith. In verse 7 the king's piety is again referred to as the source of his confidence, just as it was in Psalm 20:3. This statement of faith is emphasized by its position in the center point of the psalm.

The People Assure the King

⁸Your hand will lay hold on all your enemies;
your right hand will seize your foes.
⁹At the time of your appearing
you will make them like a fiery furnace.
In his wrath the LORD will swallow them up,
and his fire will consume them.
¹⁰You will destroy their descendants from the earth,
their posterity from mankind.
¹¹Though they plot evil against you
and devise wicked schemes,
they cannot succeed;
¹²for you will make them turn their backs
when you aim at them with drawn bow.

The People Praise the Lord

> **¹³Be exalted, O LORD, in your strength;**
> **we will sing and praise your might.**

The people assure the king of a string of future victories for God's anointed. Although these words can be applied to the victories of the kings of Judah, they are especially fitting when applied to Christ, David's greatest son. These words will be fulfilled in the fullest sense on Judgment Day when Christ accomplishes the final defeat of all the enemies of God's people.

After encouraging the king, the people turn once more to the Lord with a final word of praise for the victories he gives.

PSALM 22

Why Have You Forsaken Me?

For the director of music. To [the tune of] "The Doe of the Morning."
A psalm of David.

This psalm is one of the most important of all psalms. No psalm is quoted more frequently in the New Testament. This psalm rises above the surrounding psalms, which describe primarily the sufferings and triumphs of David, in order to give us a graphic picture of the suffering and triumph of the Messiah. The first half of the psalm portrays the humiliation and suffering of the Messiah. Only Isaiah 53 equals this psalm as an Old Testament description of the Savior's suffering. The second half describes the Messiah's exaltation.

PART ONE: THE MESSIAH'S SUFFERING

The Messiah's Plea

1 **My God, my God, why have you forsaken me?**
   Why are you so far from saving me,
so far from the words of my groaning?
²O my God, I cry out by day, but you do not answer,
   by night, and am not silent.

Jesus used these words as his own prayer on the cross
(Matthew 27:46). To the scoffers standing around the cross
it seemed that the Father had abandoned his Son. In Gethsemane Jesus had fervently prayed, "Take this cup from
me." Now it seemed that this prayer was not being answered.
Certainly God had the power to deliver his own Son. Why
wasn't he doing it? In the next sections of this prayer the
Messiah struggles to answer this question.

God's Help in the Past

³Yet you are enthroned as the Holy One;
   you are the praise of Israel.
⁴In you our fathers put their trust;
   they trusted and you delivered them.
⁵They cried to you and were saved;
   in you they trusted and were not disappointed.

The apparent failure of God to deliver his Son could not
be due to injustice or weakness on God's part. The Lord was
enthroned in heaven as the holy God, who received the
praise of Israel. Time after time he had delivered his people
when they called to him in distress. God's ability to help is
beyond question. Yet the crowd could see no evidence that
God would deliver Jesus from the cross.

God's Apparent Unconcern

> **⁶But I am a worm and not a man,**
> **scorned by men and despised by the people.**
> **⁷All who see me mock me;**
> **they hurl insults, shaking their heads:**
> **⁸"He trusts in the LORD; let the LORD rescue him.**
> **Let him deliver him, since he delights in him."**

God seems to be absent. Jesus is scorned like a slimy worm which people crush underfoot. In their mockery Jesus' enemies draw the logical conclusion, "God could rescue him if he wanted to. God isn't rescuing him. Therefore God does not want him." Could that be true?

The Mutual Love of Father and Son

> **⁹Yet you brought me out of the womb;**
> **you made me trust in you even at my mother's breast.**
> **¹⁰From birth I was cast upon you;**
> **from my mother's womb you have been my God.**
>
> **¹¹Do not be far from me, for trouble is near**
> **and there is no one to help.**

Jesus knows that the taunts of the enemy cannot be true. From the beginning of Jesus' life the Father had declared his love for him. Angels announced his future glory to Mary and Joseph even before he was born. On the day he was born angels announced the peace he would bring. The Father himself had declared his pleasure in him at his baptism and transfiguration.

In the same way Jesus had shown his love and obedience to his Father. Already as a twelve-year-old boy he had placed his Father's business first. This loyalty had continued throughout his life. Jesus would not renounce it now.

Notice how this section alternates between troubled questions (vv 1,2,6-8) and expressions of confidence which answer those questions (vv 3-5,9,10). It concludes with a word of faith (v 11) which calls for deliverance only God can give. Jesus stands alone, abandoned by his disciples. His enemies are powerful and vicious. Only God can deliver him now.

The Power of His Enemies

> ¹²Many bulls surround me;
>   strong bulls of Bashan encircle me.
> ¹³Roaring lions tearing their prey
>   open their mouths wide against me.
> ¹⁴I am poured out like water,
>   and all my bones are out of joint.
>   My heart has turned to wax;
>   it has melted away within me.
> ¹⁵My strength is dried up like a potsherd,
>   and my tongue sticks to the roof of my mouth;
>   you lay me in the dust of death.
> ¹⁶Dogs have surrounded me;
>   a band of evil men has encircled me,
>   they have pierced my hands and my feet.
> ¹⁷I can count all my bones;
>   people stare and gloat over me.
> ¹⁸They divide my garments among them
>   and cast lots for my clothing.

The mercilessness of Jesus' enemies is graphically portrayed by comparing them to vicious animals — bulls, lions and dogs. When they beat him, they are like bulls trampling a little child. When they tear his flesh, they are like lions tearing their prey. When he is on the cross, they surround him like a pack of snarling dogs.

The intensity of Jesus' suffering is described in a number of graphic pictures. He is poured out like water. He is dried up like a broken pot. These pictures and the others vividly portray the suffering which led him to cry, "I thirst." The statement, "I can count all my bones," apparently refers to the way in which he was stripped of his clothing and displayed on the cross.

In its translation of v 16, "they have pierced my hands and my feet," the NIV is suggesting a correction of an apparent copying mistake in the standard Hebrew text, which reads, "like the lion my hands and my feet." Although these translations are very different in English, the corresponding Hebrew words are very similar in appearance. A number of Greek and Hebrew manuscripts support the reading preferred by the NIV. This may be one of the comparatively rare cases in which other manuscripts preserve a better reading than the standard Hebrew text. If we accept the NIV translation, the verse is a striking description of the process of crucifixion.

The prophecy of the casting of lots for Jesus' clothes is one of the most amazing Messianic prophecies. Its fulfillment is recorded in Matthew 27:35 and John 19:24.

Though his enemies are strong and vicious, Christ is not left without help.

The Greater Power of God

> **19But you, O LORD, be not far off;**
> **O my Strength, come quickly to help me.**
> **20Deliver my life from the sword,**
> **my precious life from the power of the dogs.**
> **21Rescue me from the mouth of the lions;**
> **save me from the horns of the wild oxen.**

Although the power of the enemies is great, the power of the Lord is greater. This section of the psalm concludes with the confident prayer that the Lord will deliver Christ from the enemies.

Notice how the names of the enemies are repeated here opposite the order in which they were introduced in the preceding section.

PART TWO: THE MESSIAH'S GLORY

The Messiah's Vow

²²**I will declare your name to my brothers;**
in the congregation I will praise you.

²³**You who fear the L**ord**, praise him!**
All you descendants of Jacob, honor him!
Revere him, all you descendants of Israel!
²⁴**For he has not despised or disdained**
the suffering of the afflicted one;
he has not hidden his face from him
but has listened to his cry for help.

²⁵**From you comes the theme of my praise in the great assembly;**
before those who fear you will I fulfill my vows.

Finally we get the answer to the opening question, "Why have you forsaken me?" The Father let the Son die for the sins of his people so that he could give them eternal blessings. Christ suffered as one who was separated from God by the curse of our sins. He was forsaken by the Father as he hung dying on the cross. As we learned in Psalm 16, however, the Father did not abandon him to the grave, but raised him to life and glory. Now he is seated at the right hand of the Father in power and majesty.

In the opening and the closing verses of this section the Messiah promises to share the good news of his triumph with the assembly of God's children. This promise is fulfilled when Jesus proclaims the gospel in the church. As true man, Jesus became our brother and died for us. Through the gospel he gathers us together as the children of God who will share his glory. Read Hebrews 2:10-18 as a further explanation of the fulfillment of this prophecy.

In the middle verses of this section the Messiah invites believers to join him in praising God because the Messiah's deliverance is also their deliverance.

The Glory of Messiah's Kingdom

26The poor will eat and be satisfied;
  they who seek the Lord will praise him —
  may your hearts live forever!
27All the ends of the earth will remember and turn to the LORD,
  and all the families of the nations will bow down before him,
28for dominion belongs to the LORD
  and he rules over the nations.
29All the rich of the earth will feast and worship;
  all who go down to the dust will kneel before him —
  those who cannot keep themselves alive.
30Posterity will serve him;
  future generations will be told about the LORD.
31They will proclaim his righteousness to a people yet unborn —
  for he has done it.

Jesus' kingdom will be spread throughout the earth and through every generation till the end of time. Since he is the Savior of all people, both the rich and the poor will receive the blessings of his kingdom if they turn to him in faith. All who believe in him will be fed at the feast of eternal life. Although his enemies thought that Jesus was abandoned by God, in the end they will see the glory of his kingdom, but they will never enter it.

111

PSALM 23

Psalm 23 is the introduction of a group of psalms (23-28) which share many common themes. All of them deal in some way with God's protective shepherding of his people.

My Shepherd

This is the most familiar and best loved of the psalms. It describes God's loving care for his people in terms borrowed from the work of a shepherd. This picture was especially meaningful for David because of his own experience as a shepherd. There are many other Old Testament passages which describe God as the shepherd of Israel. Two of the most important are Isaiah 40:11 and Ezekiel 34:11-16. The meaning of this psalm is enriched for Christians by the New Testament references to Christ as their Good Shepherd. Read John 10:1-18 for the fullest development of this theme.

The Shepherd Provides for His People

A psalm of David.

1 **The LORD is my shepherd,**
I shall not be in want.
²He makes me lie down in green pastures,
he leads me beside quiet waters,
³he restores my soul.
He guides me in paths of righteousness
for his name's sake.

As a good shepherd the Lord guides his sheep, he feeds his sheep, and he gives them rest. He leads them to his word, where they find nourishment and rest for their souls. He guides them in the paths of righteousness, which lead to eternal life. These paths of gospel righteousness are not our own righteousness and good works, but the way to eternal life opened by Christ's righteousness. The Good Shepherd also guides us in paths of righteousness when he gives us the guidance and strength to live Christian lives which are pleasing to him.

Our Good Shepherd nourishes and refreshes our bodies with wholesome food and refreshing drink, but the green pastures and quiet waters in this passage are the truths of the gospel which give spiritual life and peace to our souls. The comparison of God's word to food and drink occurs in all parts of Scripture. Christ himself can also be called food and drink because he is the content of the gospel. Some of the most important examples of such passages are Isaiah 55:1,2, John 4:14 and John 6:32-59.

The Good Shepherd gives his people rest when he delivers them from the burden of sin and from futile efforts to save themselves by their own works. He says, "Come to me, all you who are weary and burdened, and I will give you rest" (Matthew 11:28). His word revives their souls whenever the assurance of forgiveness brings peace and joy to their hearts.

The Shepherd Protects His People

⁴Even though I walk through the valley of the shadow of death,
I will fear no evil,
for you are with me;
your rod and your staff, they comfort me.

A good shepherd does more than feed his sheep. He also protects them from wild animals and rustlers. The "valley of the shadow of death" may also be translated "the darkest valley." This verse may, therefore, refer to all the dangers a Christian faces, not only death. It may refer to every kind of protection God gives us, but it refers above all to deliverance from Satan, sin and eternal death.

The Shepherd King Provides for His People and Protects Them

⁵You prepare a table before me in the presence of my enemies.
 You anoint my head with oil;
 my cup overflows.
⁶Surely goodness and love will follow me all the days of my life,
 and I will dwell in the house of the LORD forever.

In this section the picture used to illustrate God's care for his people shifts from the more figurative picture of a shepherd to the more literal picture of a king. This is an easy transition because ancient Near Eastern kings were often called the shepherds of their people. A king invited his most honored associates to live in his palace. Such a king spread out rich banquet tables at which the members of his court could feast. His guests were anointed with oil as a symbol of the honor and joy of being in the royal court.

All of these scenes were common in royal courts of the ancient Near East, but in this psalm the palace is heaven, and the feasting and celebrating represent the joys of eternal life. In heaven we will feast in safety forever because we will be secure from Satan and all our enemies. No one will be able to deprive us of the joys of eternal life, which can never be interrupted or lost. There we will dwell in the presence of our Good Shepherd forever.

PSALM 24

The King of Glory

Like Psalm 23, this psalm describes the glory of Messiah's kingdom and the blessings of those who dwell there. Some commentators suggest that David wrote this psalm when the ark of the covenant was brought to Jerusalem, but there is nothing in the account of that event to connect this psalm with that memorable occasion. This psalm surely points to an event much greater than the arrival of the ark in Zion. It is fulfilled in the coming of Christ to rule.

He Owns the Whole World

Of David. A psalm.

1 **The earth is the LORD's, and everything in it,**
the world, and all who live in it;
²for he founded it upon the seas
and established it upon the waters.

The whole world belongs to Jesus, since he shares the work of creation and preservation with the Father. When this world strayed away from God in sin, Jesus returned God's flock to the fold through his work as Redeemer.

He Is Served by a Holy People

³Who may ascend the hill of the LORD?
Who may stand in his holy place?

⁴He who has clean hands and a pure heart,
who does not lift up his soul to an idol
or swear by what is false.

⁵He will receive blessing from the LORD
and vindication from God his Savior.
⁶Such is the generation of those who seek him,
who seek your face, O God of Jacob. *Selah*

The question and answer of verses 3 and 4 are similar to those in Psalm 15, which describe the person who can dwell in God's presence. Review that psalm for a further discussion of the purity of God's people. Verses 5 and 6 describe the sure blessings of those who follow the paths of righteousness and dwell in the presence of the Lord.

He Comes in Glory

> **⁷Lift up your heads, O you gates;**
> **be lifted up, you ancient doors,**
> > **that the King of glory may come in.**
>
> **⁸Who is this King of glory?**
> **The LORD strong and mighty,**
> **the LORD mighty in battle.**
>
> **⁹Lift up your heads, O you gates;**
> **lift them up, you ancient doors,**
> > **that the King of glory may come in.**
>
> **¹⁰Who is he, this King of glory?**
> **The LORD Almighty — he is the King of glory.** *Selah*

Jesus is called the King of glory because he is true God and because he has defeated all the enemies of God's people. He came in glory when he entered the world to die for our sins, but his glory was concealed, except to the eyes of faith. Many of the people of Israel did not recognize Christ's glory when he came, and they refused to welcome him. When Jesus entered the gates of Jerusalem on Palm Sunday, he received a royal welcome, but it was superficial and short-lived — yet he will not be deprived of the honor due him.

The repetition of both the invitation to welcome the King and the question and the answer which identify the King emphasize the glory of the King and our duty to honor him. When he urges the gates of Jerusalem to open wide so that the King may enter, the psalmist is really inviting all of God's people to welcome their King with joy when he comes.

Jesus comes in glory now through the gospel, and we welcome him with joy when we receive that word in faith. Jesus' glory will be more openly displayed when he comes to judge the world. When Jesus returns, the angels will gather all believers so that all of us can welcome him (1 Thessalonians 4:14). When Jesus returns in glory, he will receive from his people a royal welcome which will last forever.

These verses form the basis of the familiar Advent hymn, "Lift Up Your Heads, Ye Mighty Gates." Read that hymn as a further meditation on the meaning of this psalm.

PSALM 25

Show Me Your Ways

This psalm is an irregular acrostic (an alphabetic psalm). It is an excellent daily prayer. Although the contents of the four stanzas of the psalm overlap, each stanza does have a distinct emphasis. The first and last stanzas, which look outward, deal with the psalmist's enemies and afflictions. The middle two stanzas, which look inward, deal with the psalmist's sins and his repentance.

A Prayer for Protection

Of David.

1 **To you, O LORD, I lift up my soul;**
²in you I trust, O my God.
Do not let me be put to shame,
nor let my enemies triumph over me.
³No one whose hope is in you will ever be put to shame,
but they will be put to shame who are treacherous
without excuse.

These verses are very similar to the many prayers for protection which are typical in this section of Psalms. Note the chiastic (criss-cross) arrangement of verse three. It contrasts the fate of the ungodly and the godly in terms similar to the contrasts of Psalm 1.

A Prayer for Forgiveness

⁴Show me your ways, O LORD,
  teach me your paths;
⁵guide me in your truth and teach me,
      for you are God my Savior,
      and my hope is in you all day long.

⁶Remember, O LORD, your great mercy and love,
      for they are from of old.
⁷Remember not the sins of my youth and my rebellious ways;
  according to your love remember me,
      for you are good, O LORD.

⁸Good and upright is the LORD;
      therefore he instructs sinners in his ways.
⁹He guides the humble in what is right
      and teaches them his way.

¹⁰All the ways of the LORD are loving and faithful
      for those who keep the demands of his covenant.

¹¹For the sake of your name, O LORD,
      forgive my iniquity, though it is great.

The psalmist now turns from the consideration of his enemies to consideration of his own sins. He contrasts his own sinfulness with the goodness of God. This contrast is expressed by the striking opposites: "Remember your mercy," but "Remember not the sins of my youth." He prays for forgiveness and for renewal of his spiritual life, and he bases his plea on the grace and mercy of the Lord.

A Prayer for a Godly Life

> [12]**Who, then, is the man that fears the LORD?**
>
> **He will instruct him in the way chosen for him.**
>
> [13]**He will spend his days in prosperity,**
> **and his descendants will inherit the land.**
>
> [14]**The LORD confides in those who fear him;**
> **he makes his covenant known to them.**

The psalmist prays for guidance in godly living, a theme which was already introduced in the preceding section. A Christian who is sorry for his sins also has the desire to avoid sin and to live a life pleasing to God. Here the psalmist expresses his confidence that the Lord will instruct him so that he will grow in faith and in his dedication to the Lord.

A Second Prayer for Protection

> [15]**My eyes are ever on the LORD,**
> **for only he will release my feet from the snare.**
>
> [16]**Turn to me and be gracious to me,**
> **for I am lonely and afflicted.**
> [17]**The troubles of my heart have multiplied;**
> **free me from my anguish.**
>
> [18]**Look upon my affliction and my distress**
> **and take away all my sins.**
> [19]**See how my enemies have increased**
> **and how fiercely they hate me!**

> ²⁰Guard my life and rescue me;
>> let me not be put to shame,
>>> for I take refuge in you.

> ²¹May integrity and uprightness protect me,
>> because my hope is in you.
> ²²Redeem Israel, O God, from all their troubles!

The psalmist completes the circle of the psalm by returning to his opening theme. This time he adds more detail about his suffering and the injustice of his enemies. To his personal plea he adds a prayer for all Israel.

PSALM 26

Vindicate Me, O LORD

This declaration of innocence is similar to the one in Psalm 7. As in that psalm, David does not boast that he is without sin. He simply states that he has done nothing to deserve the hatred of his enemies. This psalm is linked to Psalms 23, 24 and 27 by its concern for God's dwelling place.

Of David.

1 Vindicate me, O LORD,
>> for I have led a blameless life;
>>> I have trusted in the LORD without wavering.

> ²Test me, O LORD, and try me,
>> examine my heart and my mind;
>>> ³for your love is ever before me,
>>>> and I walk continually in your truth.
>>> ⁴I do not sit with deceitful men,
>>>> nor do I consort with hypocrites;

⁵I abhor the assembly of evildoers
  and refuse to sit with the wicked.
⁶I wash my hands in innocence,
  and go about your altar, O LORD,
⁷proclaiming aloud your praise
  and telling of all your wonderful deeds.
⁸I love the house where you live, O LORD,
  the place where your glory dwells.

⁹Do not take away my soul along with sinners,
 my life with bloodthirsty men,
    ¹⁰in whose hands are wicked schemes,
      whose right hands are full of bribes.

¹¹But I lead a blameless life;
  redeem me and be merciful to me.
¹²My feet stand on level ground;
  in the great assembly I will praise the LORD.

David asks God to test him by examining his heart. If he is found innocent, he expects God to vindicate him by defending him against his enemies. To support his prayer David lists the evidence of his innocence. His faithfulness in worship and his abhorrence of evil men are the two main proofs of his loyalty to God. Since David has separated himself from wicked men in this life (v 5), he is confident that God will separate him from the wicked when they receive judgment in death (vv 9,10).

PSALM 27

The Stronghold of My Life

This psalm continues the themes of the preceding psalm, namely, protection from enemies and dwelling in God's presence. However, in this psalm joy in the presence of God is more prominent than concern with the enemy.

Much of the parallelism of this psalm is more complex than simple synonymous or antithetic parallelism. An attempt has been made to indicate the relationship of the thoughts by the indentation of the lines.

Of David.

Safe in God's Fortress

**1 The LORD is my light and my salvation
   — whom shall I fear?
The LORD is the stronghold of my life
— of whom shall I be afraid?**

**2When evil men advance against me to devour my flesh,
   when my enemies and my foes attack me,
      they will stumble and fall.
3Though an army besiege me,
      my heart will not fear;
   though war break out against me,
      even then will I be confident.**

David begins with a triumphant assertion of God's power in his life. Two great blessings of salvation are joy and security. In the Bible light is often a symbol of joy and happiness. In English too we sometimes speak of a "light" mood. Here the Lord, the source of our joy, is called light. Security is symbolized by calling God a stronghold under whose protection a believer is safe. No army of enemies is strong enough to deprive David of the joy and safety he has in the Lord's presence.

Happy in God's Temple

⁴One thing I ask of the LORD,
  this is what I seek:
    that I may dwell in the house of the LORD
      all the days of my life,
        to gaze upon the beauty of the LORD
        and to seek him in his temple.

⁵For in the day of trouble
    he will keep me safe in his dwelling;
    he will hide me in the shelter of his tabernacle
    and set me high upon a rock.
⁶Then my head will be exalted above the enemies
      who surround me;
  at his tabernacle will I sacrifice with shouts of joy;
  I will sing and make music to the LORD.

⁷Hear my voice when I call, O LORD;
  be merciful to me and answer me.
⁸My heart says to you, "Seek his face!"
  Your face, LORD, I will seek.
⁹Do not hide your face from me,
  do not turn your servant away in anger;
  you have been my helper.
  Do not reject me or forsake me,
      O God my Savior.
¹⁰Though my father and mother forsake me,
    the LORD will receive me.

Although David's enemies are still lurking in the background, David's joy in the presence of the Lord comes to the foreground in this section. His greatest joy comes not from his wealth or his honors, but from the freedom to worship in the Lord's tabernacle. The greatest grief David suffered during his exile was being deprived of this privilege of worship. David's greatest desire is that the Lord will preserve his freedom of worship. Do you suppose that in our country, in which we enjoy so many blessings, many people would list freedom of worship as their greatest blessing, the privilege they value above all others? By the priorities he sets in this prayer David teaches us to put first things first. Let our prayer also be, "One thing I ask of the LORD: that I may dwell in the house of the Lord all the days of my life."

Although David boldly proclaims his commitment to the Lord, he also confesses his sins. He pleads with the Lord not to forsake him, even though he deserves such treatment because of his sins. David emphasizes the greatness of God's love by declaring that it surpasses even the love of parents for their children. Earthly parents sometimes abandon their children, but the heavenly Father could never go back on his covenant and forsake his children.

Walking in God's Path

> [11]Teach me your way, O LORD;
>   lead me in a straight path
>   because of my oppressors.
> [12]Do not turn me over to the desire of my foes,
>   for false witnesses rise up against me,
>   breathing out violence.

At Home in God's Land

> [13]I am still confident of this:
>   I will see the goodness of the LORD
>   in the land of the living.

¹⁴**Wait for the LORD;**
be strong and take heart
and wait for the LORD.

The attacks of David's enemies lead him to make two requests. He asks for further instruction from God's word so that these tribulations will not shake his faith, and he asks for protection from his enemies.

David concludes with an expression of confidence in the Lord's continuing protection and eternal life. Finally, he encourages his fellow believers to join him in waiting patiently for the Lord's help.

Psalm 27 is an excellent prayer in time of adversity or sickness. Reread verses 1,4,5,13 and 14, and keep them in mind as a short prayer you may want to use in times of sickness or danger.

PSALM 28

My Rock

This psalm is connected to Psalm 27 by the references to God as a rock and fortress. It is related to Psalm 26 by its emphasis on separation from the wicked and from the judgment they will experience. The reference to God as a shepherd in the last verse connects this psalm to Psalm 23 and marks Psalms 23-28 as a collection of psalms which share many common themes.

Of David.

Protect Me from the Wicked

1 To you I call, O LORD my Rock;
do not turn a deaf ear to me.
For if you remain silent,
I will be like those who have gone down to the pit.

125

²Hear my cry for mercy
    as I call to you for help,
    as I lift up my hands toward your Most Holy Place.

³Do not drag me away with the wicked,
  with those who do evil,
    who speak cordially with their neighbors
    but harbor malice in their hearts.

As in so many of the psalms in this section, David again prays for deliverance from his enemies. He denounces the hypocrisy of his enemies who pretended to be friends. This suggests Absalom's rebellion as the occasion of this psalm.

Punish the Wicked

⁴Repay them for their deeds and for their evil work;
  repay them for what their hands have done
  and bring back upon them what they deserve.
⁵Since they show no regard for the works of the LORD
  and what his hands have done,
    he will tear them down
    and never build them up again.

David justifies his prayer by pointing out the evil deeds of his enemies. His enemies are God's enemies too, because when they were trying to destroy David, they were opposing the will and promises of God.

Then I Will Praise You

⁶Praise be to the LORD,
    for he has heard my cry for mercy.
⁷The LORD is my strength and my shield;
  my heart trusts in him, and I am helped.
My heart leaps for joy
  and I will give thanks to him in song.

126

⁸The LORD is the strength of his people,
a fortress of salvation for his anointed one.
⁹Save your people and bless your inheritance;
be their shepherd and carry them forever.

After praying to God for his own needs and thanking God for the blessings he has received, David does not forget to pray for the rest of God's people as well. Our prayers, too, should not be self-centered, but should reflect our concern for our fellow Christians.

PSALM 29

The God of Glory Thunders

Psalm 29 is quite different from the psalms which surround it. In the midst of psalms of trouble it stands as an interlude of praise just as Psalms 8 and 19 do. It appears to be the conclusion of the collection made up of Psalms 23-28.

This psalm is a beautifully balanced composition. It begins and ends with a fourfold praise of the Lord. The main body of the psalm is a fourteen-part description of God's power as it is revealed in a thunderstorm. This section refers to the voice of the Lord seven times. One line states the lesson of the psalm, "In his temple all cry, 'Glory!' "

A psalm of David.

1 Ascribe to the LORD, O mighty ones,
ascribe to the LORD glory and strength.
²Ascribe to the LORD the glory due his name;
worship the LORD in the splendor of his holiness.

³The voice of the LORD is over the waters;
the God of glory thunders,
the LORD thunders over the mighty waters.

⁴The voice of the LORD is powerful;
  the voice of the LORD is majestic.
⁵The voice of the LORD breaks the cedars;
    the LORD breaks in pieces the cedars of Lebanon.
  ⁶He makes Lebanon skip like a calf,
    Sirion like a young wild ox.
⁷The voice of the LORD strikes with flashes of lightning.
⁸The voice of the LORD shakes the desert;
  the LORD shakes the Desert of Kadesh.
⁹The voice of the LORD twists the oaks
  and strips the forests bare.

And in his temple all cry, "Glory!"

¹⁰The LORD sits enthroned over the flood;
  the LORD is enthroned as King forever.
¹¹The LORD gives strength to his people;
  the LORD blesses his people with peace.

In this psalm men and angels are admonished to worship the Lord of all creation. He rules the whole world — the sea, the forests, the deserts and the mountains. He rules over the flood of the sea because he enclosed it in boundaries on the third day of creation and returned it to those boundaries after the great flood.

God's power is displayed in the violent power of a thunderstorm, one of the most awesome forces of nature. It was important for the people of Israel to know that the Lord controls the rain and the storms, for they were often tempted to worship Baal, who was the Canaanite god of rain and storms and fertility. The Lord, not Baal, is the god who controls the storms. Unfortunately, Israel had to learn this lesson the hard way at the showdown between Elijah and the prophets of Baal at Mt. Carmel. Because Israel had not learned the lesson of this psalm, the Lord took the rain away from them until they were ready to acknowledge that the rain comes from the Lord, not from Baal.

Lebanon is the region north of Israel in which Mount Hermon, the highest mountain in the area, is located. Sirion and Lebanon are alternate names for this mountain. The Desert of Kadesh is the northern part of the Sinai wilderness south of Israel. Thus the psalm covers the entire homeland of Israel from one end of the country to the other.

"In his temple all cry, 'Glory!' " is the key line of the psalm. This line connects this psalm with the preceding psalms which emphasize the house of God. These words draw the obvious conclusion from the power of God revealed in the storm. All his creatures should stand before him in solemn awe. But believers need not stand before him in dread, for he uses his awesome power to bless his people with peace.

PSALM 30

Both Psalms 30 and 31 are concerned with deliverance from death. Both appear to be psalms written during David's old age, when he was hurrying to hand over the throne to Solomon and to complete preparations for the building of the temple before his own death. Since the principal danger he faced at this time was the conspiracy of Adonijah, the enemies referred to in these psalms may be the plotters who sided with Adonijah.

According to the heading, David submitted Psalm 30 for use at the dedication of the temple. This is surprising, since the psalm contains no obvious references to the temple building or its services. Apparently David wrote it to be used at the dedication of the temple as a prayer of thanks that his life had been lengthened so that he could complete the preparations for the temple, even though he did not live long enough to see it himself.

The opening verses of Psalm 31 are very similar to the opening verses of Psalm 71, another prayer written for old age. Thus it appears that both of these psalms were a result of David's meditation on old age and the approach of death. Psalms 6 and 18 are other psalms from this period of David's life.

You Brought Me Up from the Grave

A psalm. A song. For the dedication of the temple. Of David.

1 I will exalt you, O LORD,
for you lifted me out of the depths
and did not let my enemies gloat over me.

²O LORD my God, I called to you for help
and you healed me.
³O LORD, you brought me up from the grave;
you spared me from going down into the pit.

⁴Sing to the LORD, you saints of his;
praise his holy name.
⁵For his anger lasts only a moment,
but his favor lasts a lifetime;
weeping may remain for a night,
but rejoicing comes in the morning.

⁶When I felt secure, I said,
"I will never be shaken."
⁷O LORD, when you favored me,
you made my mountain stand firm;
but when you hid your face,
I was dismayed.

⁸To you, O LORD, I called;
to the LORD I cried for mercy:

130

Solomon Dedicates the Temple at Jerusalem

⁹"What gain is there in my destruction,
in my going down into the pit?
Will the dust praise you?
Will it proclaim your faithfulness?

¹⁰Here, O LORD, and be merciful to me;
O LORD, be my help."
¹¹You turned my wailing into dancing;
you removed my sackcloth
and clothed me with joy,
  ¹²that my heart may sing to you
  and not be silent.

O LORD my God, I will give you thanks forever.

The circumstances and major themes of this psalm are parallel to those of Psalm 6. Note especially the similarity of Psalm 30:9 and Psalm 6:5. Refer to the commentary on Psalm 6 for a further discussion of these themes. The main difference in Psalm 30 is that it seems more joyful. In Psalm 30 David calls on others to join him in praise. This more joyful tone suggests that Psalm 30 is a sequel to Psalm 6, written when David's joy had become firmer.

PSALM 31

Into Your Hands I Commit My Spirit

For the director of music. A psalm of David.

An Opening Declaration of Confidence

1 In you, O Lord, I have taken refuge;
let me never be put to shame;
deliver me in your righteousness.

²**Turn your ear to me,**
 come quickly to my rescue;
 be my rock of refuge,
 a strong fortress to save me.

³**Since you are my rock and my fortress,**
   for the sake of your name lead and guide me.
⁴**Free me from the trap that is set for me,**
   for you are my refuge.

⁵**Into your hands I commit my spirit;**
 redeem me, O Lord, the God of truth.

⁶**I hate those who cling to worthless idols;**
 I trust in the Lord.

⁷**I will be glad and rejoice in your love,**
   for you saw my affliction
   and knew the anguish of my soul.

⁸**You have not handed me over to the enemy**
 but have set my feet in a spacious place.

Most of the items in this introduction are common to many of the psalms we have studied: a plea for deliverance, a statement of confidence, a rejection of the ungodly, and a promise to praise God. Like Psalm 30, this psalm is a plea for deliverance, but Psalm 30 expresses more hope of escape from death, and Psalm 31 expresses more acceptance of God's will as death approaches. The special feature of this psalm which sets it apart is Jesus' use of the words, "Into your hands I commit my spirit," as his own prayer on the cross (Luke 23:46).

The Prayer for Deliverance

⁹Be merciful to me, O LORD, for I am in distress;
my eyes grow weak with sorrow,
my soul and my body with grief.
¹⁰My life is consumed by anguish
and my years by groaning;
my strength fails because of my affliction,
and my bones grow weak.

¹¹Because of all my enemies,
I am the utter contempt of my neighbors;
I am a dread to my friends —
those who see me on the street flee from me.
¹²I am forgotten by them as though I were dead;
I have become like broken pottery.
¹³For I hear the slander of many;
there is terror on every side;
they conspire against me
and plot to take my life.

¹⁴But I trust in you, O LORD,
I say, "You are my God."
¹⁵My times are in your hands;
deliver me from my enemies
and from those who pursue me.
¹⁶Let your face shine on your servant;
save me in your unfailing love.
¹⁷Let me not be put to shame, O LORD,
for I have cried out to you;

but let the wicked be put to shame
and lie silent in the grave.
¹⁸Let their lying lips be silenced,
for with pride and contempt they speak
arrogantly against the righteous.

Once again David contrasts his faith and innocent suffering with the hypocrisy and arrogance of his enemies. The words, "My times are in your hands," are a beautiful prayer for every Christian when death is near, as well as every day of our lives.

Closing Praise

> ¹⁹How great is your goodness,
>> which you have stored up for those who fear you,
>> which you bestow in the sight of men on those
>>> who take refuge in you.

> ²⁰In the shelter of your presence
>> you hide them from the intrigues of men;
> in your dwelling
>> you keep them safe from accusing tongues.

> ²¹Praise be to the LORD,
>> for he showed his wonderful love to me
>> when I was in a besieged city.
> ²²In my alarm I said, "I am cut off from your sight!"
> Yet you heard my cry for mercy
>> when I called to you for help.

> ²³Love the LORD, all his saints!
> The LORD preserves the faithful,
> but the proud he pays back in full.
> ²⁴Be strong and take heart,
> all you who hope in the LORD.

David bases his hope for relief from his present danger on two facts: the greatness of God's love and the many occasions when God has delivered him in the past. The reference to a besieged city may refer to Saul's attempt to trap him in Keilah (1 Samuel 23:7,8) or to Absalom's plan to besiege him in Mahanaim (2 Samuel 17 & 18). As is his custom, after David has expressed his own faith, he invites all believers to join him in this confidence. May God grant us the faith to pray with like confidence when we face death.

PSALM 32

Blessed Is He Whose Transgressions Are Forgiven

This is one of the traditional seven penitential psalms. It is one of the clearest statements of the doctrines of repentance, justification and forgiveness in the Old Testament. It is closely related to Psalm 51. It appears that this psalm, like Psalm 51, was written to express David's repentance after the prophet Nathan had confronted him with his sins of adultery and murder (2 Samuel 12).

The title *maskil* apparently identifies this as a psalm for teaching and meditation. The aim of this psalm is to teach its readers the wisdom of sincere repentance.

Of David. A *maskil*.

The Joy of Forgiveness

1 **Blessed is he whose transgressions are forgiven,**
whose sins are covered.
²Blessed is the man whose sin the Lord does not count against him

and in whose spirit is no deceit.

These verses deserve special attention for their beautiful proclamation of the doctrine of forgiveness. Paul quotes these verses in Romans 4:6-8 to show that the doctrine of salvation was the same in the Old Testament as it is in the New Testament. There has always been only one way to salvation, forgiveness through faith in Christ. David was forgiven through faith in Christ, not through his own efforts to improve his life or to make up for his sins.

The triple statement of forgiveness emphasizes the joy of the person who has been assured of God's forgiveness. The third statement, "Blessed is the man whose sin the Lord does not count against him," is especially important because it shows that forgiveness is based on a verdict of God, not on a human act or achievement. Justification or forgiveness of sins means that God, the righteous judge, has declared our sins forgiven because Christ has paid for them. Forgiveness of sins is not something we achieve by something we do, but it is a verdict of God based on Christ's work.

The last of the four members of the parallelism shows the necessity of true repentance. Although Christ has paid for the sins of all people and God has declared the sins of the whole world forgiven, only those who receive this promise with sincere repentance and faith benefit from it.

Obtaining the Joy of Forgiveness

3When I kept silent,
      my bones wasted away through my groaning all day long.
    4For day and night your hand was heavy upon me;
      my strength was sapped as in the heat of summer. *Selah*

5Then I acknowledged my sin to you
 and did not cover up my iniquity.
 I said, "I will confess my transgressions to the LORD" —
 and you forgave the guilt of my sin.   *Selah*

6Therefore let everyone who is godly pray to you
      while you may be found;
 surely when the mighty waters rise,
      they will not reach him.

⁷You are my hiding place;
you will protect me from trouble
and surround me with songs of deliverance. *Selah*

In these verses David addresses God. He contrasts his own condition before and after his repentance. During the many months when David tried to hide and excuse his sin, he was miserable. His impenitence excluded him from forgiveness, and his guilt was like a heavy burden pressing him down. When he confessed his sins and received assurance of forgiveness, he received peace and relief.

David invites all who read this psalm to follow him in confessing their sins to the Lord and receiving the peace and comfort which forgiveness brings. No burden is more painful than an awareness of guilt and the impending judgment of a holy God. No joy is greater than confidence of forgiveness and peace with God. When we have sinned, let us come boldly to the throne of grace so that we may find forgiveness and peace in time of need.

Sharing the Joy of Forgiveness

⁸I will instruct you
and teach you in the way you should go;
I will counsel you
and watch over you.

⁹Do not be like the horse or the mule,
which have no understanding
but must be controlled by bit and bridle
or they will not come to you.

¹⁰Many are the woes of the wicked,
but the LORD's unfailing love surrounds
the man who trusts in him.

> ¹¹Rejoice in the LORD and be glad, you righteous;
> sing, all you who are upright in heart!

Although some commentators understand these verses as God's reply to David, it seems best to take them as David's words of encouragement to his readers. David again contrasts the woe of the impenitent with the peace and joy of those who trust in God for forgiveness. He urges us to learn from his example. Don't be as foolish as David was when he covered up his sin and suffered needless anguish. Don't be like a stubborn mule that has to be dragged along by force. Instead, run gladly and boldly to the Lord for forgiveness. This is true wisdom.

PSALM 33

Blessed Is the Nation Whose God Is the Lord

Psalm 32 stresses the deliverance of an individual from sin. Psalm 33 describes the protection of a nation from earthly peril. In other words, Psalm 32 concerns the work of redemption which is described in the Second Article of the Creed. Its companion, Psalm 33, concerns the work of creation and preservation which is described in the First Article of the Creed.

This psalm is one of only four psalms in Book I of Psalms which are not attributed to David. It may have been written to celebrate some special occasion when Israel had experienced deliverance from an enemy or from some disaster.

Introductory Praise

1 Sing joyfully to the LORD, you righteous;
it is fitting for the upright to praise him.
²Praise the LORD with the harp;
make music to him on the ten-stringed lyre.

> [3]Sing to him a new song;
>   play skillfully, and shout for joy.
>   [4]For the word of the LORD is right and
>   true;
>   he is faithful in all he does.
>   [5]The LORD loves righteousness and justice;
>   the earth is full of his unfailing love.

God's people are invited to praise him for his faithfulness, justice and love. Specific expressions of that love are cited in the following sections of the psalm.

God's Love in Creation

> [6]By the word of the LORD were the heavens made,
>   their starry host by the breath of his mouth.
>   [7]He gathers the waters of the sea into jars;
>   he puts the deep into storehouses.
>
> [8]Let all the earth fear the LORD;
>   let all the people of the world revere him.
>   [9]For he spoke, and it came to be;
>   he commanded, and it stood firm.

These verses reaffirm the doctrine of creation taught in Genesis 1 and 2. God created the universe out of nothing, merely by speaking the command. God said, "Let there be," and it came to pass. He arranged the universe and the world in order, and he continues to maintain it to the present day. The jars and storehouses of the sea are symbols of God's control.

Therefore all the people of the earth should give him the honor he deserves as creator. Yet people continue to despise him and even to deny his work as creator. Nations defy his will, but their rebellion will fail.

God's Rule of History

¹⁰The LORD foils the plans of the nations;
  he thwarts the purposes of the peoples.
¹¹But the plans of the LORD stand firm forever,
  the purposes of his heart through all generations.

¹²Blessed is the nation whose God is the LORD,
  the people he chose for his inheritance.

¹³From heaven the LORD looks down and sees all mankind;
¹⁴from his dwelling place he watches all who live on earth —
    ¹⁵he who forms the hearts of all,
    who considers everything they do.

¹⁶No king is saved by the size of his army;
  no warrior escapes by his great strength.
¹⁷A horse is a vain hope for deliverance;
  despite all its great strength it cannot save.

¹⁸But the eyes of the LORD are on those who fear him,
  on those whose hope is in his unfailing love,
    ¹⁹to deliver them from death
    and keep them alive in famine.

God continues to rule in history so that all things work for the good of his people. In the Old Testament, God protected his chosen people Israel, so that when they were faithful to him, they defeated enemies who were much more powerful than they. When the psalmist remembered Pharaoh's army washed up on the shores of the Red Sea, the fallen walls of what had been the fortress of Jericho, and many other great victories, he could well say, "Blessed is the nation whose God is the Lord."

The vain plans of the nations could not destroy Israel or prevent God's promise of the Savior from coming true. The greatness of the armies of Egypt's Pharaoh and Assyria's Sennacherib, the number of their chariots and the speed of their horses could not save them when they stood in defiance of the Lord's will for his chosen people. Despite the smallness of their armies, the Israelites could not be defeated when the Lord stood on their side. The same mighty protection shields God's people today. Although the church has often been persecuted, it still stands, long after the tyrants and empires who opposed it lie in dust.

Today no nation is God's chosen people in the way that Israel, the bearer of the promise of the Savior, was in the Old Testament. Nevertheless, the general truths of this psalm still apply today even for nations. Already in this life, nations usually reap what they sow, just as individuals do. Nations which live in reckless defiance of God's moral standards usually experience the devastating consequences of such disobedience in the deterioration of their society. Empires which have oppressed God's people have fallen at his appointed hour. On the other hand, individuals and peoples who honor the basic moral standards of God's law and who protect the church tend to experience blessing in this life.

Although no nation, including our own, is God's people today in the same sense that Israel was in Old Testament times, we should be concerned that any society that flagrantly despises God's moral standards will eventually reap the bitter fruit of the seed it is sowing. No amount of wealth, no number of nuclear missiles, no degree of advanced technology can deliver a nation from the judgments of God. Human efforts or accomplishments are vain hopes of deliverance. The only hope for sinful people is repentance and faith.

Concluding Prayer

> ²⁰We wait in hope for the LORD;
>   he is our help and our shield.
> ²¹In him our hearts rejoice,
>   for we trust in his holy name.
>
> ²²May your unfailing love rest upon us, O LORD,
>   even as we put our hope in you.

Even though nations and many of the citizens of our land despise God's will, God's children continue to place all of their hope in him.

PSALM 34

Blessed Is the Man Who Takes Refuge in God

**Of David. When he pretended to be insane
before Abimelech, who drove him away, and he left.**

The circumstances which occasioned the writing of this psalm are described in 1 Samuel 21:10-15. In a moment of weakness of faith David, king-elect of God's people, lost his confidence in the Lord's protection against Saul and fled to Israel's enemies, the Philistines. He sought refuge with Achish, king of the Philistine city of Gath. In this heading Achish is called Abimelech, which may be an alternate name or title of his. When David realized that he had foolishly put himself in danger by going to the Philistines for help, he faked insanity to escape from them. Through this experience David learned the truth of this psalm, "Blessed is the man who takes refuge in [the Lord]," not in his own schemes. Psalm 56 is from the same period of David's life and should be read with this psalm.

This is an irregular acrostic psalm. (See introduction, p 28.)

David's Thanks for Deliverance

1 I will extol the LORD at all times;
his praise will always be on my lips.
²My soul will boast in the LORD;

An Invitation to Join David in Praise

let the afflicted hear and rejoice.
³Glorify the LORD with me;
let us exalt his name together.

The Story of David's Deliverance

⁴I sought the LORD, and he answered me;
he delivered me from all my fears.
⁵Those who look to him are radiant;
their faces are never covered with shame.
⁶This poor man called, and the LORD heard him;
he saved him out of all his troubles.
⁷The angel of the LORD encamps around those who fear him,
and he delivers them.

The Application of This Truth to All Believers

⁸Taste and see that the LORD is good;
blessed is the man who takes refuge in him.
⁹Fear the LORD, you his saints,
for those who fear him lack nothing.
¹⁰The lions may grow weak and hungry,
but those who seek the LORD lack no good thing.

¹¹Come, my children, listen to me;
I will teach you the fear of the LORD.

¹²Whoever of you loves life
and desires to see many good days,
¹³keep your tongue from evil
and your lips from speaking lies.

14Turn from evil and do good;
   seek peace and pursue it.

15The eyes of the LORD are on the righteous
   and his ears are attentive to their cry;
16the face of the LORD is against those who do evil,
   to cut off the memory of them from the earth.
17The righteous cry out, and the LORD hears them;
   he delivers them from all their troubles.
18The LORD is close to the brokenhearted
   and saves those who are crushed in spirit.
19A righteous man may have many troubles,
   but the LORD delivers him from them all;
20he protects all his bones,
   not one of them will be broken.

21Evil will slay the wicked;
   the foes of the righteous will be condemned.

22The LORD redeems his servants;
   no one will be condemned who takes refuge in him.

David invites us to learn from his experience so that we always place our trust in the Lord for deliverance from trouble. He also urges us to live day by day in a way which is in harmony with our faith (v 12,13).

This psalm contains a number of assurances of God's care, which you may want to memorize for use in difficult days. Verses 7,8, and 19 are outstanding among them. In the Old Testament "the angel of the LORD" (v 7) sometimes refers to Christ, God's messenger, but here it seems to refer to the created angels who watch over God's people. The expression, "Taste and see," in verse 8 reminds us that God's goodness is something which must be experienced before it can be truly appreciated. Verse 19 reminds us that believers

God Is Near the Afflicted

are not without troubles, but that God delivers them —either by giving them relief, or by giving them patience to endure, or by calling them to himself in heaven. In times of adversity let us take to heart the words of this psalm.

PSALM 35

David's Defender

This psalm may be treated as a summary and review of the many psalms in which David prays for help against his enemies. It therefore serves as a conclusion to the many psalms in the collection of Psalms 15 to 35 which emphasize this theme. Since nearly all the themes of Psalm 35 are discussed in the commentary on other psalms, the comments on this psalm will be limited to a few brief notes indicating the main themes of the psalm.

This psalm begins with an opening prayer in which David asks God to fight against his enemies. This is followed by three petitions in which David gives reasons for his prayer. Each petition concludes with a vow in which David promises to serve the Lord if his prayer is answered.

Opening Prayer to the Lord, Our Warrior

Of David.

**1 Contend, O Lord, with those who contend with me;
fight against those who fight against me.
²Take up shield and buckler;
arise and come to my aid.
³Brandish spear and javelin against those who pursue me.
Say to my soul, "I am your salvation."**

First Petition

**⁴May those who seek my life be disgraced and put to shame;
may those who plot my ruin be turned back in dismay.**

⁵May they be like chaff before the wind,
>with the angel of the LORD driving them away;
⁶may their path be dark and slippery,
>with the angel of the LORD pursuing them.

⁷Since they hid their net for me without cause
and without cause dug a pit for me,
⁸may ruin overtake them by surprise —
may the net they hid entangle them,
may they fall into the pit, to their ruin.

First Vow

⁹Then my soul will rejoice in the LORD
and delight in his salvation.
¹⁰My whole being will exclaim,
>"Who is like you, O LORD?
>You rescue the poor from those too strong for them,
>the poor and needy from those who rob them."

Second Petition

¹¹Ruthless witnesses come forward;
they question me on things I know nothing about.
¹²They repay me evil for good
and leave my soul forlorn.

¹³Yet when they were ill,
>I put on sackcloth
>and humbled myself with fasting.
When my prayers returned to me unanswered,
>¹⁴I went about mourning
>>as though for my friend or brother.
>I bowed my head in grief
>>as though weeping for my mother.
¹⁵But when I stumbled,
>they gathered in glee;
>attackers gathered against me when I was unaware.

They slandered me without ceasing.
¹⁶Like the ungodly they maliciously mocked;
they gnashed their teeth at me.

¹⁷O LORD, how long will you look on?
Rescue my life from their ravages,
my precious life from these lions.

Second Vow

¹⁸I will give you thanks in the great assembly;
among throngs of people I will praise you.

Third Petition

¹⁹Let not those gloat over me
who are my enemies without cause;
let not those who hate me without reason
maliciously wink the eye.
²⁰They do not speak peaceably,
but devise false accusations against
those who live quietly in the land.
²¹They gape at me and say, "Aha! Aha!
With our own eyes we have seen it."

²²O LORD, you have seen this;
be not silent.
Do not be far from me, O LORD.
²³Awake, and rise to my defense!
Contend for me, my God and Lord.
²⁴Vindicate me in your righteousness, O LORD my God;
do not let them gloat over me.
²⁵Do not let them think, "Aha, just what we wanted!"
or say, "We have swallowed him up."
²⁶May all who gloat over my distress
be put to shame and confusion;
may all who exalt themselves over me
be clothed with shame and disgrace.

> ²⁷May those who delight in my vindication
>   shout for joy and gladness;
>   may they always say, "The LORD be exalted,
> who delights in the well-being of his servant."

Third Vow

> ²⁸My tongue will speak of your righteousness
>   and of your praises all day long.

The main emphasis of all three petitions is the same. David contrasts his friendship for his enemies with their shameful betrayal of him. They were his enemies without cause, and they were repaying him evil for good. In this way David's relationship with his enemies was a type of the relationship of Christ with his enemies. This theme of unjustified hatred is treated in many other psalms, notably Psalms 38:19, 69:4, 109:3, and several verses of Psalm 119.

Jesus applied the principle of these psalms to himself in John 15:25. He truly suffered undeserved hatred, since he had shown nothing but love for his enemies. When we suffer undeserved hatred, let us follow the example of David and Christ and entrust our case to the Lord.

PSALM 36

Psalms 15-35 emphasized the blessings and victories of God's people. Psalms 36-41, which conclude Book I of Psalms, return to the theme emphasized in the opening psalms of the book, namely, the psalmist's struggle with enemies and adversity.

Concerning the Sinfulness of the Wicked

David contrasts the arrogant wickedness of the ungodly with the gracious goodness of God. He concludes with a prayer that God will continue to show his love to him and to defend him against the ungodly.

For the director of music. Of David the servant of the LORD.

The Arrogance of the Wicked

1 An oracle is within my heart
concerning the sinfulness of the wicked:

There is no fear of God before his eyes.
²For in his own eyes he flatters himself
too much to detect or hate his sin.
³The words of his mouth are wicked and deceitful;
he has ceased to be wise and to do good.
⁴Even on his bed he plots evil;
he commits himself to a sinful course
and does not reject what is wrong.

David ponders an "oracle" (a divinely revealed truth) about the maliciousness of sinners' rebellion against God. We can understand the seriousness of sin only when we measure it against the standard of God's law. God's law exposes every evil thought, word and deed as an offense against the holy God which deserves eternal punishment from him. No matter how trivial they may seem to us, all sins deserve damnation.

The heart of the problem is the corrupt nature of the sinner. The defiant sinner has no reverence for the majesty of God and no fear of his judgment. "The sinful mind is hostile to God. It does not submit to God's law" (Romans 8:7). The sinner either refuses to admit that his sin is wrong, or he brazenly ignores God's threats of judgment. Out of the sinner's corrupt heart flow evil words and deeds. He not only fails to do good, but he persists in evil in spite of God's clear warnings. Blindly, foolishly he continues down the road to destruction.

Were it not for the grace of God, these verses would be a description of us all. Only God's grace and forgiveness have freed us from the grip sin held on us. These verses remind us of what we were before God called us to faith. They portray the ugliness of the sinful nature that still lurks within us, struggling to regain the power it has lost. These verses sound a call to repentance to every sinner who continues to live in rebellion against God. They speak powerfully to the people of our day who flatter themselves with the delusion that their sinful acts are really not wrong and with the vain hope that they will escape the avenging justice of God.

The Goodness of God

5Your love, O LORD, reaches to the heavens,
  your faithfulness to the skies.
6Your righteousness is like the mighty mountains,
  your justice like the great deep.

O LORD, you preserve both man and beast.
7How priceless is your unfailing love!
Both high and low among men
    find refuge in the shadow of your wings.
8They feast on the abundance of your house;
  you give them drink from your river of delights.
    9For with you is the fountain of life;
    in your light we see light.

How sharply this beautiful description of God's love contrasts with the black picture of human sinfulness which preceded it. High as the heavens, as huge as the mountains, as deep as the sea — these comparisons give only a hint of the greatness of God's love. This love richly provides for all the physical and spiritual needs of the whole human race. These verses point beyond earthly blessings to the new heavens and the new earth where God's people will live in the light of God. They will drink of the waters of life and eat of the tree of life. Read Revelation 22:1-5 for a beautiful elaboration of these verses.

Closing Prayer

> ¹⁰**Continue your love to those who know you,**
> **your righteousness to the upright in heart.**
> ¹¹**May the foot of the proud not come against me,**
> **nor the hand of the wicked drive me away.**
> ¹²**See how the evildoers lie fallen —**
> **thrown down, not able to rise!**

After contrasting God's love with human sinfulness, David prays that God will continue to display his love to his people and to protect them against the wicked. The last verse extends comfort to the godly and a final warning to the wicked.

PSALM 37

Do Not Fret because of Evil Men

Like Psalm 36 this psalm is a study in contrasts. Throughout the psalm the fall of the wicked from prosperity to disaster is contrasted with the renewal of fortunes God's people will experience. They are enduring hardship now, but they will enjoy an eternity of peace. This psalm is very similar to Psalm 73, which warns that we should not be frustrated by the temporary prosperity of the ungodly, for they will come to a disastrous end.

An interesting stylistic feature of this psalm is the acrostic (alphabetic) pattern in which each double verse begins with a successive letter of the Hebrew alphabet until the psalmist has worked his way through the whole alphabet. This pattern is indicated in the paragraphing of the psalm. This acrostic pattern, which requires the psalmist to work through the whole alphabet, results in a psalm which is very exhaustive in its treatment of the theme, which is viewed from many different angles. Since this style results in much repetition of the same basic theme, we will not comment on each verse, but only on the basic message of the psalm. After the introduction of the theme, each section of the psalm gives one solution to the problem of being frustrated by the prosperity of the wicked. These answers are summarized in the paragraph headings.

Of David.

Introduction of the Theme

1 **Do not fret because of evil men
or be envious of those who do wrong;
²for like the grass they will soon wither,
like green plants they will soon die away.**

It is easy for believers to be frustrated when they see the ungodly prospering in spite of their sins. Why do drug pushers and pornographers get rich? If unbelievers can get away with sin, what is the use of being good? This seeming injustice may tempt the believer to say, "I might as well act like the wicked and get what I can for myself." The psalmist warns against this folly by reminding us how temporary the happiness and prosperity of the ungodly are. Even if they manage to escape the consequences of their sins throughout this life, the longest human life is shorter than the life-span of a summer plant in comparison with the eternity of anguish which will follow for the wicked.

This basic theme is woven throughout the psalm, but the psalmist brings in many subpoints and additional arguments. Although the psalm does not have a systematic outline, different sections of the psalm emphasize various reasons why the righteous should not fret because of the wicked.

Trust in God's Goodness

> [3]Trust in the LORD and do good;
> dwell in the land and enjoy safe pasture.
> [4]Delight yourself in the LORD
> and he will give you the desires of your heart.
>
> [5]Commit your way to the LORD;
> trust in him and he will do this:
> [6]He will make your righteousness shine like the dawn,
> the justice of your cause like the noonday sun.
>
> [7]Be still before the LORD and wait patiently for him;
> do not fret when men succeed in their ways,
> when they carry out their wicked schemes.

Before Christians attempt to make sense out of the moral chaos they see in the world around them, they should remind themselves of their basic relationship with God. Since he has demonstrated his goodness and love in so many ways, above all in giving his only Son to be their Savior, they should have confidence in the Lord and should continue to obey him, even when they have trouble understanding the unfairness they see in the world. When you are having trouble making sense out the apparent injustice of life, the first step is to remind yourself of God's unquestionable love.

Consider the Final Destiny of the Wicked

> [8]Refrain from anger and turn from wrath;
> do not fret — it leads only to evil.

155

⁹For evil men will be cut off,
  but those who hope in the LORD will inherit the land.

¹⁰A little while, and the wicked will be no more;
  though you look for them, they will not be found.
¹¹But the meek will inherit the land
  and enjoy great peace.

¹²The wicked plot against the righteous
  and gnash their teeth at them;
¹³but the LORD laughs at the wicked,
  for he knows their day is coming.

¹⁴The wicked draw the sword and bend the bow
  to bring down the poor and needy,
  to slay those whose ways are upright.
¹⁵But their swords will pierce their own hearts,
  and their bows will be broken.

God will punish the ungodly in his own good time. Often the schemes of the wicked backfire on them already in this life. But even if they do not, God will bring the ungodly to judgment in the end. Should we be unhappy if God in his love and mercy is giving the wicked more time for repentance? Should we not rather rejoice in this display of his love and remain confident that he will provide justice in the end?

Verse 11 of this psalm, "The meek will inherit the land [or the earth]" is echoed by Jesus in his third beatitude (Matthew 5:5).

Be Satisfied with God's Blessings

¹⁶Better the little that the righteous have
  than the wealth of many wicked;
¹⁷for the power of the wicked will be broken,
  but the LORD upholds the righteous.

¹⁸The days of the blameless are known to the LORD,
and their inheritance will endure forever.
¹⁹In times of disaster they will not wither;
in days of famine they will enjoy plenty.

²⁰But the wicked will perish:
The LORD's enemies will be like the beauty of the fields,
they will vanish — vanish like smoke.

The godly should remain content with the daily necessities the Lord provides for them. Though the godly may not be as wealthy as many of the wicked seem to be, they should remember that their heavenly Father knows their needs and gives them everything they need. It is better to enjoy the basic things of life which the Lord has enabled us to earn honestly than to live a life of luxury with wealth gained through dishonesty. It is better to be content with the good things the Lord has given us than to be envious of the ill-gotten gains of the wicked.

Continue to Live a Godly Life

²¹The wicked borrow and do not repay,
but the righteous give generously;
²²those the LORD blesses will inherit the land,
but those he curses will be cut off.

²³If the LORD delights in a man's way,
he makes his steps firm;
²⁴though he stumble,
he will not fall,
for the LORD upholds him with his hands.

²⁵I was young and now I am old,
yet I have never seen the righteous forsaken
or their children begging bread.

²⁶They are always generous and lend freely;
   their children will be blessed.

²⁷Turn from evil and do good;
   then you will dwell in the land forever.
²⁸For the LORD loves the just
   and will not forsake his faithful ones.

They will be protected forever,
   but the offspring of the wicked will be cut off;
²⁹the righteous will inherit the land and dwell in it forever.

³⁰The mouth of the righteous man utters wisdom,
   and his tongue speaks what is just.
³¹The law of his God is in his heart;
   his feet do not slip.

The godly not only appreciate what the Lord has given them, but they also share their blessings generously with the needy. They are not like the wicked who selfishly hoard for themselves. Rather, they follow the example of their heavenly Father, who pours out his blessings bountifully on the evil and on the good. Although the believer's faith is tested by the evil he sees in the world, he clings to his way of life, because his heart is strengthened and encouraged by God's word.

Believers are not promised absolute immunity from hardship in verse 25, but throughout this psalm they are assured of the Lord's continued care for them even in adversity.

Review of the Theme

³²The wicked lie in wait for the righteous,
   seeking their very lives;
³³but the LORD will not leave them in their power
   or let them be condemned when brought to trial.

³⁴Wait for the LORD
and keep his way.
He will exalt you to inherit the land;
when the wicked are cut off, you will see it.

³⁵I have seen a wicked and ruthless man flourishing
like a green tree in its native soil,
³⁶but he soon passed away and was no more;
though I looked for him, he could not be found.

³⁷Consider the blameless,
observe the upright;
there is a future for the man of peace.
³⁸But all sinners will be destroyed;
the future of the wicked will be cut off.

³⁹The salvation of the righteous comes from the LORD;
he is their stronghold in time of trouble.
⁴⁰The LORD helps them and delivers them;
he delivers them from the wicked and saves them,
because they take refuge in him.

These closing verses contrast the futures of the godly and the ungodly. When we are distressed by the evil in the world, we are to remember that there is a glorious future for the man of peace, but only an eternity of torment for the ungodly.

PSALM 38

Do Not Rebuke Me in Your Anger

This psalm, the third of the seven penitential psalms, is very similar to Psalm 6, the first penitential psalm. Compare the opening verses of these two psalms. The occasion of this psalm is not specified, but like Psalm 6, it may have been written during the plot of Adonijah recorded in 1 Kings 1. See the commentary on Psalm 6 for further details on this period of David's life.

A psalm of David. A petition.

The words "a petition" could be translated more literally "to bring to remembrance." David is pleading with the Lord to remember his gracious promises to him, to forgive his sins and to deliver him from his enemies.

Opening Plea

1 **O LORD, do not rebuke me in your anger
or discipline me in your wrath.**

Because he is conscious of his sins, most likely of his adultery with Bathsheba and his murder of Uriah, David feels that the adversity he is suffering is an expression of God's wrath. Although it was true that many of David's afflictions came as a result of his sins, these afflictions were not punishments for sins handed out by an unforgiving God, but chastening corrections from a loving Father. Nevertheless, because of the tremendous burden he feels under these afflictions, David asks the Lord to remove them so that he may receive additional assurance of God's love.

The Greatness of David's Burden

**²For your arrows have pierced me,
and your hand has come down upon me.
³Because of your wrath there is no health in my body;
my bones have no soundness because of my sin.
⁴My guilt has overwhelmed me
like a burden too heavy to bear.
⁵My wounds fester and are loathsome
because of my sinful folly.**

⁶I am bowed down and brought very low;
 all day long I go about mourning.
⁷My back is filled with searing pain;
 there is no health in my body.
⁸I am feeble and utterly crushed;
 I groan in anguish of heart.
⁹All my longings lie open before you,
 O Lord; my sighing is not hidden from you.
¹⁰My heart pounds, my strength fails me;
 even the light has gone from my eyes.

¹¹My friends and companions avoid me because of my wounds;
 my neighbors stay far away.
¹²Those who seek my life set their traps;
 those who would harm me talk of my ruin;
 all day long they plot deception.

¹³I am like a deaf man, who cannot hear,
 like a mute, who cannot open his mouth;
¹⁴I have become like a man who does not hear,
 whose mouth can offer no reply.

David feels crushed under three burdens. The first is the physical weakness and pain caused by sickness. This probably refers to David's final sickness near his life's end, but it may refer to some other unknown occasion in his life.

David's second burden is the spiritual anguish he feels because of his sins. It is likely that this refers to pangs of conscience he still felt concerning his sins of murder and adultery years after he had committed them. This anguish became especially sharp when his sons Absalom and Adonijah plotted against him, because David was aware that his own sins had been responsible for the turmoil and unhappiness in his family.

161

The third burden was betrayal by David's friends and relatives, even his own sons. Many people whom David had trusted betrayed the confidence he had placed in them. They treacherously sought to thwart his will and the Lord's by overthrowing his plans to place Solomon on the throne. The fact that two of David's sons went to their destruction in such plots must have made the pain to David especially great.

David's Confidence of Deliverance

> ¹⁵I wait for you, O LORD;
>   you will answer, O Lord my God.
> ¹⁶For I said, "Do not let them gloat
>   or exalt themselves over me when my foot slips."
> ¹⁷For I am about to fall,
>   and my pain is ever with me.
> ¹⁸I confess my iniquity;
>   I am troubled by my sin.
> ¹⁹Many are those who are my vigorous enemies;
>   those who hate me without reason are numerous.
> ²⁰Those who repay my good with evil
>   slander me when I pursue what is good.
>
> ²¹O LORD, do not forsake me;
>   be not far from me, O my God.
> ²²Come quickly to help me, O Lord my Savior.

Although David is still bearing a heavy burden, he has become confident that the Lord will deliver him in due time. He confesses that his sins make him unworthy of deliverance and that his weakness makes him incapable of saving himself. Nevertheless, he remains confident that the Lord will deliver him, for he is being unjustly persecuted only because he obeyed the Lord's command to make Solomon his successor. David's final plea expresses both the intensity of his pain and his continuing trust in God his Savior for deliverance.

This psalm shows us that even true believers may feel crushed by physical pain and spiritual anguish in times of suffering and trial. Such anguish is not necessarily a sign of unbelief. Indeed, those with very sensitive consciences like David's may be most prone to such agonizing self-reflection. If you are ever crushed with such pain in your life, recognize such afflictions as a powerful testimony of the awfulness of sin. Accept even these sufferings as a warning from the Lord, given in love and intended for your good. But, like David, cling to God's promises and pray fervently to him for relief in the time and hour which he knows best.

PSALM 39

Show Me My Life's End

For the director of music. For Jeduthun. A psalm of David.

Jeduthun is the temple musician to whom David entrusted this psalm. He is mentioned in 1 Chronicles 16:41 and 25:1-3.

This psalm is a lament concerning death and the shortness of human life. Psalm 90 is a similar meditation. Even for Christians death is a feared enemy they must overcome. In spite of the fear and anguish thoughts of death bring to him, David maintains his faith. He prays that meditating on the end of his own life will give him a true perspective on time and eternity. Perhaps this psalm was written near the end of David's life, at the same time as Psalm 38.

The Psalmist's Anguish

1 I said, "I will watch my ways
 and keep my tongue from sin;
I will put a muzzle on my mouth
  as long as the wicked are in my presence."

²But when I was silent and still,
  not even saying anything good,
  my anguish increased.
³My heart grew hot within me,
  and as I meditated, the fire burned;
  then I spoke with my tongue:

Thinking about death filled David with fear and distress. He was hesitant to express these thoughts openly, for fear that his enemies might pounce on these feelings as evidence of unbelief. But suppressing his anguish was no solution, because it brought David no relief from his distress. David resolved his conflict by taking his burden to the Lord.

The Shortness of Human Life

⁴"Show me, O LORD, my life's end and the number of my days;
  let me know how fleeting is my life.
⁵You have made my days a mere handbreadth;
  the span of my years is as nothing before you.
  Each man's life is but a breath.   *Selah*
⁶Man is a mere phantom as he goes to and fro:
  He bustles about, but only in vain;
  he heaps up wealth, not knowing who will get it.

The Enduring Goodness of God

⁷"But now, Lord, what do I look for?
  My hope is in you.
⁸Save me from all my transgressions;
  do not make me the scorn of fools.
⁹I was silent;
  I would not open my mouth,
      for you are the one who has done this.
¹⁰Remove your scourge from me;
  I am overcome by the blow of your hand.
¹¹You rebuke and discipline men for their sin;
  you consume their wealth like a moth —
  each man is but a breath.   *Selah*

Since human life is so short, we must put our hope in God alone. David realized that he, like all of us, was deserving of death because of his sins. He recognized death and the fear of death as God's judgments on sin. For this reason David did not lash out against God, but accepted his suffering and the threat of death as divine discipline.

Therefore, in the face of death's threats, David asked for three blessings from God. He asked for his sins to be forgiven so that death would lose its sting. He asked that his enemies, who were also enemies of the gospel promise, not be allowed to triumph as a result of David's death. Finally, he asked to be delivered from the impending threat of death so that he could complete his work of establishing the dynasty of kings from whom Christ would descend. Then he would be ready to die in peace.

Closing Prayer

> 12"Hear my prayer, O LORD,
>   listen to my cry for help;
>   be not deaf to my weeping.
>   For I dwell with you as an alien,
>   a stranger, as all my fathers were.
> 13Look away from me,
>   that I may rejoice again
>   before I depart and am no more.

David's prayer can also be our prayer at times when we are oppressed by fear of death. Such fears are natural even for a Christian. But when they strike us, we do well to express them to the Lord in prayer as David did so that, with his help, we may overcome them. Like David, we must confess, "My hope is in you, Lord."

PSALM 40

For the director of music. Of David. A psalm.

I Desire to Do Your Will

This psalm brings further resolution to the fears of death expressed in Psalm 39, but it goes beyond David's thoughts as he faces death. Verses 6-8 are quoted in the New Testament as an expression of Christ's willing submission to death when he came to be our Savior.

Messiah's Prayer of Thanks

1 **I waited patiently for the LORD;**
he turned to me and heard my cry.
²He lifted me out of the slimy pit,
out of the mud and mire;
he set my feet on a rock
and gave me a firm place to stand.
³He put a new song in my mouth.
a hymn of praise to our God.
Many will see and fear
and put their trust in the LORD.

⁴Blessed is the man who makes the LORD his trust,
who does not look to the proud,
to those who turn aside to false gods.

⁵Many, O LORD my God, are the wonders you have done.
The things you planned for us no one can recount to you;
were I to speak and tell of them,
they would be too many to declare.

In these verses the psalmist expresses thanksgiving for deliverance from death. These words would be a meaningful prayer during any of the many crises when David escaped from death. They would be a beautiful prayer anytime a Christian experiences deliverance from death after an accident or serious illness. However, they are most meaningful as a prayer of the Messiah after his resurrection. When God the Father raised Christ from the pit of death, Jesus sent the "new song" of the gospel throughout the world, so that many would put their trust in the Lord. Of all the many wonders God has done, none is greater than the wonder of salvation accomplished through Jesus' death and resurrection.

Messiah's Willing Sacrifice

> **⁶Sacrifice and offering you did not desire,**
> **but my ears you have pierced;**
> **burnt offerings and sin offerings you did not require.**

> **⁷Then I said, "Here I am, I have come —**
> **it is written about me in the scroll.**
> **⁸I desire to do your will, O my God;**
> **your law is within my heart."**

God had indeed commanded blood sacrifices for sin in the Old Testament ceremonial law. But he had never intended that they should be a substitute for obedience, as Saul had attempted to make them (1 Samuel 15). The sacrifices were not intended to be misused as a way of earning God's favor or of paying for sin as the people of Israel did. Old Testament believers benefited from the sacrifices only through faith in the Savior to whom the sacrifices pointed. Only Christ, the Lamb of God, could offer the real payment for sin. The animal sacrifices only pointed to it. Read Hebrews 10:1-10 as a New Testament statement of this truth.

Verses 6-8 of Psalm 40 are quoted in Hebrews 10:5-7, but if you look at this quotation in Hebrews, you will see one significant difference from the Old Testament text. Where Psalm 40 reads, "My ears you have pierced," Hebrews reads,

"A body you prepared for me." Although these two translations sound quite different, the basic meaning is the same in both cases. Literally translated, the Hebrew of Psalm 40:6 would read, "My ears you have dug out."

Some commentators interpret this as a reference to the ceremony described in Exodus 21:6, in which a person had his ear pierced when he voluntarily became the lifelong servant of his master. It is more likely, however, that this verse refers to two creative acts of God: 1) when he creates a human being with ears that are capable of hearing God's word, and 2) when he "opens the ears" of the believer so that he is willing to obey the word of God that he hears. Either or both of these acts of God are appropriate to this context.

The interpretation, "A body you prepared for me," which Hebrews 10 adopted from the Greek translation of the Old Testament, really includes both of these points. The words, "a body you have prepared," point first of all to the act of incarnation by which Jesus received a true human nature, which included a real human body. When taken together with the following verses, these words also indicate Jesus' obedient fulfillment of the purpose for which he had received a human body, that he might die as our Savior from sin.

Therefore, although the Greek translation of Psalm 40:6 is not a literal translation of the Hebrew text, the writer of Hebrews retained it because it was familiar to his readers and because it accurately reflected the main point of the prophecy: Christ's willing obedience which led him to sacrifice his body on the cross in payment for our sins.

Although many of the thoughts in this psalm would be appropriate to David, only Christ received a body to sacrifice for sin. Only Christ was foretold in the prophetic scroll of Scripture as the Savior who was to come. Only Christ became obedient unto death, even death on the cross. Only Christ prayed in Gethsemane, "Not my will, but your will be done." It is primarily on the basis of these verses, which only Christ could fulfill, that we classify Psalm 40 as one of the most important Messianic psalms.

Messiah's Preaching of Good News

⁹I proclaim righteousness in the great assembly;
I do not seal my lips, as you know, O Lord.
¹⁰I do not hide your righteousness in my heart;
I speak of your faithfulness and salvation.
I do not conceal your love and your truth
from the great assembly.

Like the opening verses of this psalm, these words would be appropriate as the prayer of any child of God. But we can pray these words only because Christ, the risen and ascended Savior, fulfilled them when he sent the gospel throughout the world so that we too would receive it. We now reveal to others the love and truth of God which he has revealed to us.

Messiah's Prayer in Distress

¹¹Do not withhold your mercy from me, O Lord;
may your love and your truth always protect me.
¹²For troubles without number surround me;
my sins have overtaken me, and I cannot see.
They are more than the hairs of my head,
and my heart fails within me.

¹³Be pleased, O Lord, to save me;
O Lord, come quickly to help me.
¹⁴May all who seek to take my life be put to shame and confusion;
may all who desire my ruin be turned back in disgrace.
¹⁵May those who say to me, "Aha! Aha!" be appalled
at their own shame.

> [16]**But may all who seek you rejoice and be glad in you;**
> **may those who love your salvation always say,**
> **"The LORD be exalted!"**
> [17]**Yet I am poor and needy;**
> **may the Lord think of me.**
> **You are my help and my deliverer;**
> **O my God, do not delay.**

Again, there is nothing in this portion of the prayer which would not be appropriate for any believer, but because of the overall Messianic character of the psalm, we understand these words first of all as the prayer of the Messiah during his suffering. In this respect they are parallel to the beginning of Psalm 22. These words may seem out of order at the end of this psalm, since they follow the worldwide preaching of the gospel described in verses 9 and 10. However, it should be noted that, already before his death, Jesus had begun the faithful preaching of the gospel described in those verses. It is only the worldwide spread of this message to us through his apostles which was subsequent to his death and resurrection. Strictly speaking, then, verses 9 and 10 probably foreshadow the worldwide preaching of the gospel which occurred already during Jesus' ministry.

Many see the words of verse 12, "My sins have overtaken me" as an insurmountable obstacle to the Messianic interpretation of this psalm. But this really is no problem when we remember that Scripture describes Jesus as one who was made "to be sin for us" (2 Corinthians 5:21). When he willingly assumed the guilt of our sins, our burden became his, and he bore all the consequences of our sins. He was counted as a sinner so that we could be counted as children of God.

PSALM 41

Even My Friend

This psalm also contains a Messianic prophecy. The psalmist speaks of betrayal by a close friend who shared his bread. This was fulfilled by Judas when he betrayed Jesus. This prophecy seems to be typical, rather than direct, because all the circumstances and statements of the psalm are appropriate to the life of David, and there is nothing in the psalm which is uniquely Messianic.

David experienced this sort of betrayal twice in his life. The first was when his advisor Ahithophel betrayed him and went over to Absalom (2 Samuel 16,17). Like Judas, Ahithophel committed suicide when his plans fell apart.

David experienced a second betrayal when his closest supporter, Joab, who had shared his many battles and campaigns, betrayed him by supporting Adonijah against Solomon (1 Kings 1). Most commentators connect this psalm with Ahithophel, but the reference to sickness and the special closeness of Joab to David may indicate that this psalm belongs to the time of Adonijah's plot, rather than Absalom's. Ahithophel's suicide makes him a more appropriate type of Judas than Joab, but this point is not reflected in this psalm. See 1 Kings 1 and the commentary on Psalms 6 and 38 for more information about the plot of Adonijah.

For the director of music. A psalm of David.

David's Confidence of Deliverance

**1 Blessed is he who has regard for the weak;
the LORD delivers him in times of trouble.
2 The LORD will protect him and preserve his life;
he will bless him in the land
and not surrender him to the desire of his foes.**

³The LORD will sustain him on his sickbed
  and restore him from his bed of illness.
⁴I said, "O LORD, have mercy on me; heal me,
  for I have sinned against you."

Because David has confessed his sins and entrusted his life to the Lord, he is confident of delivery from death and from the conspirators.

The Treachery of the Conspirators

⁵My enemies say of me in malice,
  "When will he die and his name perish?"
⁶Whenever one comes to see me, he speaks falsely,
  while his heart gathers slander;
  then he goes out and spreads it abroad.
⁷All my enemies whisper together against me;
  they imagine the worst for me, saying,
⁸"A vile disease has beset him;
  he will never get up from the place where he lies."
⁹Even my close friend, whom I trusted,
  he who shared my bread, has lifted up his heel against me.

The treachery of the conspirators and their opposition to the Messianic line of Solomon form a further basis for David's confidence that God will deliver him.

Closing Prayer

¹⁰But you, O LORD, have mercy on me;
  raise me up, that I may repay them.
¹¹I know that you are pleased with me,
  for my enemy does not triumph over me.
¹²In my integrity you uphold me
  and set me in your presence forever.

In these verses David repeats his prayer and reaffirms his confidence in the Lord. This confidence extends not only to the preservation and lengthening of his life on earth, but to an eternal presence with the Lord after death.

Closing Doxology

> **¹³Praise be to the LORD, the God of Israel,**
> **from everlasting to everlasting. Amen and Amen.**

This doxology apparently applies not just to this psalm, but to the entire first book of psalms (Psalms 1-41). This forms a fitting conclusion to the whole book, which is concerned with the glorious future of the Davidic kingship, which found its fulfillment in Christ.

BOOK II
PSALMS 42-72

Like Book I, this second division of the Book of Psalms is arranged on the basis of authorship. Although this book ends with the note, "This concludes the prayers of David, son of Jesse," this collection also includes eight psalms by the Sons of Korah, three anonymous psalms, and single psalms by Asaph and Solomon. Perhaps this book originated as a collection of psalms of David and his musicians and was motivated by the building of Solomon's temple.

The book is also arranged partially on the basis of psalm type and subject matter. Psalms 52-55 are *maskil*. Psalms 56-60 are *miktam*. Psalms 52-60 are mostly from the time of David's flight from Saul.

A peculiar characteristic of this book is a preference for the divine name "God" rather than the name "LORD" (the covenant name Jehovah or Yahweh), which is favored in the other divisions of Psalms. Some commentators have suggested that this is due to the later date at which these psalms were collected or to the fact that they were collected in the Northern Kingdom of Israel, but there is no clear evidence for either of these assertions.

Others suggest that the name "God" is used because of the reluctance of the Jews to pronounce the divine name Yahweh or Jehovah. This led to the custom of pronouncing this name "LORD." This practice, which is followed also in the English Bible, had developed fully by the time these psalms were collected. However, the fact that the name "LORD" is retained even in such a late psalm as Psalm 137 casts serious doubt on the validity of this explanation. We conclude that the reason for this difference of usage of the divine names remains uncertain.

PSALM 42

Psalms 42-49 were written by the Sons of Korah, who were a group of Levites whom David had placed in charge of music in the temple. They apparently were descendants of the Korah who had led the rebellion against Moses in Numbers 16. Since the Sons of Korah were a group who served as temple musicians over a long period of time, it is possible that some of their psalms were written later than the psalms of David. A number of them do seem appropriate to later times, but there is nothing in these psalms which demands a late date. The overall theme of these psalms is a longing for the glory of Jerusalem, the temple and the Davidic King.

We will discuss Psalms 42 and 43 as a unit, since they are united by a common theme, a common refrain, and a single heading. We do not know whether they were written at one time and then divided into two parts or whether Psalm 43 was added later — much as certain hymns have had stanzas added by subsequent hymnwriters.

This psalm is a lament of a Levite who is separated from his beloved temple in Jerusalem. Because Mt. Hermon, which is in the northern Transjordan, is mentioned in this psalm, it has been suggested that this psalm was written by a Levite living near Mt. Hermon, perhaps in the Levitical city of Golan in Bashan or in the upper Jordan Valley. It has also been suggested that this psalm was written during the divided monarchy when such Levites might be cut off from Jerusalem either by the secession of the Northern Kingdom under Jeroboam or by the later invasions of Israel's territory in the Transjordan by the Arameans.

As the Deer Pants for Streams of Water

The psalm certainly is also appropriate to David's lifetime since it may have been occasioned by the disruptions caused by Absalom's rebellion or by one of the several brief invasions of the Transjordan by the Arameans which occurred during David's reign, for example, in 2 Samuel 10.

For the director of music. A *maskil* of the Sons of Korah.

Longing for the Temple

1 **As the deer pants for streams of water,**
  so my soul pants for you, O God.
 ²My soul thirsts for God, for the living God.
  When can I go and meet with God?
³My tears have been my food day and night,
  while men say to me all day long,
   "Where is your God?"

⁴These things I remember as I pour out my soul:
   how I used to go with the multitude,
   leading the procession to the house of God,
   with shouts of joy and thanksgiving among the festive throng.

Refrain

⁵Why are you downcast, O my soul?
Why so disturbed within me?
Put your hope in God,
  for I will yet praise him, my Savior and my God.

Remembrance of the LORD

⁶My soul is downcast within me;
   therefore I will remember you from the land of the Jordan,
  the heights of Hermon — from Mount Mizar.
  ⁷Deep calls to deep in the roar of your waterfalls;
  all your waves and breakers have swept over me.

⁸By day the LORD directs his love,
  at night his song is with me —
  a prayer to the God of my life.
⁹I say to God my Rock, "Why have you forgotten me?
  Why must I go about mourning, oppressed by the enemy?

¹⁰My bones suffer mortal agony
      as my foes taunt me, saying to me all day long,
      "Where is your God?"

Refrain

¹¹Why are you downcast, O my soul?
  Why so disturbed within me?
  Put your hope in God,
      for I will yet praise him, my Savior and my God.

PSALM 43

A Plea for Vindication

1 Vindicate me, O God,
  and plead my cause against an ungodly nation;
  rescue me from deceitful and wicked men.

²You are God my stronghold.
  Why have you rejected me?
  Why must I go about mourning, oppressed by the enemy?

³Send forth your light and your truth,
  let them guide me;
  let them bring me to your holy mountain,
  to the place where you dwell.

⁴Then will I go to the altar of God,
  to God, my joy and my delight.
  I will praise you with the harp, O God, my God.

Refrain

> ⁵**Why are you downcast, O my soul?**
> **Why so disturbed within me?**
> **Put your hope in God,**
> > **for I will yet praise him, my Savior and my God.**

Each of the three sections of the psalm closes with a refrain which expresses the psalmist's dismay at being cut off from the festivals of the Lord which were celebrated in the temple in Jerusalem. This refrain also expresses the hope that he will soon be able to join in those festivals once again. Although there is sorrow in each of the three stanzas, there seems to be a strengthening of hope as the psalmist progresses through the three stanzas.

In the first stanza longing and sorrow predominate. Hope is confined largely to the refrain. It is difficult for us to understand the intense longing Israel had for the temple in Jerusalem, since our worship is not so attached to one city or one building. But the sacrifices and many of the most important religious celebrations of Old Testament worship could be celebrated only in the temple. So to be cut off from the temple was to be denied participation in some of the most meaningful and important parts of worship. That is why a believer who longed for God as intensely as a thirsty deer longs for water would intensely desire to reach the city of Jerusalem and its temple.

The second stanza continues the lament at being cut off from Jerusalem and at the taunts of the enemy who mock the psalmist's God. The waves that sweep over the psalmist may refer to the falls and rapids of the upper Jordan, but here they are a figure for the sorrows that overwhelm him. Although the psalmist's dismay continues throughout this stanza, the sorrow is broken by the interlude of hope in verse 3. It is very likely that this word of faith and hope was deliberately placed in the middle of the middle stanza of the double psalm.

In the third stanza (that is, Psalm 43) the light of hope shines more brightly. Clouds of sorrow still remain because God's deliverance has not yet arrived, but confidence in God's light and truth, which will lead the psalmist back to the temple, shines through more clearly. The psalmist hopes that he will soon express his joy and thanksgiving at God's altar. But even if a literal return to God's altar is slow in coming, the psalmist is being restored to faith and peace.

When we are overwhelmed by sorrow, it will be helpful to ask ourselves the psalmist's question, "Why are you downcast, O my soul?" Talking to ourselves and reminding ourselves of the promises of God can help us put our sorrows into perspective. We should ask ourselves, "Is such depression really necessary if God is still in control of things? Will such sorrow do any good? Can it make things any better? Is it not better to hope in God and trust in his promises?" Like the psalmist, we may have to struggle long and repeat the same truths over and over again in order to conquer our sorrows or depressions, but, like him, we should struggle and persevere until God's light and truth guide us into his presence.

PSALM 44

Past Victory — Present Defeat

This psalm is closely related to the preceding psalm in that it too is a puzzled lament over defeat and exile. In Psalms 42-43 the tone is more personal and individual. Here the lament is more for the nation. Psalm 44 expresses the bewilderment of the faithful in Israel in the face of some crushing defeat after which Israelites were carried off into captivity.

Many commentators suggest one of the defeats Judah suffered during the reigns of Jehoshaphat or Hezekiah as the occasion of this psalm, but it could just as easily refer to the defeats Israel experienced early in the life of David, while Saul was still king. The fact that the triumphs of David's reign are not cited among the glorious past victories strengthens the impression that this psalm reflects conditions early in the life of David, but this argument is not conclusive.

Another possibility is that this psalm was written during the time of David, but that it was intended for future use, just as in Deuteronomy Moses wrote songs that were intended to be used in the future, long after his death.

For the director of music. Of the Sons of Korah. A *maskil*.

Past Victory

1 We have heard with our ears, O God;
our fathers have told us what you did
in their days, in days long ago.

**2 With your hand you drove out the nations
and planted our fathers;
you crushed the peoples and made our fathers flourish.
3 It was not by their sword that they won the land,
nor did their arm bring them victory;
it was your right hand, your arm,
and the light of your face,
for you loved them.**

Present Trust

**4 You are my King and my God,
who decrees victories for Jacob.**

⁵Through you we push back our enemies;
  through your name we trample our foes.
⁶I do not trust in my bow,
  my sword does not bring me victory;
⁷but you give us victory over our enemies,
  you put our adversaries to shame.
⁸In God we make our boast all day long,
  and we will praise your name forever.   *Selah*

In the first two sections of the psalm the writer gives two reasons why Israel could be confident of victory. First, God gave Israel victory in the past, especially when Joshua led them into the land of Canaan. Second, the people of Israel have faith in God to give them victory in the present.

Although this psalm was written by a Levite, the first person singular references to battle indicate that it was probably written to be used as a prayer of the king. This second section apparently was based on similar thoughts in many of the psalms of David.

Present Defeat

⁹But now you have rejected and humbled us;
  you no longer go out with our armies.
¹⁰You made us retreat before the enemy,
  and our adversaries have plundered us.
¹¹You gave us up to be devoured like sheep
  and have scattered us among the nations.
¹²You sold your people for a pittance,
  gaining nothing from their sale.
¹³You have made us a reproach to our neighbors,
  the scorn and derision of those around us.
¹⁴You have made us a byword among the nations;
  the peoples shake their heads at us.
¹⁵My disgrace is before me all day long,
  and my face is covered with shame

¹⁶at the taunts of those who reproach and revile me,
because of the enemy, who is bent on revenge.

¹⁷All this happened to us, though we had not forgotten you
or been false to your covenant.
¹⁸Our hearts had not turned back;
our feet had not strayed from your path.
¹⁹But you crushed us and made us a haunt for jackals
and covered us over with deep darkness.
²⁰If we had forgotten the name of our God
or spread out our hands to a foreign god,
²¹would not God have discovered it,
since he knows the secrets of the heart?

²²Yet for your sake we face death all day long;
we are considered as sheep to be slaughtered.

The psalmist is perplexed that Israel has suffered a crushing defeat in spite of God's promises and their faith in him. He cannot understand why this should be. Since idolatry was present at almost every point of Israel's history, the denial of idolatry must be understood as the assertion of the faithful among Israel. It is they who cannot understand why they are suffering in spite of their faith in God's promises.

Verse 22 suggests the resolution of this enigma. For the faithful among Israel the defeats the nation suffered were not a punishment as they were for the unbelievers among the people. For the faithful these defeats at the hands of the heathen were persecution they endured for the Lord's sake. Paul reinforces this interpretation when he quotes this verse in Romans 8:36 as part of a discussion of the hardships Christians endure for the faith.

Present Plea

> 23Awake, O Lord! Why do you sleep? Rouse yourself!
>   Do not reject us forever.
> 24Why do you hide your face
>   and forget our misery and oppression?
> 25We are brought down to the dust;
>   our bodies cling to the ground.
> 26Rise up and help us;
>   redeem us
>   because of your unfailing love.

The psalm concludes with a plea that God would grant victory to Israel in order to relieve their sufferings and to uphold the honor of his name. God's unfailing grace and mercy are the basis for their plea. The answer to this plea is found in the next psalm.

PSALM 45

The Wedding of the Victorious King

Psalm 45 is an answer to the plea of Psalm 44 because it pictures the Messianic King who brings victory to his people.

Introduction

> For the director of music. To [the tune of] "Lilies."
> Of the Sons of Korah. A *maskil*. A wedding song.

> 1 My heart is stirred by a noble theme
>   as I recite my verse for the king;
>   my tongue is the pen of a skillful writer.

In the opening verse the poet declares the greatness of his theme. He is not writing about an ordinary king or composing a wedding march for a royal wedding of Israel. By inspiration he is writing for Christ, the Messianic King, and for his wedding to his bride, the church. The quotation of this psalm in Hebrews 1 and many of its details which will be discussed below make it clear that this psalm is not a mere "royal psalm" written for a king of Israel, but a Messianic psalm which refers to Christ.

THE GLORY OF THE ROYAL GROOM
His Beautiful Words

²**You are the most excellent of men**
  and your lips have been anointed with grace,
    since God has blessed you forever.

This verse was the inspiration for the familiar hymn "Beautiful Savior." Jesus' beauty was not a physical attractiveness, but his pure, sinless character and the beautiful words of truth, grace, and forgiveness which he spoke. Addressed to an earthly king these words would be idle flattery. Addressed to Christ they express true worship. Romans 9:5, which calls Christ "God over all, forever praised," is probably a reference to this verse.

His Powerful Rule

³**Gird your sword upon your side, O mighty one;**
  clothe yourself with splendor and majesty.
⁴**In your majesty ride forth victoriously**
    in behalf of truth, humility and righteousness;
  let your right hand display awesome deeds.
⁵**Let your sharp arrows pierce the hearts of the king's enemies;**
  let the nations fall beneath your feet.

Although Christ once came to Jerusalem in lowliness, riding on a donkey, he will return in majesty to subdue all the enemies of his kingdom. On Judgment Day every knee will bow to him. Satan and all his followers will be confined to hell. The King's people will then live in eternal peace and security because of his rule. Read Revelation 19 for a fuller development of this theme.

His Just Rule

⁶Your throne, O God, will last for ever and ever;
a scepter of justice will be the scepter of your kingdom.
⁷You love righteousness and hate wickedness;
therefore God, your God, has set you above your companions
by anointing you with the oil of joy.

No sin and no sinners will be allowed to enter Jesus' eternal kingdom. Only his friends, whose sins have been covered by the wedding garment of their Savior's righteousness, will be able to share in his eternal joy.

Verse 6 is very important as one of the clearest Old Testament testimonies to Christ's deity. The Messianic King is called God, and he rules an eternal kingdom. However, in verse 7 he is also distinguished from God. This distinction is meaningful only in light of the doctrines of the Trinity and of Christ's incarnation. Although the Messianic King is true God, he is also the obedient Son who became a man in obedience to his Father's will. Jesus is set above all other human beings because he is exalted in joy at the right hand of God. He is worthy of the exalted position because as the God-man he has completed the work of our salvation.

Many recent commentators and translations try to set aside the testimony of these verses to Jesus' deity. They produce such renderings as "The eternal and everlasting God has enthroned you" or "The throne God has given you will last forever." Such translations are based more on the assumption that the psalms could not contain a true prophecy of Christ's deity than on any evidence in the text. Such translations ignore the simple sense of the Hebrew text, the renderings of the most ancient translations, and the quotation of these verses in Hebrews 1:8,9 as a testimony of Christ's divine superiority to the angels. The Messianic interpretation is clear and should not be set aside.

The Beauty of Life with Him

> 8All your robes are fragrant
> with myrrh and aloes and cassia;
> from palaces adorned with ivory
> the music of the strings makes you glad.
> 9Daughters of kings are among your honored women;
> at your right hand is the royal bride in gold of Ophir.

These verses use images taken from a life of earthly luxury to represent the beauty of life in Christ's presence. The King is dressed in beautiful robes, perfumed with the most expensive spices. His palace is decorated with ivory carvings and filled with music. His bride is dressed in gold from Ophir, which is the unknown location in Arabia or Africa from which Solomon obtained his gold. The daughters of kings symbolize the truth that all the members of Christ's household are royalty. These verses are a transition to the next section of the psalm, which describes the beauty of the King's bride, the church of believers.

The Beauty of the Bride

> 10Listen, O daughter, consider and give ear;
> Forget your people and your father's house.
> 11The king is enthralled by your beauty;
> honor him, for he is your Lord.
>
> 12The Daughter of Tyre will come with a gift,
> men of wealth will seek your favor.

189

¹³**All glorious is the princess within her chamber;**
   her gown is interwoven with gold.
¹⁴**In embroidered garments she is led to the king;**
   her virgin companions follow her and are brought to you.
¹⁵**They are led in with joy and gladness;**
   they enter the palace of the king.

In marriage a man and woman leave their parents and enter a bond with each other which takes precedence over all others. When we become God's children through faith in Christ, this too is a relationship which demands exclusive loyalty and which must take precedence over all others. We must put away all other gods. We are to love nothing or no one more than God. The bride's dedication to her beloved in these verses represents our dedication to God. In 2 Corinthians 11:2 Paul applies this picture to the Corinthians. He tells them, "I promised you to one husband, to Christ, so that I might present you as a pure virgin to him."

The bride is the church. Her ladies-in-waiting, the men who seek her favor, and her children will represent individual believers who are brought to Christ through the church. Because it was a heathen city which was famous for its great wealth, Tyre is mentioned as an example of those who pay homage to the bride. The rich garments and the treasures of the bride represent the spiritual riches she has from Christ, namely, the forgiveness of sins and the joys of eternal life.

The description of Christ and his bride is developed more fully in Ephesians 5:26,27, which describes the church as radiant, without stain or wrinkle or any blemish, holy and blameless. The prophecy of these verses is fulfilled when people enter the church through faith and when the church is finally gathered together in heaven.

The Glory of the King's Children

¹⁶Your sons will take the place of your fathers;
 you will make them princes throughout the land.
¹⁷I will perpetuate your memory through all generations;
 therefore the nations will praise you for ever and ever.

The masculine grammatical endings of the Hebrew words make it clear that these verses are addressed to the king, rather than the queen. The King's sons are the believers who flock into the church, especially those from among the Gentiles. The King makes them rulers with him. Read Isaiah 60:1-9 for another poetic description of the Gentiles' flocking to Christ. The relationship of Christ and his children is also described in Hebrews 2:10-13, which describes Jesus as the one who brings many sons to glory.

It seems strange to refer to the King's "fathers" in the plural if the King is Christ, who has only one heavenly Father and no earthly father. This term probably refers to the Messiah's ancestors in the Davidic line and, in a more general sense, to Israel as a whole. Although Christ was the everlasting Father of Israel, he was also the child who was born to them. In this sense the people of Israel were Christ's "fathers." This prophecy is fulfilled when the "children" who come to Christ from the Gentiles replace the "fathers" from Israel who rejected him.

Jesus' name and memory will be perpetuated through all generations by the believers who praise him on earth and in heaven. This psalm teaches us to appreciate the present glory we have as members of Christ's church and to anticipate the joy we will have when we are welcomed to the eternal wedding feast of the Lamb.

PSALM 46

The King's Reign

Although this psalm does not specifically mention the Messiah as a distinct person of the Godhead, it is nevertheless an appropriate follow-up to Psalm 45, since it provides a further description of God's rule over the world, which is exercised by Christ. This psalm was the basis for Luther's famous hymn, "A Mighty Fortress Is Our God." Nothing in the text specifies the occasion when it was written, but the destruction of the Assyrian army of Sennacherib (2 Kings 19:35) was a dramatic example of the way in which this psalm is fulfilled during the history of this world.

This psalm could have provided comfort for God's people at many specific crises in Israel's history, but its scope extends far beyond any one fulfillment in history. The peace established by Christ's return completes the fulfillment of this psalm.

For the director of music. Of the Sons of Korah.
According to *alamoth*. A song.

Alamoth is a musical instruction which seems to refer to the way in which the accompanying musical instruments were to be tuned.

1 **God is our refuge and strength,**
   an ever-present help in trouble.
²Therefore we will not fear,
      though the earth give way
      and the mountains fall into the heart of the sea,
      ³though its waters roar and foam
      and the mountains quake with their surging.   *Selah*

Believers can remain calm even in the midst of the greatest calamities, since God is their strong fortress. His help is ever-present even to the end of the world. The upheavals described in these verses may represent all of the various kinds of calamities which strike the world. All of these are signs of the end. However, these verses will be fulfilled literally and completely on the last day, when this universe is destroyed by fire.

The earth and its mountains seem solid and indestructible. But these too will be dissolved. Even then, believers will be secure in the hand of God. For believers Christ's appearance will be a cause for joy, not dread. Jesus says, "When these things begin to take place, stand up and lift up your heads, because your redemption is drawing near" (Luke 21:28).

> ⁴There is a river whose streams make glad the city of God,
>   the holy place where the Most High dwells.
> ⁵God is within her, she will not fall;
>   God will help her at break of day.
>
> ⁶Nations are in uproar, kingdoms fall;
>   he lifts his voice, the earth melts.
>
> ⁷The LORD Almighty is with us;
>   the God of Jacob is our fortress.   *Selah*

The heavens and the earth can be shaken, but God's city cannot fall. The city of God is the church, especially as it is at peace in heaven. In Revelation 21 our eternal home is described as a strongly fortified city in which God's people dwell in complete security. The waters of the sea are restless and dangerous, but the river of God is peaceful and life-giving. This river reminds us of the rivers of Eden which sustained life there. In this psalm and in Revelation the river represents the life-giving power of God which will sustain us throughout eternity. Revelation 22:1-5 describes our eternal home as a new Eden, watered by the river of the water of life, as clear as crystal, flowing from the throne of God.

We begin to experience the fulfillment of these verses already in this life. The Lord preserves his city, the church, from destruction. Since God's word sustains our faith, it is often compared to waters of life. Nevertheless, the ultimate fulfillment of the promises of these verses will come only in the new heavens and the new earth.

> 8Come and see the works of the LORD,
>   the desolations he has brought on the earth.
> 9He makes wars cease to the ends of the earth;
>   he breaks the bow and shatters the spear,
>   he burns the shields with fire.
>
>   10"Be still, and know that I am God;
>   I will be exalted among the nations,
>   I will be exalted in the earth."
>
> 11The LORD Almighty is with us;
>   the God of Jacob is our fortress.   *Selah*

We can point to many occasions in history when the Lord intervened to protect his people from destruction. The destruction of the Egyptian army of Pharaoh at the Red Sea and of the Assyrian army of Sennacherib as it surrounded Jerusalem are but two examples. God's protection of the church and the spiritual peace which is brought through the conquests made by the gospel provide another level of fulfillment to these words. The complete fulfillment will occur only in the new heavens and the new earth. There all wars will have come to an end, and perfect, uninterrupted spiritual peace will endure forever.

As the people of Jerusalem could take comfort from the psalm when they were surrounded by hostile armies, as

Luther could take comfort from the psalm when he was threatened by pope and emperor, so we too can take comfort from this psalm through any danger even to the end of the world. The words "Be still" are both a rebuke to a world in rebellion against God and an assurance of peace to his people.

PSALM 47

The King's Empire

Psalm 47 continues the theme of Messianic rule, which was introduced in Psalm 45 and continued in Psalm 46. Psalm 47 emphasizes the King's rule over all people. The conquests of the gospel will spread throughout the world. On Judgment Day the entire world will have to submit to the Messiah's rule.

For the director of music. Of the Sons of Korah. A psalm.

**1 Clap your hands, all you nations;
shout to God with cries of joy.**

**²How awesome is the LORD Most High,
the great King over all the earth!
³He subdued nations under us,
peoples under our feet.
⁴He chose our inheritance for us,
the pride of Jacob, whom he loved.   *Selah***

**⁵God has ascended amid shouts of joy,
the LORD amid the sounding of trumpets.**

**⁶Sing praises to God, sing praises;
sing praises to our King, sing praises.
⁷For God is the King of all the earth;
sing to him a psalm of praise.**

⁸God reigns over the nations;
   God is seated on his holy throne.
⁹The nobles of the nations assemble
      as the people of the God of Abraham,
            for the kings of the earth belong to God;
            he is greatly exalted.

Although this king is an awesome conqueror and judge, the predominant tone of this psalm is joy. This king is no tyrant, but a gracious Savior. The conquest by which the nations come under the rule of Israel is the spread of the gospel throughout the world. When they are conquered by the gospel, heathen who were aliens to God's kingdom become citizens of his spiritual Israel (Ephesians 2:11-20). In the words of the psalm, "The nobles of the nations assemble as the people of the God of Abraham."

Israel celebrated with shouts of joy and the sounding of trumpets when God "ascended" to Jerusalem when the ark of the covenant was brought up by David (2 Samuel 6). We should celebrate the exaltation of Christ and his coming into all lands with the gospel with the same kind of joy. The chief application of this psalm is indicated by the repeated admonition, "Sing praises." We rejoice when Christ is exalted through the preaching of the gospel in every land.

PSALM 48

The King's Holy City

This psalm continues the theme of Psalms 46 and 47. Most of the comments on those psalms apply to this psalm as well. Here too God's people rejoice because of his rule over his city, the church.

A song. A psalm of the Sons of Korah.

1 Great is the LORD, and most worthy of praise,
   in the city of our God, his holy mountain.
²It is beautiful in its loftiness,
      the joy of the whole earth.
   Like the utmost heights of Zaphon is Mount Zion,
      the city of the Great King.
³God is in her citadels;
   he has shown himself to be her fortress.

⁴When the kings joined forces,
   when they advanced together,
⁵they saw her and were astounded;
   they fled in terror.
⁶Trembling seized them there,
   pain like that of a woman in labor.
⁷You destroyed them like ships of Tarshish
      shattered by an east wind.

⁸As we have heard, so have we seen
      in the city of the LORD Almighty,
      in the city of our God:
   God makes her secure forever.   *Selah*

⁹Within your temple, O God,
   we meditate on your unfailing love.
¹⁰Like your name, O God,
   your praise reaches to the ends of the earth;
   your right hand is filled with righteousness.

¹¹Mount Zion rejoices,
   the villages of Judah are glad
      because of your judgments.
¹²Walk about Zion, go around her, count her towers,
¹³consider well her ramparts, view her citadels,
      that you may tell of them to the next generation.

¹⁴For this God is our God for ever and ever;
   he will be our guide even to the end.

In the Bible the city of God is Jerusalem, but it is Jerusalem on three levels: the earthly city, the church on earth, and the church in heaven.

We should not minimize the importance of the earthly Jerusalem. It was the place God chose for his earthly dwelling place, the temple. It was the only place where sacrifices could be made to him. It was the place where God's Son, the Messianic King, gave his life for us. Jerusalem was the launching pad from which the gospel went out to the whole world. Yet the city itself was not large. Mount Zion, the mountain on which it was built, was not particularly high. Many of the surrounding hills were much higher. Mount Hermon (Zaphon), on the northern border of Israel, is more than three times as high.

The importance of Jerusalem is not its size or majesty, but the majesty of the King who gave his life there and whose kingdom went out from Jerusalem. The empire of the kings of Israel was never large or impressive compared to other world empires, but the kingdom of Christ includes the whole world.

The real importance of the earthly city Jerusalem is that it is a type of the Jerusalem above, which is the mother of us all (Galatians 4:26). Many of the words of this psalm are appropriate to the love and protection God gave to the Old Testament Jerusalem, but this Jerusalem, which is the joy of the whole earth, is not the earthly city, but the church which was born in Jerusalem.

In Revelation 20:9 the attack of the kings against God's city represents the final onslaught made by the enemies of the church before Christ's return. Their attack will fail. God's "Jerusalem" will exist forever as Mount Zion, the heavenly Jerusalem, the city of the living God (Hebrews 12:22). This psalm leads us to meditate on the unfailing love of God, who protects his church. It increases our longing for the day we will enter the gates of the eternal city of our King.

PSALM 49

The folly of Riches

Psalm 49, the concluding psalm of the Sons of Korah collection, is different from the psalms which precede it. It seems to be more closely related to the psalms that follow it, which all deal with human weakness in some way. This psalm has a dual theme, riches and death. Since death is inevitable, it is foolish to trust in riches. You can't take them with you.

Psalms 36, 37 and 39 are similar to Psalm 49. The message of this psalm is very similar to that of the book of Ecclesiastes.

For the Director of Music. Of the Sons of Korah. A psalm.

Introduction

1 Hear this, all you peoples;
listen, all who live in this world,
²both low and high,
rich and poor alike:
³My mouth will speak words of wisdom;
the utterance from my heart will give understanding.
⁴I will turn my ear to a proverb;
with the harp I will expound my riddle:

This is a teaching psalm addressed to people rather than a psalm of praise addressed to God. The psalmist's message is for everyone, rich and poor alike, Israelite and Gentile. It applies to all, for all must die. The rich are warned not to place too much confidence in their riches. The poor are warned against being envious of the rich and against discouragement because of the prosperity of the wicked.

The psalmist's teaching is called a proverb and a riddle because it deals with one of the central problems of life, which fascinates people but nevertheless remains a mystery to them, namely, the riddle of the meaning of life and the relationship of life and death. This riddle can be answered with wisdom and understanding only when it is considered in light of mankind's relationship to God and eternity.

The Limitations of Riches

⁵Why should I fear when evil days come,
  when wicked deceivers surround me —
⁶those who trust in their wealth
  and boast of their great riches?

⁷No man can redeem the life of another
  or give to God a ransom for him —
⁸the ransom for a life is costly,
  no payment is ever enough —
⁹that he should live on forever and not see decay.
¹⁰For all can see that wise men die;
  the foolish and the senseless alike perish
    and leave their wealth to others.
¹¹Their tombs will remain their houses forever,
  their dwellings for endless generations,
    though they had named lands after themselves.
¹²But man, despite his riches, does not endure;
  he is like the beasts that perish.

¹³This is the fate of those who trust in themselves,
  and of their followers, who approve their sayings. *Selah*
¹⁴Like sheep they are destined for the grave,
  and death will feed on them.
  The upright will rule over them in the morning;
  their forms will decay in the grave,
    far from their princely mansions.

The psalmist's enemies are rich and powerful. Such wealth is a great advantage in earthly power struggles. The rich can hire the best lawyers. They can influence public officials. They can hire ruthless men to enforce their will. But the power of riches is limited. Although riches can buy much land, the only real estate the rich can occupy permanently is the grave.

Even though riches can buy the best medical care, money cannot buy an extra day of life on earth. When God summons them from this world, the rich must come without delay. Their wealth will do nothing for them in eternity. They cannot take it with them. They cannot bribe their way into heaven or escape hell by making advance payment for their sins while they are still on earth. They cannot hire a lawyer who will get them through the judgment on a technicality.

Only one man could pay a ransom for sin. Only one could redeem a life. And the ransom he paid is beyond price. It is a gift of God, given freely to all who believe in Jesus, the man God sent to pay for sin. This ransom was paid for rich and poor without distinction.

When the psalmist compares the death of the rich to that of an animal and when he speaks of the permanency of death, he is not denying the doctrine of the resurrection or the doctrine of hell. He is stressing the finality of death. Except for a few miraculous exceptions such as Moses and Elijah at Jesus' transfiguration, no one can return to earth once God has called him from this world. "Man is destined to die once, and after that to face judgment" (Hebrews 9:27). Once a person is gone from this world, no amount of money can bring him back. Death is final.

Since no one can see or measure the soul, the death of a man closely resembles the death of an animal. The bodies of men and of animals are made of the same elements. Both decay and return to the ground from which they came. Without faith man is no better off than an animal when he dies. In fact, he is much worse off, because unlike animals, he must face judgment and damnation. No amount of riches will do him any good then.

In Verse 14 the psalmist hints at the resurrection of the ungodly when he declares that the righteous will rule over them in the morning. The psalmist's belief in the resurrection is made clear in verse 15.

The Limitless Power of God

> **15But God will redeem my life from the grave;**
> **he will surely take me to himself.** *Selah*

This verse is one of the high points of the Old Testament in its clear confession of the resurrection and eternal life. Because of their evolutionary view of religion many critical commentators insist on dating all Old Testament references to the resurrection late in the Old Testament period. For this reason many classify this psalm as post-exilic.

Limiting the resurrection references to late in the Old Testament period can be done only by an arbitrary redating of Old Testament books. Many of the clearest Old Testament references to life after death and the resurrection are early. In addition to the references we find in psalms of David, such as Psalms 16:11 and 17:15, Job 19:26 and Ecclesiastes 12:7 are other early references to the eternal life of believers.

Although the doctrine of the resurrection to eternal life is not taught as explicitly in the earliest books of the Old Testament as it is in the New Testament, it is clearly present. This is affirmed by Jesus in Matthew 22:29-32, where he declares that the resurrection was taught by Moses in Exodus 3:6.

Review and Conclusion

> **16Do not be overawed when a man grows rich,**
> **when the splendor of his house increases;**

¹⁷**for he will take nothing with him when he dies,**
   his splendor will not descend with him.
¹⁸**Though while he lived he counted himself blessed —**
   and men praise you when you prosper —
¹⁹**he will join the generation of his fathers,**
   who will never see the light of life.

²⁰**A man who has riches without understanding**
   is like the beasts that perish.

This section repeats and emphasizes truths already stated earlier in the psalm. Though riches are often a great advantage on earth, they will not help an unbeliever on Judgment Day. Though unbelievers too will rise to be judged, they will never see the light of life in heaven. Therefore, their eternal existence in hell is called eternal death, not eternal life. Though unbelievers will have a conscious existence throughout eternity, that existence, lived in separation from God's grace, is more appropriately called "death" than "life."

PSALM 50

The Folly of Formalistic Worship

This psalm of Asaph, who was a leader of the temple musicians, expands on the theme of Psalm 49. If trust in riches is folly, so is trust in an empty formalistic religion. In this psalm Israel is on trial for turning the temple worship, which was intended to be a joyful willing service to the Lord, into an empty ritual, which was done out of habit and to gain reward.

A psalm of Asaph.

The Summons

1 **The Mighty One, God, the L**ORD**, speaks**
   and summons the earth

from the rising of the sun
to the place where it sets.
²From Zion, perfect in beauty, God shines forth.

³Our God comes and will not be silent;
a fire devours before him,
and around him a tempest rages.

⁴He summons the heavens above, and the earth,
that he may judge his people:
⁵"Gather to me my consecrated ones,
who made a covenant with me by sacrifice."
⁶And the heavens proclaim his righteousness,
for God himself is judge. *Selah*

These verses summon the people of Israel to appear before God to be judged for their spiritual indifference and self-centered worship. God's condemnation of formalistic worship includes all the worship of the heathen because their worship was based on self-interest rather than on love for God. However, Israel's guilt was even greater than that of the heathen because Israel had greater knowledge of God and because they had made a covenant to serve the Lord. The form of God's summons to Israel is very effective because in the first three verses it sounds as if the heathen are being summoned to Mount Zion to be judged. The complacent among Israel must have smiled at the thought.

Suddenly in verse 4 it becomes clear that Israel is the main target of judgment. What a jolt this sudden turn must have given to the hearers! What a jolt this should give us! We must recognize that, like Israel, we too have been given much. Of us, too, much will be expected. "From everyone who has been given much, much will be demanded" (Luke 12:48).

Heaven and earth are called to appear as witnesses at Israel's trial because they are portrayed as the witnesses who have observed Israel's half-hearted worship. This picture is based on the very similar summons issued by Moses in Deuteronomy 4:26 and 32:1. Isaiah 1:2 uses the same figure of speech.

Israel is complacent and feels that it will never be called to account. The Israelites think that when God comes, it will be good for them and bad for their heathen enemies. For this reason they are eager for the day of the Lord's judgment, but when the Lord comes, it will not be to bless them, but to judge them. His anger is burning against them because of their indifference.

The Accusation

> [7]"Hear, O my people, and I will speak,
> O Israel, and I will testify against you:
>> I am God, your God.
> [8]I do not rebuke you for your sacrifices
> or your burnt offerings, which are ever before me.
> [9]I have no need of a bull from your stall
> or of goats from your pens,
> [10]for every animal of the forest is mine,
> and the cattle on a thousand hills.
> [11]I know every bird in the mountains,
> and the creatures of the field are mine.
> [12]If I were hungry I would not tell you,
> for the world is mine, and all that is in it.
> [13]Do I eat the flesh of bulls
> or drink the blood of goats?
>
> [14]Sacrifice thank offerings to God,
> fulfill your vows to the Most High,
> [15]and call upon me in the day of trouble;
> I will deliver you,
> and you will honor me."

> ¹⁶**But to the wicked, God says:**
> **"What right have you to recite my laws**
> **or take my covenant on your lips?**
> ¹⁷**You hate my instruction**
> **and cast my words behind you.**
> ¹⁸**When you see a thief, you join with him;**
> **you throw in your lot with adulterers.**
> ¹⁹**You use your mouth for evil**
> **and harness your tongue to deceit.**
> ²⁰**You speak continually against your brother**
> **and slander your own mother's son.**

The accusation in these verses is rather indirect. We have to read between the lines. It was not the outward form of Israel's worship that was inadequate. They were continuing to offer the sacrifices at the temple which the Lord had commanded through Moses. For this reason God does not criticize the sacrifices they were offering. The problem was with the evil attitudes in the hearts of the worshipers.

Two major problems were apparent. The people of Israel were setting aside the first table of the law. Many in Israel thought they were doing God a favor with their offerings, imagining that he had need of their services. The logical conclusion of such thinking was that if God needed their offerings, he owed them something in return for their offerings. The Lord destroys this kind of thinking with two arguments: God is not like a human being who needs food. He is self-sufficient.

Secondly, even if he needed offerings, he would not have to ask the Israelites for them, since everything in the world was already his. All the offerings Israel gave to the Lord already belonged to him. The obvious conclusion was that God owed Israel nothing for their offerings, so they should not place any confidence in the mere fact that they were offering the prescribed sacrifices.

The second wrong attitude on the part of many worshipers in Israel was ignoring the second table of the law. This is expressed in the last paragraph of the accusation. Many in Israel offered sacrifices for their sins, even though they fully intended to continue with the same sins. They were offering sacrifices without real repentance. They wanted to go through the motions of worship and to be thought of as religious, but they did not want to take to heart the admonitions and teachings of God's word, which they hated.

Strictly speaking, the middle paragraph of the accusation is not an accusation, since it gives a positive statement of the characteristics and results of true worship. As such, it anticipates the admonition of the last section of the psalm. Nevertheless, the placement of this section in the midst of the accusation is appropriate because it shows what was lacking in the worship of many of the Israelites.

Their offerings were not real thank offerings, because they were not offered with a thankful heart. Their vows were not real vows, because they had no intentions of correcting their sinful lives. They were not calling on God in the humble recognition that they were the needy ones; they were treating God as if he were the needy one who owed them a favor for their service to him. They were not honoring God by their worship, but trying to make a business deal with him. Such worship deserved God's judgment and would surely receive it.

The Verdict

> 21These things you have done and I kept silent;
>   you thought I was altogether like you.
>   But I will rebuke you and accuse you to your face.
> 22"Consider this, you who forget God,
>   or I will tear you to pieces, with none to rescue;

Because God's judgment did not come immediately, the complacent in Israel thought they were dealing with God successfully and that he condoned or at least tolerated their lifeless, formalistic worship. They imagined that God was like them. They were trying to create God in their own image, rather than conforming to God's image. This mistake has been repeated countless times by the inventors of heathen religions and by many modern theologians.

Israel was complacent, but judgment for Israel was looming just over the horizon. God was giving them time for repentance. Through his prophets he continued to warn them. Jeremiah 7, Micah 6:1-8 and Amos 5:18-6:7 are three of the many admonitions of the prophets against formalistic worship. But when Israel failed to heed these warnings, their formalistic worship was swept away through the devastating invasions of the Assyrians and Babylonians. But at the time this psalm was written it was not yet too late to escape.

The Way to Escape

> **[23]He who sacrifices thank offerings honors me,**
> **and he prepares the way**
> **so that I may show him the salvation of God."**

True sacrifices, offered in faith and thankfulness, would please and honor God. Although they would not earn anything, such sacrifices would yield the blessings the Lord promised to his people: the forgiveness of sins, deliverance from their enemies, and the preservation of the people in the land until they would see the arrival in the land of the Messiah, who would bring salvation from the Lord. These blessings would not be earned rewards, but gracious gifts of God to his people.

This psalm has many obvious applications to our stewardship and worship. We should beware of giving our offerings to certain needs with the feeling that God needs us to do his work. God did not need Israel's offerings, and he obviously doesn't need ours either. He already owns the whole world. He has thousands of angels who could deliver his word for him.

God invites us to join in the work of missions, not because he needs us, but to give us the privilege of working with him. When Israel did not take the gospel to the nations, Paul's work went on without them. If we throw away our chances, the work will go on without us, and only we will be the poorer for it. God's kingdom will come, and his will shall be done — either with us or without us.

We should beware of thinking that God owes us anything for our worship. We should not serve God just to get something for ourselves. Today many people worship God as a way to financial prosperity or peace of mind. We are to serve God because we love him, not because we love ourselves.

We should beware of thinking that merely carrying out the right forms of worship or belonging to the right church is of any value in itself. No one will be saved by belonging to an orthodox church, by regularly attending church and the Lord's Supper, or by confessing pure doctrine. All of these things are valuable as confessions of faith and as opportunities for faith to be nourished by the means of grace. But none of these things are substitutes for faith. God wants worship which is an expression of faith and love. Only such worship is pleasing to him.

PSALM 51

Cleanse Me from My Sin

This psalm is a transition between Psalms 49-50 and Psalms 52-60. Like Psalms 49 and 50 it deals with true

God-pleasing sacrifices and the true payment for sin. Like most of the psalms that follow, it is tied to a historical incident in the life of David.

Psalm 51 is the best known of the penitential psalms. It has had an important influence on our liturgy.

For the director of music. A psalm of David. When the prophet Nathan came to him after David had committed adultery with Bathsheba.

The historical circumstances which occasioned this psalm are recorded in 2 Samuel 11 and 12 and may be reviewed there. This psalm expresses David's true repentance after his sin. Although this psalm was written for a specific occasion, it expresses general truths which are universal and timeless in their application.

The Plea for Forgiveness

1 Have mercy on me, O God,
    according to your unfailing love;
    according to your great compassion
blot out my transgressions.
2 Wash away all my iniquity
and cleanse me from my sin.

By heaping up repetitions David expresses the intensity of his plea.

David's plea is based on God's mercy, his unfailing love and his great compassion, not on any action of David. It is by grace that we are forgiven, not by deeds we have done or payments we have made.

The deep stain of sin is emphasized by the heaping up of terms — transgression, iniquity, and sin. Sin is rebellion against God, it is hatred for God, it is violation of his Law, it is failing to live up to the standards he has set. Sin is a perverse rejection of God and his will. Sin produces an ugly distortion of God's good creation.

Although the disastrous effects of sin are great, the cleansing from sin is thorough and complete. Sin is blotted out, it is washed away, we are cleansed from it. "The blood of Jesus, his Son, purifies us from all sin" (1 John 1:7).

These verses are one of the clearest and most beautiful statements of the doctrine of forgiveness in the Old Testament. They closely parallel beautiful statements in Paul's epistles, especially Romans, and show that there has always been only one way to peace with God. From Adam to the end of the world the one way to salvation has been and always will be through forgiveness based on God's grace and delivered through faith.

The Confession

> ³For I know my transgressions,
> and my sin is always before me.
> ⁴Against you, you only, have I sinned
> and done what is evil in your sight,
>   so that you are proved right when you speak
>   and justified when you judge.
> ⁵Surely I was sinful at birth,
> sinful from the time my mother conceived me.

In this beautiful confession David first confesses his actual sins, which in this case were murder and adultery. He recognizes that his sins were not merely sins against Bathsheba, with whom he had committed adultery, against Uriah, whom he had treacherously murdered, and against the people who were offended or misled by his sin. His sin was above all an offense against the holy God. His sin was gross ingratitude for the many blessings and privileges God had given him. The offense of his sin was compounded by the hypocrisy with which he had tried to cover up his sin. His shameful record fully justified the strong verdict God delivered to him through Nathan and the chastisements the Lord had imposed on him.

In this confession David also acknowledges original sin. Corrupt actions flow from a corrupt nature. Like all of us, David had been conceived and born with a corrupt nature inherited from Adam. He had been born as an enemy of God, whose will was opposed to God. He had been born as a condemned sinner, worthy of damnation. Although David had been freed from the rule of his sinful nature, he had allowed it to regain control over him, and he had fallen into terrible sin.

Though it was an extreme example, David's sin was no fluke, no accident, no surprise. It was an expression of the corrupt nature which lurks within, even when it is covered with a veneer of decency. David realized that his need for forgiveness extended beyond forgiveness for a few gross sins, horrible as those may have been. He recognized a need for complete renewal.

His Need

> **⁶Surely you desire truth in the inner parts;
> you teach me wisdom in the inmost place.**

David realized that dealing with sin requires more than cleaning up your act and behaving a little better than before. God wants more than improved outward performance. He wants a change of heart. But this change of heart David could never produce. Nor can we. This change of heart and renewal must come from God. David prays for such renewal. So do we.

The Plea for Renewal

> [7]Cleanse me with hyssop, and I will be clean;
> wash me, and I will be whiter than snow.
> [8]Let me hear joy and gladness;
> let the bones you have crushed rejoice.
> [9]Hide your face from my sins
> and blot out all my iniquity.
> [10]Create in me a pure heart, O God,
> and renew a steadfast spirit within me.
> [11]Do not cast me from your presence
> or take your Holy Spirit from me.
> [12]Restore to me the joy of your salvation
> and grant me a willing spirit, to sustain me.

David prays for cleansing from sin. The cleansing with hyssop was part of the cleansings required by the Old Testament ceremonial law. Hyssop was a plant the priest used as a sort of sponge or sprinkler to apply the cleansing blood or water of Old Testament ceremonies to the worshiper (Numbers 19:18, Leviticus 14:6). The application of blood with hyssop symbolized the cleansing David received in reality by the application of the blood of Christ to him before the throne of God.

God's forgiveness of our sin is also described as God's hiding his face from sin so that he no longer sees it, as God's blotting out of sin from his record book, and as God's washing us whiter than snow. This last picture especially emphasizes the completeness of forgiveness. "The blood of Jesus, his Son, purifies us from all sin" (1 John 1:7).

The result of such forgiveness will be joy and gladness in place of the fear and grief caused by unforgiven sin. Another result will be love which produces an eagerness to serve God out of gratitude for sin forgiven. David prays for such a cleansed heart and willing spirit so that he will be eager to

213

serve God and remain faithful to him. This psalm itself is the best evidence that his prayer was answered. How different is the David who speaks in this psalm from the hypocritical schemer trying to cover up his sin who is described in 2 Samuel 11. What a testimony this psalm is to the power of the Spirit working through the word.

The last verses of this section are very familiar as *The Offertory* we use in our regular Sunday worship. In this prayer David recognizes his unworthiness and his weakness. With the words, "*Create* in me," David is praying for a miraculous act which can be performed by God alone. His prayer can be answered only through the work of the Holy Spirit, who alone can work in him repentance, faith and willing service. The Holy Spirit not only creates in us faith through which we receive forgiveness, but also a willingness to serve God, so that we begin to keep God's law. Because this renewal is never perfect in this life, David prays that the Spirit will keep him steadfast and sustain him so that he will not fall again.

In general, the NIV rendering of this section is quite close to the translation we have used in worship for many years. The only significant difference is that the NIV understands verse 12 as a reference to the willing spirit the Holy Spirit places into us rather than as a reference to the Holy Spirit, who makes us willing, as the King James Version did. Either thought is correct, but on the basis of the Hebrew the translation of the NIV seems preferable.

Although the preceding verses are translated as a prayer, several of the verses could be translated as statements of what God will do in the future rather than as wishes or pleas. In any case, we should see in these verses not only a plea, but also an expression of confidence that God will answer David's prayer, because the prayer is followed immediately by a promise of what David will do when his prayer is answered.

The Pledge of Renewed Service

¹³Then I will teach transgressors your ways,
and sinners will turn back to you.
¹⁴Save me from bloodguilt, O God,
the God who saves me,
and my tongue will sing of your righteousness.
¹⁵O Lord, open my lips,
and my mouth will declare your praise.

¹⁶You do not delight in sacrifice,
or I would bring it;
you do not take pleasure in burnt offerings.
¹⁷The sacrifices of God are a broken spirit;
a broken and contrite heart, O God, you will not despise.

¹⁸In your good pleasure make Zion prosper;
build up the walls of Jerusalem.
¹⁹Then there will be righteous sacrifices,
whole burnt offerings to delight you;
then bulls will be offered on your altar.

Genuine repentance produces an intention to avoid sin and to serve God more faithfully. David promises that if God gives him a renewed heart, he will praise God joyfully, he will offer sacrifices motivated by true repentance, and he will share God's word with others. The promise that his worship will not be mere formality is the chief connecting link between this psalm and Psalm 50. God is not pleased with sacrifices which are a mere going through the motions, but only with worship that flows from a repentant heart.

The last verses of the psalm broaden it from a personal prayer for David to a prayer which includes all of God's people. David prays that the Lord will bless his people, so that all of them will worship him in a way that is pleasing to him. The prosperity and building of the walls of Jerusalem which David prayed for are more spiritual than physical.

Nathan Reproaches David

This doctrinal psalm is one of the richest and most important of all the psalms. It displays both the extreme depths of sin and the perfect cleansing of forgiveness. It contains petitions and thoughts that we will want to use frequently, both in our public services and in our private devotions. May God grant to each of us the repentant spirit and renewed heart such as David displays in this psalm.

PSALM 52

Psalms 52-60 are joined together by the headings that link most of them to historical events in the life of David. All of them have to do with David's dealings with his enemies. Many of them come from the time when David was fleeing from Saul.

Your Tongue Is a Razor

For the director of music. A *maskil* of David.
When Doeg the Edomite had gone to Saul and told him:
"David has gone to the house of Ahimelech."

The circumstances behind this psalm are described in 1 Samuel 21:1-10 and 22:6-23. When David was fleeing from Saul, he had gone to the priest Ahimelech and obtained food and Goliath's sword from him. Ahimelech did not know that David was fleeing from Saul, because David had concealed that fact. In order to gain a reward from Saul, Doeg told Saul that the priests had helped David, but he did not tell Saul that they had done so unknowingly. Doeg then massacred the priests when none of Saul's other men were willing to carry out this atrocity.

Doeg's Sin

1 Why do you boast of evil, you mighty man?
Why do you boast all day long,
   you who are a disgrace in the eyes of God?

²Your tongue plots destruction;
it is like a sharpened razor;
you who practice deceit.
³You love evil rather than good,
falsehood rather than speaking the truth.   *Selah*
⁴You love every harmful word,
   O you deceitful tongue!

Doeg's tongue was as deadly as his sword, because it was his dishonest report to Saul that led to the death of the priests. Both his deceptive report and his heartless massacre of the priests were motivated by his greedy desire to enrich himself. Doeg was proud of his deceitful scheming. He thought he was a mighty man in the eyes of Saul, but he was a disgrace in the eyes of the Lord.

Doeg's Judgment

⁵Surely God will bring you down to everlasting ruin:
He will snatch you up and tear you from your tent;
he will uproot you from the land of the living. *Selah*

⁶The righteous will see and fear;
they will laugh at him, saying,
⁷"Here now is the man
      who did not make God his stronghold
      but trusted in his great wealth
      and grew strong by destroying others!"

David was confident that the Lord would punish Doeg in due time and deprive him of his dishonest gain. Then the judgment against Doeg would be a warning to the godly not to follow in Doeg's treacherous ways. The books of Samuel do not report the final outcome of God's dealings with Doeg, but, like David, we are confident that he received his judgment in due time.

David's Deliverance

**[8]But I am like an olive tree flourishing in the house of God;
I trust in God's unfailing love for ever and ever.
[9]I will praise you forever for what you have done;
in your name I will hope, for your name is good.
I will praise you in the presence of your saints.**

David was confident that the Lord would continue to preserve him during his flight from Saul so that he would live to praise God among his people both in time and in eternity.

This psalm is a prayer against those who treacherously disregard the Eighth Commandment in order to advance themselves at the expense of others. Those who report Christians to oppressive governments, those who spread false rumors about their rivals in business, and those who cut down their neighbors with gossip are among the many examples of those who "use their tongue like a razor" today.

PSALM 53

The Fool

This psalm is a near duplicate of Psalm 14. See the commentary on that psalm for remarks which apply to this psalm as well. The differences between Psalm 53 and 14 are indicated by italics. The most significant differences are the replacement of the divine name "LORD" by the name "God" in Psalm 53 and a substantial revision of verse 5. The other variations are minor stylistic changes.

For the director of music. According to *mahalath*. A *maskil* of David.

The musical directions are not present in Psalm 14. The term *mahalath* refers to a sad melody used during sickness or affliction.

1 The fool says in his heart, "There is no God."
They are corrupt, *and* their *ways* are vile;
there is no one who does good.

²*God* looks down from heaven on the sons of men
to see if there are any who understand,
any who seek God.

³*Everyone has turned away,*
they have together become corrupt;
there is no one who does good, not even one.

⁴Will the evildoers never learn —
those who devour my people as men eat bread
and who do not call on *God?*

⁵There they *were,* overwhelmed with dread,
where there was nothing to dread,
God scattered the bones of those who attacked you;
you put them to shame, for God despised them.

⁶Oh, that salvation for Israel would come out of Zion!
When *God* restores the fortunes of his people,
let Jacob rejoice and Israel be glad!

The main questions raised by this psalm are why two versions of the psalm occur in Psalms and who made the changes which distinguish the two versions from each other. The appearance of nearly identical material in two different psalms is not unique to Psalms 14 and 53, although in the other cases it is only parts of a psalm that are reproduced in another place. These duplications are called "doublets." Examples are Psalm 40:13-17 and Psalm 70:1-5, Psalm 57:7-11 and Psalm 108:1-5, and Psalm 60:5-12 and Psalm 108:6-13.

It is possible that a later inspired writer revised material originally written by David. Isaiah's account of Sennacherib's attack on Jerusalem (Isaiah 36) appears in slightly different form in 2 Kings 18, which was probably written by Jeremiah, and in 2 Chronicles 32, which was probably written by Ezra. Jude seems to adapt material from 2 Peter in his epistle. However, since Psalms 14 and 53 both have headings listing them as psalms of David, it is probable that David produced both versions himself.

Even today it is not uncommon for an author to produce more than one version of the same basic work. Often an author will revise something he has written to make it appropriate to a new occasion. For example, a pastor who was reusing a graduation sermon which he had originally written for a college graduation might revise it if he was using it for a grade school graduation. At any rate, it appears from the doublets in Psalms that on more than one occasion David reworked and reused material which he had originally composed for different occasions.

It is not clear what circumstances moved David to write Psalms 14 and 53. The changes in verse 5 suggest that Psalm 53 was revised from Psalm 14 to celebrate deliverance from a siege. David's victory over Absalom when he crossed the Jordan to trap David in the city of Mahanaim (2 Samuel 18) may be the occasion for Psalm 53. The time when Saul tried to trap David in Keilah (1 Samuel 23:7) is another possible occasion for writing one of these psalms. Since this psalm has no historical heading, the circumstances of its writing remain uncertain. The reference to Zion implies that both psalms, in their present form, date from a time after David had captured Jerusalem and had brought the ark there.

Psalm 53 is probably placed between Psalm 52, which refers to Doeg, and Psalm 54, which refers to the Ziphites, because it is intended to remind us of a fool named Nabal whom David encountered during his flight from Saul. The Hebrew word for fool in Psalm 53 is *nabal*, the same word as the name Nabal. Between his trouble with Doeg (1 Samuel 22) and his escape from the Ziphites (1 Samuel 26) David nearly killed Nabal because of his scornful treatment of David, but he was prevented from doing this by the wise intervention of Nabal's wife Abigail (1 Samuel 25).

We have spent some time on the circumstances of the composition of Psalms 14 and 53 in order to illustrate the way inspired writers sometimes used and adapted previously written materials. Scripture itself indicates the adaptation and use of such materials by the inspired writers. This is something quite different from the source theories of the negative critics, who divorce the biblical materials from their proper historical settings and from the inspired writers. It is important to distinguish between these two things.

PSALM 54

Ruthless Men Seek My Life

For the director of music. With stringed instruments.
A *maskil* of David. When the Ziphites had gone to Saul and said,
"Is not David hiding among us?"

The occasion of this psalm is reported in 1 Samuel 23:19-29 and 26:1-5. The Ziphites, who were members of David's own tribe of Judah, twice tried to betray David, apparently to win Saul's favor. This psalm has the same basic elements which we have observed in many of the previous psalms David wrote while fleeing from his enemies.

The Plea

1 **Save me, O God, by your name;
vindicate me by your might.
²Hear my prayer, O God;
listen to the words of my mouth.**

The Problem

**³Strangers are attacking me;
ruthless men seek my life —
men without regard for God.** *Selah*

The Solution

**⁴Surely God is my help;
the Lord is the one who sustains me.
⁵Let evil recoil on those who slander me;
in your faithfulness destroy them.**

The Outcome

**⁶I will sacrifice a freewill offering to you;
I will praise your name, O LORD, for it is good.
⁷For he has delivered me from all my troubles,
and my eyes have looked in triumph on my foes.**

PSALM 55

My Friend Betrays Me

This psalm was apparently written at the time of Absalom's rebellion, when David was betrayed by his friend and advisor Ahithophel. If so, this psalm should be compared to Psalm 41, which evidently deals with the same circumstances. These events are described in 2 Samuel 15 to 18.

For the director of music. With stringed instruments.
A *maskil* of David.

Opening Plea

1 Listen to my prayer, O God,
do not ignore my plea;
²hear me and answer me.

The Problem

My thoughts trouble me
and I am distraught
³at the voice of the enemy,
at the stares of the wicked;
for they bring down suffering upon me
and revile me in their anger.
⁴My heart is in anguish within me;
the terrors of death assail me.
⁵Fear and trembling have beset me;
horror has overwhelmed me.

⁶I said, "Oh, that I had the wings of a dove!
I would fly away and be at rest —
⁷I would flee far away and stay in the desert;   *Selah*
⁸I would hurry to my place of shelter,
far from the tempest and storm."

⁹Confuse the wicked, O Lord,
confound their speech,
for I see violence and strife in the city.
¹⁰Day and night they prowl about on its walls;
malice and abuse are within it.
¹¹Destructive forces are at work in the city;
threats and lies never leave its streets.

¹²If an enemy were insulting me,
I could endure it;

if a foe were raising himself against me,
    I could hide from him.
¹³But it is you, a man like myself,
    my companion, my close friend,
      ¹⁴with whom I once enjoyed sweet fellowship
      as we walked with the throng at the house of God.

Everything in this psalm fits with the time of Absalom's conspiracy. Verses 9-11 describe the slanders and plots passed around by Absalom and his co-conspirators. It was a special grief when David realized that his advisor Ahithophel had betrayed him and gone over to Absalom.

A sad irony of David's prayer is the fact that Uriah could have said about David many of the same things David said about Ahithophel.

In verse 6 David desires to fly away and escape the conspiracy. This feeling contrasts sharply with Psalm 11, in which David rejects such advice to flee. During Absalom's conspiracy David fled from the city into the wilderness. 2 Samuel 15:14 makes it clear that concern to avoid needless bloodshed in Jerusalem was the key factor in David's decision to flee the city. The desire to flee does not reflect despair so much as grief at being betrayed by a son and a friend. It is not so much a desire to hide in the wilderness, as a wish to take refuge in God.

The urge to flee from trouble is always a danger for a Christian. Elijah gave in to it (1 Kings 19). Jeremiah battled against it (Jeremiah 9:2 and 10:17). Giving in to such a desire is often a cowardly refusal to suffer for the gospel. But at other times there may be valid reasons to withdraw in the face of danger. We need guidance from God to recognize the difference.

225

At different times in his ministry Paul followed both courses. There were times when he had to stay and face trial. There were times when a prudent withdrawal was best for the young Christian church. It takes enlightened judgment to distinguish courage from wasteful foolhardiness and a reasonable concern for others from selfish cowardice. We pray that God will always help us know the difference.

Plea for Judgment

15Let death take my enemies by surprise;
   let them go down alive to the grave,
   for evil finds lodging among them.

Confidence in Judgment

16But I call to God,
      and the LORD saves me.
17Evening, morning and noon I cry out in distress,
      and he hears my voice.
18He ransoms me unharmed from the battle waged against me,
      even though many oppose me.
19God, who is enthroned forever,
      will hear them and afflict them —   *Selah*
      men who never change their ways
      and have no fear of God.

In these verses David prays for the defeat of the betrayer and his allies. This prayer was answered when Ahithophel committed suicide after Absalom rejected his advice. Absalom and many of his co-conspirators also came to their deserved end when they were killed in battle.

The Traitor's Treachery

20My companion attacks his friends;
   he violates his covenant.

²¹His speech is smooth as butter,
>   yet war is in his heart;
>   his words are more soothing than oil,
>   yet they are drawn swords.

This second description of the traitor emphasizes his cunning and his hypocrisy. In this Ahithophel resembled Judas, who hypocritically concealed his treachery and then betrayed Jesus with a kiss of friendship. David's anguish in these circumstances gives us insight into Christ's anguish in circumstances that were even more painful.

God's Solution

²²Cast your cares on the LORD
>   and he will sustain you;
>   he will never let the righteous fall.
²³But you, O God, will bring down the wicked
>   into the pit of corruption;
>   bloodthirsty and deceitful men will not live out
>   half their days.

But as for me, I trust in you.

David repeats his confidence that the Lord will deliver him. Verse 22 is well known and often memorized because it is a general statement of God's care, which can be applied in almost any circumstances. This psalm, like many of the other psalms of David, teaches us to trust in the Lord in any adversity and to remain confident that God will judge the wicked.

PSALM 56

When I Am Afraid

For the director of music. To [the tune of] "A Dove on Distant Oaks."
Of David. A *miktam*. When the Philistines had seized him in Gath.

This psalm is the first of five *miktam*. The circumstances which caused it to be written are described in 1 Samuel 21:10-15. During his flight from Saul, David panicked and in weakness of faith left Israel and sought safety by joining himself to the Philistine king Achish of Gath. When Achish's men seized David because he had killed Goliath, David escaped death by faking insanity. This psalm is an expression of faith, written by David after his act of weakness.

STANZA ONE
The Enemies

1 **Be merciful to me, O God, for men hotly pursue me;**
all day long they press their attack.
²My slanderers pursue me all day long;
many are attacking me in their pride.

David's Trust

³When I am afraid, I will trust in you.
⁴In God, whose word I praise, in God I trust;
I will not be afraid.
What can mortal man do to me?

STANZA TWO
The Enemies

⁵All day long they twist my words;
they are always plotting to harm me.
⁶They conspire, they lurk,
they watch my steps, eager to take my life.

David's Trust

> **⁷On no account let them escape;**
> **in your anger, O God, bring down the nations.**
>
> **⁸Record my lament;**
> **list my tears on your scroll —**
> **are they not in your record?**
>
> **⁹Then my enemies will turn back when I call for help.**
> **By this I will know that God is for me.**
>
> **¹⁰In God, whose word I praise,**
> **in the LORD, whose word I praise —**
> **¹¹in God I trust; I will not be afraid.**
> **What can man do to me?**

David's Promise

> **¹²I am under vows to you, O God;**
> **I will present my thank offerings to you.**
> **¹³For you have delivered me from death**
> **and my feet from stumbling,**
> **that I may walk before God in the light of life.**

In two stanzas which end with a very similar refrain David gives a double description of his enemies and of his trust in God. The plotters and liars who are condemned in this psalm may include not only the Philistines, but also the liars and plotters among Saul's men, like Doeg, since it was their treachery which had forced David to flee in the first place.

David's double expression of confidence contains some beautiful phrases which apply to almost any danger. The words "When I am afraid, I will trust in you" are a fitting prayer in sickness, in storms, in war, in persecution and in any other danger. When it seems that we are alone in our sorrows, what a comfort to know that God has counted and kept a record of our every tear. If we trust in the Lord, why should we be afraid of what man can do to us?

As is his custom, David closes his prayer with a promise to praise God for answering his prayer.

PSALM 57

Refuge in the Shadow of Your Wings

**For the director of music. To [the tune of] "Do Not Destroy."
Of David. A *miktam*. When he had fled from Saul into the cave.**

This psalm was written when David hid from Saul in a cave. This happened at least two times — first at Adullam in 1 Samuel 22:1 and later at En Gedi in 1 Samuel 24, when David had an opportunity to kill Saul but refused to do so. It is likely that the second of these two incidents is the one referred to here.

This psalm is the first of three psalms which are sung to the same tune. The last verses of this psalm are nearly identical to the first verses of Psalm 108. This doublet will be discussed in the comments on Psalm 108.

The Opening Plea

1 Have mercy on me, O God,
have mercy on me,
    for in you my soul takes refuge.
    I will take refuge in the shadow of your wings.
        until the disaster has passed.

²I cry out to God Most High,
    to God, who fulfills his purpose for me.
³He sends from heaven and saves me,
    rebuking those who hotly pursue me;   *Selah*
    God sends his love and his faithfulness.

These verses are typical of the opening pleas which are characteristic of so many of David's psalms. The psalmist compares God's protecting power to the sheltering wings of a mother bird protecting her babies. This comparison of the protecting and carrying power of God's wings occurs early in the Old Testament in Exodus 19:4 and Deuteronomy 32:11. It appears several times in the psalms (Psalms 17:8; 36:7; 61:4; 63:7; 91:4) and is used again by Jesus in one of his last appeals to Jerusalem (Matthew 23:37). The figure of wings conveys the impression of both soaring majesty and power as well as intimate shelter.

The Problem

> 4I am in the midst of lions;
> I lie among ravenous beasts —
> men whose teeth are spears and arrows,
> whose tongues are sharp swords.
>
> 5Be exalted, O God, above the heavens;
> let your glory be over all the earth.
>
> 6They spread a net for my feet —
> I was bowed down in distress.
>
> They dug a pit in my path —
> but they have fallen into it themselves. *Selah*

David's enemies are described as ferocious beasts, tearing their prey, and as trappers, trying to catch an animal. These descriptions emphasize both the viciousness and the cunning of David's enemies. The embarrassment of Saul, who trapped himself in the cave, may be reflected in the irony of the second half of verse 6.

A noteworthy feature of this description is the exclamation of praise which separates the two pictures of the enemy. Even in the midst of distress David thinks of the glory of God. These thoughts change his distressed heart to a steadfast heart.

David's Confidence

> [7]My heart is steadfast, O God,
>   my heart is steadfast;
>   I will sing and make music.
> [8]Awake, my soul!
>   Awake, harp and lyre!
>   I will awaken the dawn.
> [9]I will praise you, O Lord, among the nations;
>   I will sing of you among the peoples.
>   [10]For great is your love, reaching to the heavens;
>   your faithfulness reaches to the skies.
>
> [11]Be exalted, O God, above the heavens;
>   let your glory be over all the earth.

As usual, David promises to praise God after he has been delivered. He is confident that even though he has spared Saul's life, God will keep him safe until he becomes king. He has this confidence because the God who is always faithful to his promises had declared this to him.

The closing exclamation of praise is the same as the exclamation in the middle of the psalm (v 5). David reaffirms the confidence he had expressed earlier.

PSALM 58

Do You Rulers Speak Justly?

**For the director of music. [To the tune of] "Do Not Destroy."
Of David. A *miktam*.**

This psalm is not linked to a specific situation in David's life as other psalms in this section are. It could be a condemnation of Saul's corrupt regime, but it is general enough to apply to any misgovernment. Psalm 82 is similar in theme.

Unjust Rulers

1 **Do you rulers indeed speak justly?
Do you judge uprightly among men?**

**²No, in your heart you devise injustice,
and your hands mete out violence on the earth.
³Even from birth the wicked go astray;
from the womb they are wayward and speak lies.
⁴Their venom is like the venom of a snake,
like that of a cobra that has stopped its ears,
⁵that will not heed the tune of the charmer,
however skillful the enchanter may be.**

The word translated "rulers" often means "gods" or "heavenly beings." This word emphasizes that even corrupt rulers are servants of God and are his representatives on earth. But at the instigation of Satan such corrupt rulers misuse the power God has given them. The judgment against such corrupt rulers will be especially severe because they are God's servants who have the responsibility to punish evil and reward good (Romans 13:1-7). It is an abomination when rulers do the opposite and punish the innocent and protect the wicked. Since much has been given to them, their punishment for misusing that authority will be correspondingly severe. Like snakes that do not hear the music of the charmer, they carry out their evil, undeterred by either strong warnings or kind appeals.

The most enormous crimes in history have been carried out by governments. Corrupt rulers are so common in the world that such corruption sometimes seems normal. In a sense it is, since corrupt rulers are simply the prominent examples of a human race which is corrupt from birth. The evil they harbor in their hearts is expressed by the violence of their hands. By comparing the corrupt rulers to snakes, David may be making a subtle reference to their master the devil, who taught them their evil ways. Though many take such corrupt rulers for granted, the God who distinguishes right from wrong cannot let their wickedness pass unnoticed. Neither can his people.

The Curse on Unjust Rulers

> **6Break the teeth in their mouths, O God;**
> **tear out, O LORD, the fangs of the lions!**
> **7Let them vanish like water that flows away;**
> **when they draw the bow, let their arrows be blunted.**
> **8Like a slug melting away as it moves along,**
> **like a stillborn child, may they not see the sun.**
>
> **9Before your pots can feel the heat of the thorns —**
> **whether they be green or dry —**
> **the wicked will be swept away.**

David denounces corrupt rulers with harsh curses. See the introduction to this volume for comments on the imprecatory passages in the psalms. The comparison in verse 9 emphasizes the swiftness of their destruction.

Portions of verses 7 and 9 are very difficult to translate, but none of the suggested alternate translations seem to offer any significant improvement over the NIV.

The Joy of the Righteous

¹⁰The righteous will be glad when they are avenged,
when they bathe their feet in the blood of the wicked.
¹¹Then men will say, "Surely the righteous still are rewarded;
surely there is a God who judges the earth."

Although Christians pray for the repentance of their enemies, it is also proper that they rejoice when God's judgment triumphs and justice is done. Compare this psalm with Revelation 19 for a further demonstration of this truth. The reason for the saints' rejoicing is not personal revenge, but joy that God's honor is upheld, sin is deterred, and the righteous are rewarded.

This psalm condemns every unjust ruler. Sad to say, David himself was such a ruler during a brief period of his reign. Other examples in Scripture are Ahab and Jezebel, who persecuted God's prophets and people of God like Naboth; Herod, who killed the babies of Bethlehem; and Pilate and Caiaphas, who sent Christ to his death. Examples from our time include Nazi and Communist persecutors, and democratic rulers who allow innocent unborn to be killed even while they allow murderers to live.

PSALM 59

They Lie in Wait

For the director of music. [To the tune of] "Do Not Destroy."
Of David. A *miktam*. When Saul had sent men to watch
David's house in order to kill him.

The setting of this psalm is given in 1 Samuel 19. Saul had given his daughter Michal to David in marriage, hoping

that she would help him against David. However, she loved
David and took his side against her father. When Saul sent
men to their house, Michal helped David escape. She put a
dummy in David's bed and let him escape out the window.

The psalm can be divided into two parts, each of which
ends with a nearly identical refrain. The enemies are described in very similar terms in each half of the psalm, but
there is a definite progression in the psalm. Prayer for
deliverance is dominant in the first half, and a confident
description of deliverance is emphasized in the second half.

STANZA ONE
Opening Plea

1 **Deliver me from my enemies, O God;**
   protect me from those who rise up against me.
²Deliver me from evildoers
   and save me from bloodthirsty men.

The Viciousness of the Enemy

³See how they lie in wait for me!
   Fierce men conspire against me
      for no offense or sin of mine, O LORD.
   ⁴I have done no wrong,
   yet they are ready to attack me.

   Arise to help me;
   look on my plight!
⁵O LORD God Almighty, the God of Israel,
   rouse yourself to punish all the nations;
   show no mercy to wicked traitors. *Selah*

⁶They return at evening, snarling like dogs,
   and prowl about the city.
⁷See what they spew from their mouths —
   they spew out swords from their lips,
   and they say, "Who can hear us?"

Conclusion and Refrain

> **⁸But you, O LORD, laugh at them;**
> **you scoff at all those nations.**
> **⁹O my Strength, I watch for you;**
> **you, O God, are my fortress, my loving God.**

In the first stanza David emphasizes three points: the viciousness, treachery and arrogance of the enemy; his own innocence, which makes him undeserving of persecution; and the power and willingness of God to judge the enemies. The harshness of David's description of the enemies as a pack of snarling dogs is not surprising, since these men stooped so low as to attack him in his own home under cover of darkness and even expected David's wife to help them.

STANZA TWO
Opening Confidence

> **¹⁰God will go before me**
> **and will let me gloat over those who slander me.**

The Judgment of the Enemies

> **¹¹But do not kill them, O LORD our shield,**
> **or my people will forget.**
> **In your might make them wander about,**
> **and bring them down.**
> > **¹²For the sins of their mouths,**
> > **for the words of their lips,**
> **let them be caught in their pride.**
> > **For the curses and lies they utter,**
> **¹³consume them in wrath,**
> **consume them till they are no more.**
> **Then it will be known to the ends of the earth**
> > **that God rules over Jacob.** *Selah*

237

¹⁴**They return at evening, snarling like dogs,**
and prowl about the city.
¹⁵**They wander about for food**
and howl if not satisfied.

Conclusion and Refrain

¹⁶**But I will sing of your strength,**
in the morning I will sing of your love;
for you are my fortress,
my refuge in times of trouble.
¹⁷**O my Strength, I sing praise to you;**
you, O God, are my fortress, my loving God.

The pattern of the second stanza is similar to the first, except that David has progressed to greater certainty of victory. David issues a strong call for the punishment of the ungodly. He asks that their punishment be both public and prolonged so that it will serve as a lesson to others both in Israel and in the whole world. He also asks that their punishment include final destruction. These are harsh words, but they agree with God's own verdict on impenitent sinners.

The pronouncements of Judgment Day will include both a public vindication of God's justice and an announcement of eternal destruction. The only difference between the judgments of the Last Day and what David is praying for is that David is speaking of preliminary judgments which take place in time and which can still serve as a lesson to others.

Every part of stanza two shows progression in thought from stanza one. The enemies are still snarling, but in stanza two their arrogance has been subdued. In the refrain of stanza one David is waiting for the Lord. In stanza two David is already praising the Lord, because he has been carried from great danger, in which his own house was a death trap, to safety in the fortress of God.

David's reference to "the ends of the earth" expands the application of this psalm from the experiences of David's early life which motivated him to write the psalm to the experiences of believers throughout the world until the end of time. The same principles of judgment and justice which applied to God's dealings with Saul and his cronies apply to all evildoers and persecutors of all time.

PSALM 60

You Have Rejected Us

For the director of music. To [the tune of] "The Lily of the Covenant." A *miktam* of David. For teaching. When he fought Aram Nahsraim and Aram Zobah, and when Joab returned and struck down twelve thousand Edomites in the Valley of Salt.

The circumstances which lie behind this psalm are described in 2 Samuel 8 and 10. The Arameans were the inhabitants of the country we today call Syria. Aram Naharaim is the northeastern part of the country near the Euphrates River. Zobah is in central Syria, probably in the Bekaa Valley. Saul and David conducted campaigns against the Arameans and subjected the region to tribute.

The exact time and circumstances of the battles mentioned in the heading of this psalm are uncertain, but it may refer to the resurgence of the Arameans against Israel later in David's reign when they came to help the Ammonites in their defiance of Israel (2 Samuel 10). The battle against the Edomites probably refers to an attack which rebelling Edomites made against Israel through the Arabah Valley south of the Dead Sea in an attempt to take advantage of Israel's conflict with the Ammonites and Arameans to the north and east.

The last verses of this psalm are nearly identical to the last verses of Psalm 108. This doublet will be discussed in the comments on that psalm.

David's Prayer

1 **You have rejected us, O God,**
and burst forth upon us;
you have been angry —
    now restore us!
²You have shaken the land and torn it open;
mend its fractures, for it is quaking.
³You have shown your people desperate times;
you have given us wine that makes us stagger.

⁴But for those who fear you,
you have raised a banner to be unfurled
    against the bow. *Selah*

⁵Save us and help us with your right hand,
that those you love may be delivered.

David first speaks of the desperate predicament in which Israel finds itself. Since it is being attacked simultaneously by several enemies, humanly speaking it seems likely that Israel will be defeated. It looks as if David's kingdom will be torn apart. David and the people are perplexed. What has happened to God's promises of victory? Are God's people being rejected for sins they have committed?

David sets these fears aside with a statement of confidence. God's promise is like a battle flag which will lead them to victory. David asks God to demonstrate his love for them by delivering them.

God's Reply

⁶God has spoken from his sanctuary:
"In triumph I will parcel out Shechem
and measure off the Valley of Succoth.
⁷Gilead is mine, and Manasseh is mine;
Ephraim is my helmet, Judah my scepter.
⁸Moab is my washbasin, upon Edom I toss my sandal;
over Philistia I shout in triumph."

This assurance from God seems to be based on the past victory he gave Israel when he allowed them to conquer the land under Joshua. Shechem was the city in Samaria which was the first "capital" of Israel after the conquest. The Valley of Succoth is the area along the Jabbok River east of the Jordan. Gilead is a region in the northern Transjordan which was occupied by the tribe of Manasseh. These Transjordan territories had been conquered and divided among the tribes of Israel under the leadership of Moses.

Ephraim and Judah were the two most powerful and influential tribes of Israel, who led them in war. Taken together, the places named represent the whole land of Israel. Moab, Edom and Philistia were Israel's enemies on their eastern, southern and western borders, respectively. They are described in terms which show that they have been subjected to Israelite rule.

Some commentators suggest that David may here be quoting from an ancient psalm in some non-canonical book, such as the "Book of the Wars of the Lord" mentioned in Numbers 21:14. If so, he is using past victories given by the Lord as an assurance that he will help his people now. In any case, the quotation with its references to territory on both sides of the Jordan fits the struggle against the Arameans and Edomites in which the control of Israel's tribal territory east of the Jordan was at stake.

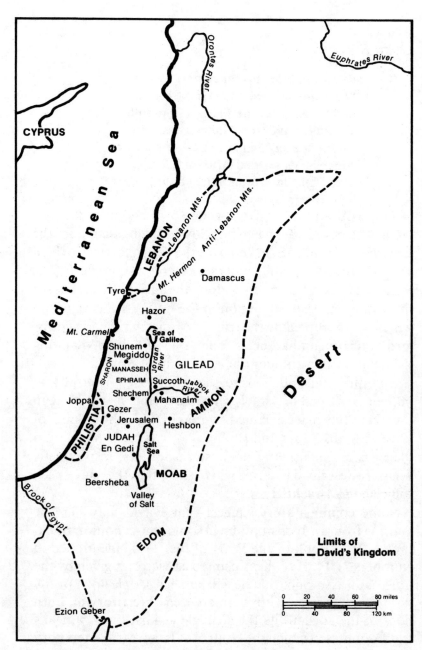

Israel and Neighboring Nations

David's Prayer

> [9]Who will bring me to the fortified city?
> Who will lead me to Edom?
> [10]Is it not you, O God, you who have rejected us
> and no longer go out with our armies?
> [11]Give us aid against the enemy,
> for the help of man is worthless.
> [12]With God we will gain the victory,
> and he will trample down our enemies.

In light of God's proclamation of past victories David asks, "Who will give us victory in the present? Who will let us hold on to the territories east of the Jordan?" To David the answer is obvious: "Although God has allowed us to suffer reverses, he will relent and grant us the victory." In the battle against the Arameans and Ammonites God did give such a victory, and David's kingdom was preserved.

PSALM 61

Although Psalms 61-64 do not have specific historical headings like those of the preceding psalms, they are closely related to them in theme. These four psalms continue the theme of Psalms 59 and 60: trust in God in time of danger.

A Soldier's Prayer from the Ends of the Earth

For the director of music. With stringed instruments. Of David.

> **1** Hear my cry, O God;
> listen to my prayer.
> [2]From the ends of the earth I call to you,
> I call as my heart grows faint;
> lead me to the rock that is higher than I.
> [3]For you have been my refuge,
> a strong tower against the foe.

⁴I long to dwell in your tent forever
and take refuge in the shelter of your wings.   *Selah*
⁵For you have heard my vows, O God;
you have given me the heritage of those
who fear your name.

⁶Increase the days of the king's life,
his years for many generations.
⁷May he be enthroned in God's presence forever;
appoint your love and faithfulness to protect him.

⁸Then will I ever sing praise to your name
and fulfill my vows day after day.

We cannot be sure when this psalm was written, but it may come from the time of Absalom's revolt, when David was in exile at "the ends of the earth," when he was driven away from the temple and his dynasty seemed to be in danger of falling. Or perhaps it was written during another of David's foreign campaigns.

David is confident that God, who has been his refuge and tower in the past, will deliver him again. He renounces trust in his own power when he confesses that God is the rock who is higher than he is.

Dwelling in God's tent forever, receiving a heritage from God and dwelling in the protection of his wings are more intimate terms than the preceding figures of a rock and a tower. These terms look beyond earthly security and the establishing of David's dynasty in Jerusalem to the Messiah's eternal kingdom. David's prayer for the king also reaches beyond David himself, beyond Solomon and all the other members of the dynasty to King Messiah, that is, to Christ and his eternal kingdom. David himself will praise this king descended from him.

The opening verses of this psalm would be an appropriate prayer for a soldier or anyone else in danger far from home. Abraham, Jacob, Joseph and Daniel come to mind as people for whom this prayer would have been appropriate. Far from home, we too must trust in the rock that is higher than we.

PSALM 62

My Soul Rests in God Alone

For the director of music. For Jeduthun. A psalm of David.

This psalm is the first of a series of seven "psalms" in the strict sense of the term. "For Jeduthun" might better be translated "according to the style of Jeduthun," the temple musician.

1 My soul finds rest in God alone;
  my salvation comes from him.
²He alone is my rock and my salvation;
 he is my fortress,
 I will never be shaken.

³How long will you assault a man?
 Would all of you throw him down —
   this leaning wall, this tottering fence?
⁴They fully intend to topple him from his lofty place;
 they take delight in lies.
 With their mouths they bless,
 but in their hearts they curse.   *Selah*

The picture of God as a rock of protection connects this psalm with the preceding one. Since God is David's fortress, it is futile for his enemies to try to overthrow him, even though he himself is as weak as a tottering wall. The enemies are cowardly bullies who boldly attack the weak. They are envious of their superiors and eager to attack those in lofty positions. They are the opposite of the godly who strengthen the weak and rejoice with those who have been richly blessed. Though the enemies practice hypocrisy, their schemes will not succeed.

> 5Find rest, O my soul, in God alone;
>   my hope comes from him.
> 6He alone is my rock and my salvation;
>   he is my fortress,
>   I will not be shaken.
> 7My salvation and my honor depend on God;
>   he is my mighty rock, my refuge.
>
> 8Trust in him at all times, O people;
>   pour out your hearts to him,
>   for God is our refuge.   *Selah*
> 9Lowborn men are but a breath,
>   the highborn are but a lie;
>   if weighed on a balance,
>   they are nothing;
>   together they are only a breath.
> 10Do not trust in extortion
>   or take pride in stolen goods;
>   though your riches increase,
>   do not set your heart on them.
>
> 11One thing God has spoken,
>   two things have I heard:
>   that you, O God, are strong,
> 12and that you, O Lord, are loving.
>   Surely you will reward each person
>   according to what he has done.

The second half of the psalm starts with an expression of confidence very similar to that which began the psalm.

David's main concern in this half of the psalm is that others will share his confidence in God as the only rock of protection. He advocates a patient, quiet waiting for God. He invites all people to join him in this confidence.

He warns against two undependable sources of help. Don't trust in people as your ultimate source of help. They are too short-lived and fickle to be a dependable help. Riches are undependable and fleeting, whether they are gained by honest or dishonest means.

David concludes with a meditation on two attributes of God which are a comfort to believers. God is almighty, but he uses this power to protect his people, not to crush them. God is loving and faithful, and he has the power to fulfill his loving promises for his people. These two characteristics combined give God's people peace and comfort in every circumstance. They can await his just judgment with confidence.

This psalm is one of the most general and universal prayers of David. We can easily apply it to our lives as a beautiful expression of the truths we study in the First Commandment and the First Article of the Creed.

PSALM 63

My Soul Thirsts for You

A psalm of David. When he was in the Desert of Judah.

Like Psalm 61, this psalm suggests a time of exile. In this respect it is also similar to Psalms 41-43. Perhaps it was written as a reflection on David's flight through the wilderness of Judah when he had to escape Absalom. His flight from Saul would be another possibility, but then the references to the king would have to be references which look ahead in faith to David's kingship.

1 O God, you are my God,
earnestly I seek you;
my soul thirsts for you,
my body longs for you,
in a dry and weary land
where there is no water.

²I have seen you in the sanctuary
and beheld your power and your glory.

David expresses a longing for God and his temple. His prayer is the prayer of an intimate friend of God. He addresses his God, not a stranger. His eagerness is that of a lover, longing to be reunited with the one he loves. He is eager to be restored from exile so that he can worship in God's presence. He promises to join eagerly in such worship when he is restored.

³Because your love is better than life,
my lips will glorify you.
⁴I will praise you as long as I live,
and in your name I will lift up my hands.
⁵My soul will be satisfied as with the richest of foods;
with singing lips my mouth will praise you.
⁶On my bed I remember you;
I think of you through the watches of the night.
⁷Because you are my help,
I sing in the shadow of your wings.
⁸My soul clings to you;
your right hand upholds me.

Praising God is David's food and drink. Earlier he was thirsty, now he is satisfied. Meditation and praise nourish his life. Praise will be in his mind and on his lips day and night. He will rest in the shadow of God's wings, but for his enemies the situation will be quite different.

⁹They who seek my life will be destroyed;
  they will go down to the depths of the earth.
¹⁰They will be given over to the sword
  and become food for jackals.

¹¹But the king will rejoice in God;
  all who swear by God's name will praise him,
  while the mouths of liars will be silenced.

Physical and eternal death await the ungodly. The gruesome picture of scavengers feeding on their bodies is only a pale foreshadowing of the grim reality of hell. Those who clamor against God will be silenced, but the mouths of God's people will praise him eternally.

PSALM 64

Hide Me from the Conspiracy

For the director of music. A psalm of David.

This psalm, which has no specific historical setting, can serve as a summary or review of the many psalms of David we have studied which are prayers against his enemies.

Opening Plea

1 Hear me, O God, as I voice my complaint;
  protect my life from the threat of the enemy.
²Hide me from the conspiracy of the wicked,
  from that noisy crowd of evildoers.

The Enemies' Wickedness

³They sharpen their tongues like swords
  and aim their words like deadly arrows.
⁴They shoot from ambush at the innocent man;
  they shoot at him suddenly, without fear.

⁵They encourage each other in evil plans,
  they talk about hiding their snares;
  they say, "Who will see them?"
⁶They plot injustice and say, "We have devised a perfect plan!"

Surely the mind and heart of man are cunning.

God's Judgment

⁷But God will shoot them with arrows;
  suddenly they will be struck down.
⁸He will turn their own tongues against them
  and bring them to ruin;

The Joy of the Godly

all who see them will shake their heads in scorn.
⁹All mankind will fear;
  they will proclaim the works of God
  and ponder what he has done.

¹⁰Let the righteous rejoice in the LORD
  and take refuge in him;
  let all the upright in heart praise him!

All the familiar elements of David's prayers against his enemies are here: an opening plea, a description of the treachery, viciousness and arrogance of the enemy, the innocence of the persecuted, an assurance of God's victory, and the thankfulness of the righteous. This psalm echoes the denunciation of cutting tongues which we first heard in Psalm 52. This psalm thus provides a fitting conclusion to this group of psalms concerning David's suffering, which began with Psalm 52.

"Surely the heart and mind of man are cunning." These words describe all of Saul's futile scheming against David.

These words characterize the treachery of Absalom as well. These words are an apt summary of the schemes of sinners of every time and place. In spite of all such schemes the ungodly will fail. In spite of such schemes the upright in heart will live to praise the Lord.

PSALM 65

Psalms 65-68 are all classified as "songs." All of them seem appropriate for use at festivals and in processions.

A Thanksgiving Psalm
You Crown the Year with Bounty

This psalm would be especially appropriate during pilgrimages to Jerusalem for the harvest festival of Pentecost and Tabernacles. It gives thanks for God's spiritual blessings to his people, for his governing of the nations, and for the harvest. This psalm is especially appropriate for our Thanksgiving Day, which emphasizes the same three themes.

For the director of music. A psalm of David. A song.

Introduction

**1 Praise awaits you, O God, in Zion;
to you our vows will be fulfilled.
²O you who hear prayer,
to you all men will come.**

The translation of the first line is uncertain. As the NIV note indicates, it may be translated, "Praise befits you, O God." Either thought fits the context. The references to vows in this section and to forgiveness in the next section may suggest that this psalm was composed after delivery from a drought or famine.

This prayer has an underlying mission theme. It speaks of the increase of the Lord's worship as his circle of worshipers grows from those Jews who come to his festivals in Jerusalem to the larger number of people who come to him from all nations. The psalmist foresees the day promised to Abraham when the blessings on Abraham's seed will be blessings for all the families of the earth.

Spiritual Blessings

> ³**When we were overwhelmed by sins,**
> **you forgave our transgressions.**
> ⁴**Blessed are those you choose**
> **and bring near to live in your courts!**
> **We are filled with the good things of your house,**
> **of your holy temple.**

These verses were especially fitting when the festival crowds of priests and pilgrims flocked to the temple. These words also express the joy we find in the festivals we celebrate with our fellow Christians in our churches. The richest fulfillment of these words will come when we are gathered together as one congregation in the festival of eternal life. The mention of forgiveness is fitting in a festival song, because without forgiveness we would have nothing to celebrate and could not come into God's presence.

Blessings on the Nations

> ⁵**You answer us with awesome deeds of righteousness,**
> **O God our Savior,**
> **the hope of all the ends of the earth**
> **and of the farthest seas,**
> ⁶**who formed the mountains by your power,**
> **having armed yourself with strength,**
> ⁷**who stilled the roaring of the seas,**
> **the roaring of their waves,**
> **and the turmoil of the nations.**

**⁸Those living far away fear your wonders;
where morning dawns and evening fades
you call forth songs of joy.**

God puts the unruly in their place. He rules over the restless waves of the sea and over the restless turmoil of the nations. He confined the seas in boundaries at creation. He turned them loose in the flood and then returned them to their places. He confines nations and empires to the boundaries he sets for them. When they become too proud, he breaks their power. He demonstrated this again and again during Israel's history, especially during the Exodus from Egypt. The psalmist looked ahead to the day when God would show such awesome deeds to all the people of the world. This day has come, and we rejoice in it. The awesome deeds Christ accomplished for our salvation are being preached where the morning dawns and the evening fades away.

Our Savior rules this world. He is our rock and fortress. Therefore, we do not trust in the strength of the mountains as our security. Nor do we fear the wild waves of the sea. The awesome deeds of God are our hope.

Blessings of the Harvest

**⁹You care for the land and water it;
you enrich it abundantly.
The streams of God are filled with water
to provide the people with grain,
for so you have ordained it.
¹⁰You drench its furrows and level its ridges;
you soften it with showers and bless its crops.
¹¹You crown the year with your bounty,
and your carts overflow with abundance.
¹²The grasslands of the desert overflow;
the hills are clothed with gladness.**

¹³The meadows are covered with flocks
   and the valleys are mantled with grain;
   they shout for joy and sing.

Sometimes God works by spectacular miracles. More often he works in a gentle rain. Without the cycle of the rains God has ordained, life would vanish from the earth. When God sends rain even the deserts bloom. Through the rain our Father sends he richly provides our daily bread. All creation rejoices in his blessings. This beautiful description of the rain and its blessings reminds us to praise the bountiful God who gives them all.

PSALM 66

How Awesome Are Your Deeds

This psalm expands on the theme of part two of the preceding psalm. It focuses on God's awesome deeds by which he delivered his people Israel from Egypt. However, it is general enough to apply to all of the awesome deeds by which God delivers his people.

For the director of music. A song. A psalm.

The Praise of the World

1 Shout with joy to God, all the earth!
²Sing the glory of his name;
   make his praise glorious!
³Say to God, "How awesome are your deeds!
   So great is your power that your enemies cringe before you.
⁴All the earth bows down to you;
   they sing praise to you,
   they sing praise to your name."   *Selah*

254

All the peoples of the earth are invited to join Israel in praising God for the great deeds he has done. The Egyptians and all the surrounding nations were filled with awe for the Lord over the great deeds by which he delivered Israel. But now he will be the gracious God of all people who turn to him.

God's Awesome Deeds to Deliver His People

> [5]**Come and see what God has done,**
>> **how awesome his works in man's behalf!**
>> [6]**He turned the sea into dry land,**
>>> **they passed through the waters on foot —**
>> **come, let us rejoice in him.**
>
> [7]**He rules forever by his power,**
> **his eyes watch the nations —**
> **let not the rebellious rise up against him.** *Selah*
>
> [8]**Praise our God, O peoples,**
> **let the sound of his praise be heard;**
> [9]**he has preserved our lives**
> **and kept our feet from slipping.**
>> [10]**For you, O God, tested us;**
>> **you refined us like silver.**
>> [11]**You brought us into prison**
>> **and laid burdens on our backs.**
>> [12]**You let men ride over our heads;**
>> **we went through fire and water,**
> **but you brought us to a place of abundance.**

This section is based on Israel's deliverance from their suffering in Egypt. It may also be applied to all trials of God's people, since the Exodus is a type and pattern of all of God's acts of deliverance.

Actually the major emphasis of this section is not on the final deliverance, but on the benefits of the trials which God

Praying in the Temple

allowed to precede that deliverance. God uses trials to test and refine his people. We do not know the author or date of this psalm, but this thought of refining through suffering would be appropriate either to David or to another individual at some later point in Israel's history. Isaiah 43 develops a very similar theme.

His People's Praise

> [13]I will come to your temple with burnt offerings
> and fulfill my vows to you —
> [14]vows my lips promised
> and my mouth spoke when I was in trouble.
> [15]I will sacrifice fat animals to you
> and an offering of rams;
> I will offer bulls and goats. *Selah*

> [16]Come and listen, all you who fear God;
> let me tell you what he has done for me.
> [17]I cried out to him with my mouth;
> his praise was on my tongue.

> [18]If I had cherished sin in my heart,
> the Lord would not have listened;
> [19]but God has surely listened
> and heard my voice in prayer.

> [20]Praise be to God, who has not rejected my prayer
> or withheld his love from me!

The surprising thing about this section is the personal, individual character of the prayer and praise, since the preceding section was national or congregational. It appears that the psalmist was applying to his own personal experience the lesson he had learned from the deliverance of the nation. Like the nation, he has been forgiven and delivered in spite of his sins. For this he praises God and invites others to join him in his praise.

Although we direct people's attention primarily to God's great acts which won salvation for all people, it is also appropriate that we testify to the significance these acts have had in our own lives. Our examples and our experiences can be an encouragement to others.

PSALM 67

Thy Kingdom Come

For the director of music. With stringed instruments. A psalm. A song.

This psalm makes an excellent mission prayer. The psalmist prays that all people may experience the same grace and blessing which God placed upon his people Israel in the benediction he gave to Moses and Aaron. This psalm prays for the fulfillment of the promise to Abraham. The harvest in this psalm is primarily the harvest of souls through the gospel, rather than the harvest of the crops of the fields. This psalm is especially appropriate for Pentecost, which began as an Old Testament harvest festival but today is celebrated as the beginning of the harvest which the church gathers through the preaching of the gospel.

This psalm has a balanced poetic form. It begins with a four-line prayer that God will bless his people. The middle prayer, that all people will join in the praise of God, begins and ends with the same words. The psalm ends with a four-line answer to the prayer.

The Prayer

1 **May God be gracious to us and bless us
and make his face shine upon us,** *Selah*

²that your ways may be known on earth,
your salvation among all nations.

³May the peoples praise you, O God;
  may all the peoples praise you.
⁴May the nations be glad and sing for joy;
      for you rule the peoples justly
      and guide the nations of the earth.   *Selah*
⁵May the peoples praise you, O God;
  may all the peoples praise you.

The Answer

⁶Then the land will yield its harvest,
  and God, our God, will bless us.
⁷God will bless us,
  and all the ends of the earth will fear him.

When God is gracious to us and blesses us, we want to share his word with all people. Our praise of God will lead others to praise him. God's blessings to us will be a source of blessing to others. If we joyfully praise God and tell the nations of his righteousness, the earth will yield a rich harvest of souls won for Christ and for eternal life.

Psalms 65-67 teach us that the truth about God is our personal property, it is not our private property. It will be no less ours when we have shared it with others. In fact, we will be enriched by such sharing. God is just as generous with his grace as he is with the harvest he provides in nature. He wants us to share his grace with others. May God bless us and our work so that the earth yields a rich spiritual harvest.

PSALM 68

The Procession of My God

For the director of music. Of David. A psalm. A song.

Like the three preceding psalms, Psalm 68 is very appropriate for use at a festival in the temple. It describes a procession of God from Mount Sinai, where the ark of the covenant was constructed, to the temple on Mount Zion in Jerusalem, where the ark found its home. This psalm may have been written for the procession when David brought the ark of the covenant to Jerusalem (2 Samuel 6) or for some occasion when the ark accompanied Israel into battle, such as 2 Samuel 11:11. However, it is appropriate for any festive procession to the temple. In the Christian church this psalm is often read on the festival of Jesus' ascension and on Pentecost.

Judgment on God's Enemies

1 May God arise, may his enemies be scattered;
may his foes flee before him.
2 As smoke is blown away by the wind,
may you blow them away;
as wax melts before the fire,
may the wicked perish before God.

If this psalm was written shortly after David conquered Jerusalem, it is natural that David would pray that the God of victory would continue to subdue his enemies just as he had done during the exodus from Egypt, during the conquest of the Promised Land, during the days of the judges, and during the victories of David which culminated in the capture of Jerusalem.

It is apparent that David is looking to the past for comfort in the present and in the future, since the opening verses of Psalm 68 are very similar to the prayer which was recited whenever the people of Israel marched out of their camp in the wilderness with the ark of God leading the way (Numbers 10:35). The main difference is that in Numbers 10 the words must be translated as a wish or a prayer. In the psalm these verses may just as properly be translated as an affirmation of faith, "God will arise and his enemies will be scattered."

With the many enemies the people of God face today —atheistic Communism, militant Islam, humanism and materialism, false teachers within the church — it often seems that the church is fighting a losing battle. But we can be as confident of final victory as David was. Before the Almighty God even great armies are as fragile as smoke which the wind blows away, as soft as wax that melts in the white-hot fury of the Lord. As it was when the Egyptian army floated ashore at the Red Sea, as it was when Sennacherib's army was destroyed in a night, so it will be for all God's enemies when Christ returns.

Blessing on God's People

> ³But may the righteous be glad and rejoice before God;
>   may they be happy and joyful.
> ⁴Sing to God, sing praise to his name,
>   extol him who rides on the clouds —
>   his name is the LORD —
>   and rejoice before him.
>
> ⁵A father to the fatherless, a defender of widows,
>   is God in his holy dwelling.
> ⁶God sets the lonely in families,
>   he leads forth the prisoners with singing;
>   but the rebellious live in a sun-scorched land.

261

What a contrast between the disaster experienced by God's enemies and the blessings enjoyed by his children! Although he is a mighty God, whose rule over nature is pictured by his riding on the clouds, he is a gentle father to his children. Although the clouds at Mount Sinai and the clouds of Judgment Day are tokens of the awesome judgments of God, even when he comes in judgment his coming will be a blessing for his people.

God has a special concern for the physically weak, for the oppressed and for widows and orphans. These terms refer not only to earthly circumstances, but also to the spiritual plight of Israel and the church in the world. Israel was not strong or numerous among the nations of its day. Today, too, the true church is not powerful or numerous in comparison to its enemies in the world. The poor and the lonely described in this psalm are the same people who are described as poor, mourning, meek and hungry in the Beatitudes (Matthew 5).

Sometimes the prisons of God's people are literal prisons, like the slave camps of Egypt or the prison of Herod. Sometimes they are the prisons of sin or oppression. God sets his people free from all such prisons through the message of the gospel of forgiveness and through the deliverance from physical distress which he brings to his people. God unites his people into one family, the church of believers. They will have a pleasant inheritance both in this world and in eternity. For God's enemies there will be only the barrenness of a sun-scorched land, now and eternally.

The general principle of God's care outlined in the preceding verses is applied to some specific historical situations in the following verses.

God Brings His People into His Land

⁷When you went out before your people, O God,
when you marched through the wasteland, *Selah*
⁸the earth shook,
the heavens poured down rain,
before God, the One of Sinai,
before God, the God of Israel.
⁹You gave abundant showers, O God;
you refreshed your weary inheritance.
¹⁰Your people settled in it,
and from your bounty, O God, you provided for the poor.

These verses refer to the blessings God gave his people as he led them through the wilderness from Mount Sinai to the Promised Land. There were real thunder and clouds at Mount Sinai, and the earth shook when God came down, but it seems most likely that the shaking of the earth and the showers of rain in these verses are symbols of the protecting power of God and the "showers of blessing" which accompanied Israel throughout the wilderness years and as they settled in the rich land he provided for them.

This providence of God as he led his people through the wilderness and into their inheritance is the model for the way in which God provides for his people through all time, whether he provides by spectacular miracle or quiet providence. Like Israel, we too can say, "From your bounty, O God, you provided for the poor."

God Defeats the Kings of the Land

¹¹The Lord announced the word,
and great was the company of those who proclaimed it:
¹²"Kings and armies flee in haste;
in the camps men divide the plunder.

263

13Even while you sleep among the campfires,
the wings of my dove are sheathed with silver,
its feathers with shining gold."

14When the Almighty scattered the kings in the land,
it was like snow fallen on Zalmon.

These verses describe the victories over their enemies which God gave his people through the judges. They are loosely based on the song sung by Deborah after her victory over the army of Sisera (Judges 5). In the closing verses of her song, Deborah makes an ironic comment on the plans of Israel's enemies to divide the plunder they expected to get from Israel. The irony both in Deborah's song and in this psalm is that in spite of the treacherous attacks of the enemy it is God's people who divide the plunder, not their enemies.

In Deborah's song the mother of Sisera, waiting for him at home, keeps telling herself that Sisera and his army are late in returning only because they have so much booty to divide. But at that very moment the bodies of Sisera's soldiers are scattered on the battlefield like drifts of snow, and it is Israel that is collecting the booty.

David echoes this song of Deborah because it expresses a truth which is applicable in every age of the history of God's people. Although this section is based on a specific historical event, the principles it sets forth are timeless and applicable to the victories of God and his people from the day of Deborah to the Day of Judgment.

Since verse 13 is difficult to translate and to interpret, you may find some translations which render it quite differently than the NIV. Nevertheless, we will confine our comments to the NIV translation, since none of the other translations are a marked improvement.

The reference to those who sleep among the campfires is apparently a rebuke to the negligent and weak in faith who stayed home and did not participate in the battle against the Lord's enemies. It is patterned after the rebuke to the tribe of Reuben in Judges 5:16.

Many different interpretations have been suggested for the beautiful wings of the dove. They have been understood as a figurative description of Israel basking in prosperity and enjoying the riches of the plunder, a description of the women of Israel dressing in the recently won plunder, a description of a trophy captured from the enemy, a description of the flight of the enemy, or a description of God's glory. A combination of the first two explanations seems most likely.

Zalmon means "Black Mountain" and may refer either to a mountain in the middle of Samaria or to one in Bashan.

The Lord Makes His Dwelling in Zion

> [15]The mountains of Bashan are majestic mountains;
> rugged are the mountains of Bashan.
> [16]Why gaze in envy, O rugged mountains,
> at the mountain where God chooses to reign,
> where the LORD himself will dwell forever?
>
> [17]The chariots of God are tens of thousands
> and thousands of thousands;
> the Lord has come from Sinai into his sanctuary.
> [18]When you ascended on high,
> you led captives in your train;
> you received gifts from men,
> even from the rebellious —
> that you, O LORD God, might dwell there.

The mountains of Bashan are the high mountains northeast of the Sea of Galilee, near the territory of Sisera.

Although these mountains are much higher than Mount Zion in Judah, Mount Zion surpasses them in beauty and glory, since the temple and the ark of the true God are there.

The chariots of God represent the angels who always serve in his presence. They accompanied him to Mount Sinai (Deuteronomy 33:2). Statues of cherubim hovered over the ark of the covenant (Exodus 25:20). The angels will accompany Christ when he returns in glory (Matthew 25:31).

God "ascended on high" when the ark was enshrined in the temple in Jerusalem. This move completed the conquest of the Promised Land, which was now ruled by a king after God's own heart. God had received gifts from men, since his temple now occupied the center of the land Israel had taken from their enemies.

But this "ascension" to Zion, great as it was, pointed to a greater ascension. In Ephesians 4:7-13 Paul applies these words to Christ's ascension after his death and resurrection. Christ's ascension marks the completion of God's conquest of the earth. Christ has defeated and subjected sin, death and Satan. Christ now has all power in heaven and in earth. He is King of kings and Lord of lords.

In agreement with the Greek translation of the Old Testament, Paul modifies the quotation somewhat from its Hebrew form. Instead of saying, "You received gifts from men," Paul says, "He gave gifts to men." Paul does this to stress the application of this passage to us. Christ has not only received gifts, but he shares with us the power he has received. He gives us gifts which enable us to join in the work of bringing people into his kingdom by announcing his victory to them. He gives us his word. He gives the church pastors, teachers and missionaries.

By the faithful use of these gifts we bring people into God's kingdom of grace so that God dwells in their hearts through faith. Through the faithful preaching of the gospel we prepare ourselves and others for the day when Christ will return to claim the kingdom that is already his. Then we and all who are his will ascend to his glorious kingdom with him.

God's Daily Care

> **¹⁹Praise be to the Lord, to God our Savior,**
> **who daily bears our burdens.**   ***Selah***

This beautiful little prayer summarizes all that God does for us. He gives us our daily bread. He daily forgives our sins. He daily gives us peace of mind through his word. He watches over us and preserves our lives. He protects the church from destruction. Praise be to the Lord, to God our Savior!

God's Future Victories

> **²⁰Our God is a God who saves;**
> **from the Sovereign LORD comes escape from death.**
> **²¹Surely God will crush the heads of his enemies,**
> **the hairy crowns of those who go on in their sins.**
> **²²The Lord says, "I will bring them from Bashan;**
> **I will bring them from the depths of the sea,**
> **²³that you may plunge your feet in the blood of your foes,**
> **while the tongues of your dogs have their share."**

This section includes devastating defeats God inflicts on the enemies of his people, such as the destruction of Sisera's army, but it points especially to the eternal judgments of hell. Verse 23 is not a pretty picture, but hell is not a pretty place. Revelation 19:17,18 also describes damnation as a body-strewn battlefield where scavengers feed on the corpses.

If we think of the most horrible pictures of disaster which we can imagine from earthly life, we have only a pale reflection of the terribleness of hell. These gruesome pictures warn us to beware that we never experience these terrible consequences of impenitence and unbelief. God wants all people to be saved and to come to the knowledge of the truth, but those who refuse and go on in their sins will experience the horrors of eternal judgment.

God's Procession into the Temple

24Your procession has come into view, O God,
  the procession of my God and King into the sanctuary.
25In front are the singers,
  after them the musicians;
  with them are the maidens playing tambourines.

26Praise God in the great congregation;
  praise the LORD in the assembly of Israel.

27There is the little tribe of Benjamin, leading them,
  there the great throng of Judah's princes,
  and there the princes of Zebulun and of Naphtali.

After the preceding sections, which review the history of God's march to Zion, this section describes the actual procession into Jerusalem. The singers and musicians are the priests who fulfilled those roles in the worship in the temple. Women playing tambourines often participated in victory processions as they did when David returned from killing Goliath (1 Samuel 18:6). Several of the tribes of Israel, mentioned as participants in the procession, represent the lay people of Israel. Benjamin may be given special prominence because the city of Jerusalem was located in the tribal territory of Benjamin.

Prayer for Future Victory

28Summon your power, O God;
  show us your strength, O God,
  as you have done before.

This section returns to a historical view of God's victories. It prays that the victories of the past will be continued in the future. The next section responds to this prayer with the assurance of great victories in the future.

God Rules the Nations

> ²⁹**Because of your temple at Jerusalem**
> **kings will bring you gifts.**
> ³⁰**Rebuke the beast among the reeds,**
> **the herd of bulls among the calves of the nations.**
> **Humbled, may it bring bars of silver.**
> **Scatter the nations who delight in war.**
> ³¹**Envoys will come from Egypt;**
> **Cush will submit herself to God.**
>
> ³²**Sing to God, O kingdoms of the earth,**
> **sing praise to the Lord,** ***Selah***
> ³³**to him who rides the ancient skies above,**
> **who thunders with mighty voice.**
> ³⁴**Proclaim the power of God,**
> **whose majesty is over Israel,**
> **whose power is in the skies.**

This section refers to the spiritual submission of the nations to the gospel. This type of figurative language, in which the progress of the gospel is described in terms of nations coming to Jerusalem, is very common in the prophets, especially in Isaiah. The beast among the reeds is a crocodile or hippopotamus. Here it represents Egypt, which up to the time of David had been Israel's greatest enemy. The bulls and calves are other nations, great and small, which are enemies of Israel. Cush is the region just south of Egypt.

These nations come under Israel's rule and bring gifts to God's temple when people of those nations become citizens of God's spiritual Israel through faith in Christ. Egypt, which once had been Israel's greatest enemy, became one of the greatest centers of Christianity during the early history of the church. We have lived to see the day when this section has been and is being fulfilled through the worldwide spread of the gospel.

Closing Praise

> 35You are awesome, O God, in your sanctuary;
>   the God of Israel gives power and strength to his people.
>
> **Praise be to God!**

These words are an appropriate conclusion to the psalm, since they are an apt summary of God's relationship to his people throughout history. For his awesome deeds we too say, "Praise be to God."

PSALM 69

The Messiah's Prayer: Save Me, O God

This psalm is matched only by Psalm 22 as a graphic prophetic description of Christ's suffering. Like Psalm 22, it is frequently referred to in the New Testament.

For the director of music. To [the tune of] "Lilies." Of David.

The Messiah's Troubles

1 Save me, O God,
    for the waters have come up to my neck.
2I sink in the miry depths, where there is no foothold.
    I have come into the deep waters;
    the floods engulf me.
3I am worn out calling for help;
    my throat is parched.
    My eyes fail, looking for my God.

In the Old Testament, raging flood waters and deep mud often symbolize troubles too difficult for the believer to overcome by himself. Here they symbolize the overwhelming burden of our sin and the depths of suffering Christ endured. Verse 3 reflects the urgency of Christ's prayer in Gethsemane and the anguished cry on the cross, "My God, my God, why have you forsaken me?" These verses describe Christ's inner turmoil. The following section directs our attention to the hostility of his enemies.

The Unfairness of Messiah's Enemies

> **⁴Those who hate me without reason outnumber the hairs of my head;**
> **many are my enemies without cause, those who seek to destroy me.**
> **I am forced to restore what I did not steal.**

The words, "They hated me without reason," are used in John 15:25 as a fitting description of Jesus' enemies. Jesus went around doing good — preaching the gospel of forgiveness, comforting the afflicted, healing the sick, feeding the hungry, and even raising the dead. In spite of this, yes, even because of this, the leaders of Israel hated him. The more good he did, the more they were determined to put him to death. Though Pilate admitted he found no fault with Jesus, he caved in to the demands that Christ be crucified. Christ was forced to pay for crimes he had not committed.

Messiah's Guilt

> **⁵You know my folly, O God;**
> **my guilt is not hidden from you.**

This verse presents the greatest difficulty to the Messianic interpretation of this psalm. How can this verse be applied to Christ, the sinless Son of God? This verse would seem to provide the strongest support for the claim that Psalm 69 must refer primarily to David or some other human being.

It is not difficult to counter this argument. Christ, though he had committed no sin, was indeed a sinner before the judgment of God. Paul says, "God made him who had no sin to be sin for us" (2 Corinthians 5:21). He tells the Galatians, "Christ redeemed us from the curse of the law by becoming a curse for us" (Galatians 3:13). Even the Old Testament tells us, "The LORD has laid on him the iniquity of us all" (Isaiah 53:6). The Messiah could properly speak of his guilt, since our guilt was transferred to him.

But how can foolishness be attributed to Christ, the infinitely wise Son of God? "Folly" may be just a synonym for sin in this passage. If so, the explanation given above covers this word as well. However, if "folly" is to be understood here in the normal sense of the word, it is used in the ironic sense used so often in 1 Corinthians.

The gospel Christ died to establish is foolishness to the unbelieving world (1 Corinthians 1:21). In the eyes of this world, any message which preaches free forgiveness is foolish, and anyone who gives himself for others is a fool. So by this world's standard of judgment Christ was a fool. How foolish to die for the wicked, for the ungrateful, and for the lowly!

But what the world regards as foolishness we, by the grace of God, recognize as the wisdom of God. The one whom they thought a fool we recognize as the very heart of God's wisdom — that is, our righteousness, redemption and salvation. We are told to become "fools" by following Christ's example (1 Corinthians 3:18; 4:10). This we gladly do, rejoicing that the innocent one became guilty so we could become innocent in him and that the wise one became a "fool" so that we could become wise in him.

The Offense of the Messiah

⁶May those who hope in you not be disgraced because of me,
O Lord, the LORD Almighty;
may those who seek you not be put to shame because of me,
O God of Israel.

Christ's humble appearance and wretched death turned off many in Israel. How could such a miserable man be their Messiah? Christ's humble life and the simplicity of the gospel message are also an offense to many today. Many are ashamed of the gospel and embarrassed by what they regard as the impossible claims of Scripture. We pray that we may never be ashamed of Jesus or his message, for only he can enable us to stand before God's judgment without shame.

The Messiah's Shame

⁷For I endure scorn for your sake,
and shame covers my face.
⁸I am a stranger to my brothers,
an alien to my own mother's sons;
⁹for zeal for your house consumes me,
and the insults of those who insult you fall on me.

¹⁰When I weep and fast,
I must endure scorn;
¹¹when I put on sackcloth,
people make sport of me.
¹²Those who sit at the gate mock me,
and I am the song of the drunkards.

Jesus' suffering did not begin on Maundy Thursday and Good Friday. He had endured scorn throughout his ministry. The people laughed when he said that Jairus's daughter was only sleeping (Matthew 9:24). The proud Pharisees sneered when Jesus rebuked their covetousness (Luke 16:14). Saddest of all, his own brothers looked on his work with skepticism and tried to interfere with his ministry (John 7:5, Mark 3:21).

Both halves of verse 9 are quoted in the New Testament as prophecies of Christ. John 2:17 connects Jesus' zeal for his Father's house with the first cleansing of the temple. Both times Jesus cleansed the temple he incurred the hostility and reproach of the Jewish leaders. Romans 15:3 quotes the second half of the verse as a general statement concerning the willingness of Christ to suffer because of his loyal obedience to his Father's will.

During his suffering Jesus was scorned both by the "cream" of Jewish society, the religious and political leaders, and by the "bottom of the barrel" like the criminals with whom he was crucified.

An Interlude of Prayer

> 13But I pray to you, O LORD,
>   in the time of your favor;
>   in your great love, O God,
>   answer me with your sure salvation.
>
> 14Rescue me from the mire,
>   do not let me sink;
>   deliver me from those who hate me,
>   from the deep waters.
> 15Do not let the floodwaters engulf me
>   or the depths swallow me up
>   or the pit close its mouth over me.
>
> 16Answer me, O LORD, out of the goodness of your love;
>   in your great mercy turn to me.
> 17Do not hide your face from your servant;
>   answer me quickly, for I am in trouble.
> 18Come near and rescue me;
>   redeem me because of my foes.

The description of Messiah's suffering is interrupted by a prayer for deliverance which echoes and expands upon his opening prayer. The prayer emphasizes three points: the greatness of his affliction, the bitter hatred of his enemies, and the goodness and mercy of God, which is the basis for his prayer.

The Messiah's Shame

> 19You know how I am scorned, disgraced and shamed;
>   all my enemies are before you.
> 20Scorn has broken my heart and has left me helpless;
>   I looked for sympathy, but there was none,
>   for comforters, but I found none.
> 21They put gall in my food
>   and gave me vinegar for my thirst.

After the interlude of prayer the psalmist resumes the description of the scorn the Messiah suffers from his enemies. The fulfillment of this prophecy is obvious in the gospel accounts of Jesus' suffering. The mockery of the soldiers during Jesus' trial, the taunts of his enemies gathered around the cross, the flight of his disciples and Peter's denial — all of these contributed to the loneliness and anguish of Christ during his passion. The references to bitter gall and vinegar to drink in Matthew 27:34 and 48 make it clear that the suffering of Christ fulfilled this psalm.

We look in vain for a literal fulfillment of these words in the life of David. David was a type of Christ, but some of the statements of the Messianic psalms exceed any experiences of David's life, and the psalms containing such statements are direct prophecies of Christ.

The Messiah's Curse

> 22May the table set before them become a snare;
>   may it become retribution and a trap.

²³May their eyes be darkened so they cannot see,
   and their backs be bent forever.
²⁴Pour out your wrath on them;
   let your fierce anger overtake them.
²⁵May their place be deserted.
   let there be no one to dwell in their tents.
²⁶For they persecute those you wound
   and talk about the pain of those you hurt.

²⁷Charge them with crime upon crime;
   do not let them share in your salvation.
²⁸May they be blotted out of the book of life
   and not be listed with the righteous.

The words of this prayer are horrifying; they are nothing less than a prayer for the damnation of one's enemies. To many people this prayer seems incompatible with Jesus' prayer on the cross, "Father, forgive them." Even many evangelical commentators have been distressed by this prayer and have tried to separate it from Christ by classifying it as an Old Testament prayer which is outdated in the New Testament era. However, when the New Testament applies these words to Judas in Acts 1:20, it shows that this is the prayer of the Messiah against his enemies.

The scriptural basis for such prayers was discussed in the section of the introduction which dealt with the imprecatory psalms. You may want to review that section at this time.

God has revealed his will to us: "Whoever believes and is baptized will be saved, but whoever does not believe will be condemned" (Mark 16:15). Our prayers must be in harmony with this revealed will of God. Jesus' will certainly was in harmony with that of his Father, who wants all people to be saved. Jesus did pray for the repentance of his enemies. Jesus had repeatedly warned Judas and appealed to him to turn back from his sin. But when Judas closed his heart to

God's love, he placed himself under the curse of God's law. The God who does not want anyone to perish is the same God who will cast those who reject his will into hell. This prayer reflects that grim reality.

In one sense the wounds and pain Christ suffered were imposed on him by his Father, since he was permitting Christ to suffer for our sins. But the enemies who were imposing Christ's suffering and mocking him as he endured it did not understand this. They were afflicting Christ for their own malicious purposes. Even as he was bearing the sins of the world, they were mocking his claim to be God's Son and scorning him as a worthless, self-appointed Messiah. Because they blasphemously and defiantly rejected the only payment for sin, nothing remained for them but God's condemnation as described in this psalm.

Messiah's Closing Prayer

> [29]I am in pain and distress;
> may your salvation, O God, protect me.
>
> [30]I will praise God's name in song
> and glorify him with thanksgiving.
> [31]This will please the LORD more than an ox,
> more than a bull with its horns and hoofs.
> [32]The poor will see and be glad —
> you who seek God, may your hearts live!
>
> [33]The LORD hears the needy
> and does not despise his captive people.
>
> [34]Let heaven and earth praise him,
> the seas and all that move in them,
> [35]for God will save Zion
> and rebuild the cities of Judah.
> Then people will settle there and possess it;
> [36]the children of his servants will inherit it,
> and those who love his name will dwell there.

277

This psalm ends as it began, with a prayer for deliverance. But the closing prayer differs from the opening prayer in that it passes beyond the suffering to the deliverance and the final victory. The Messiah promises to praise God with heartfelt thanksgiving when the victory has been won. This closing prayer moves beyond the loneliness of the Messiah during his suffering to the joy he shares with those who become one with him through faith.

The Messiah's victory is not for him alone. It is for his people who will share the joy of his victory in the eternal Zion. His victory is our victory because we are among the spiritually poor who have seen what he has done and rejoice in it. We join our victorious Savior in praising God's name with thanksgiving.

PSALM 70

Hasten to Save Me

For the director of music. Of David. A petition.

The NIV calls this psalm "a petition." The term translated "petition" is literally "a psalm for remembrance." This probably means that it is a petition for God to remember the psalmist's plight and deliver him. However, it may also mean that it is a prayer which reminds the psalmist of God's power and goodness.

This psalm is nearly identical to the conclusion of Psalm 40. It substitutes the divine name "God" for "LORD" in several places and omits the opening words, "*Be pleased* to save me," but otherwise it reproduces Psalm 40:13-17 almost exactly. We might ask, "Why would the same verses appear twice in the psalter?" We cannot answer this question precisely, but it appears that the verses as they appear here have been detached from Psalm 40 to make them into a more general prayer.

We do the same thing when we use only certain verses of a longer hymn as a closing hymn or an evening prayer. In Psalm 40 these verses are the conclusion of a longer prayer of the Messiah to God. It seems significant that these verses are placed after Psalm 69, which is also a Messianic psalm and which has several thoughts very similar to portions of Psalm 40. These verses link up very well with Psalm 69, which is a plea for deliverance.

1 **Hasten, O God, to save me;**
O LORD, come quickly to help me.

²May those who seek my life
  be put to shame and confusion;
 may all who desire my ruin
  be turned back in disgrace.
³May those who say to me, "Aha! Aha!"
  turn back because of their shame.

⁴But may all who seek you
  rejoice and be glad in you;
 may those who love your salvation
  always say, "Let God be exalted!"

⁵Yet I am poor and needy;
 come quickly to me, O God.
 You are my help and my deliverer;
 O LORD, do not delay.

This prayer is marked by urgency and simplicity. It begins and ends with cries for speedy help. In between, it briefly asks for judgment against the enemies of God and deliverance for his people. It bases this plea on the psalmist's need and God's power. Because it is so lacking in details and specific circumstances, it is applicable to any time of oppression or danger.

PSALM 71

Do Not Cast Me Away When I Am Old

The words of verse 12, "Come quickly to help me," link this psalm to Psalm 70, but this psalm is more specific, since it applies especially to old age. No author is listed, but it may be placed here at the end of a Davidic collection, just before a psalm of Solomon, because it was a psalm of David's old age. The opening verses are very similar to the beginning of Psalm 31, a psalm of David which deals with the end of life.

Opening Prayer

1 **In you, O LORD, I have taken refuge;**
let me never be put to shame.

2Rescue me and deliver me in your righteousness;
turn your ear to me and save me.
3Be my rock of refuge, to which I can always go;
give the command to save me,
for you are my rock and my fortress.
4Deliver me, O my God, from the hand of the wicked,
from the grasp of evil and cruel men.

The opening line could well serve as the motto of David's life. In his boyhood he had trusted God when he fought the bear and the lion and when he stood alone against Goliath. When he fled from Saul and Absalom, God had been his refuge. When God had delivered him from these enemies, David wrote Psalm 18, which begins with some very similar thoughts, as a psalm of thanks. Now he asks God to remain his refuge and fortress as his life draws to a close.

Remembrance of Past Help and Statement of Present Need

> [5]For you have been my hope, O Sovereign LORD,
>   my confidence since my youth.
> [6]From birth I have relied on you;
>   you brought me forth from my mother's womb.
>
> I will ever praise you.
>
> [7]I have become like a portent to many,
>   but you are my strong refuge.
>
> [8]My mouth is filled with your praise,
>   declaring your splendor all day long.

This section moves quickly from one thought to another. David speaks first of the past help of God, which began already before his birth. (Incidentally, these verses are also a powerful testimony against those who deny that children and babies can believe.) Twice David refers briefly to his present praise and thanksgiving for God's past and present care, but he does not dwell on this theme either time.

The only problem of interpretation in this section is the word "portent" in verse 7. Does this mean that David is a sign of God's loving care to many because of the many times God has helped him, or is "portent" here a negative term which points ahead to the derogatory judgment of his enemies, which is described more fully in the next section? The second interpretation seems more likely. Here even in the midst of his memories of God's past help, David briefly refers to present troubles. But he also refers briefly to the solution, trust in God as a refuge. Both of these themes will be developed more fully in the following sections.

Plea for Help in Present Trouble

> ⁹Do not cast me away when I am old;
>   do not forsake me when my strength is gone.
>
> ¹⁰For my enemies speak against me;
>   those who wait to kill me conspire together.
> ¹¹They say, "God has forsaken him;
>   pursue him and seize him,
>   for no one will rescue him."
>
> ¹²Be not far from me, O God;
>   come quickly, O my God, to help me.
> ¹³May my accusers perish in shame;
>   may those who want to harm me be covered
>   with scorn and disgrace.

In this section two pleas for deliverance "sandwich" a brief description of David's trouble. We do not know for certain who the enemies are to whom he is referring, but Adonijah and his co-conspirators in 1 Kings 1 are the most likely suspects. At the time Adonijah conspired to seize the throne, David had grown very feeble. The conspirators had every reason to think they could win easily. Since David had trusted in God for victory even when he still had the strength of his youth, he had all the more reason to do so now in his old age.

Present and Future Praise

> ¹⁴But as for me, I will always have hope;
>   I will praise you more and more.
> ¹⁵My mouth will tell of your righteousness,
>   of your salvation all day long,
>   though I know not its measure.

¹⁶I will come and proclaim your mighty acts,
   O Sovereign LORD;
 I will proclaim your righteousness, yours alone.
¹⁷Since my youth, O God, you have taught me,
   and to this day I declare your marvelous deeds.

¹⁸Even when I am old and gray, do not forsake me, O God,
   till I declare your power to the next generation,
   your might to all who are to come.
¹⁹Your righteousness reaches to the skies, O God,
   you who have done great things.
   Who, O God, is like you?

This is a beautiful prayer for every Christian, but especially for aged Christians. Although David speaks movingly of his personal experience, the focus of this prayer is not David, but God. Mighty acts and marvelous deeds, righteousness and salvation too great to measure — these are the theme of David's song. These are the theme of his message for all generations to follow.

Like David, we have experienced love from God which is too great to measure. The love of Christ which surpasses knowledge — who can know how wide and how long and how high and how deep it is? Who is like our God? Who else can save? His righteousness — his alone — is the way to salvation. This saving love of God is to be the theme of our songs and of our message for the next generation and for all generations to come.

The last years of life are often difficult for Christians today, just as they were for David. The pains and weaknesses of old age often make Christians eager or even impatient to leave this life. But if God leaves us here only to declare his goodness, which we have experienced through a lifetime, that is reason enough for us to be here.

If we have no power left to do anything but declare God's power to the next generation, that is reason enough to be content until he calls us to himself.

Closing Confidence

²⁰**Though you have made me see troubles, many and bitter,**
you will restore my life again;
from the depths of the earth
you will again bring me up.
²¹**You will increase my honor**
and comfort me once again.

Some Hebrew texts have "us" and "our" in verse 20 instead of the singular "my" and "me." Many commentators, therefore, see these verses as nothing more than a prayer for deliverance from personal and national crises for the enjoyment of a longer life. Although David certainly hopes for deliverance from his present troubles so that he can finish the work God has given him to do, I believe he also looks beyond deliverance from this one difficult situation to freedom from all grief and pain in eternity.

Certainly the knowledge of the resurrection expressed in these verses is not as explicit and clear as that expressed in the New Testament. Nevertheless, David expresses a knowledge and hope of the resurrection in the conclusions of Psalms 16, 17 and 23. Is it unthinkable or even surprising that he should express the same hope in a psalm which may be the last one he wrote? Deliverance from specific crises in his life reminded David of the coming deliverance from every danger. What would be more natural than turning his thoughts heavenward as the end of his life approached?

When our last days draw near, may we direct our thoughts heavenward and to the resurrection as David did and as Paul did when his death drew near, so that we may be confident of deliverance, either by longer earthly life or through death, which ushers us into the Lord's presence.

Closing Praise

> [22]I will praise you with the harp for your faithfulness,
>   O my God;
>   I will sing praise to you with the lyre,
>   O Holy One of Israel.
> [23]My lips will shout for joy when I sing praise to you —
>   I, whom you have redeemed.
> [24]My tongue will tell of your righteous acts all day long,
>   for those who wanted to harm me
>   have been put to shame and confusion.

In these verses the psalmist speaks as if the crisis is now past. It may be that after the crisis was over David added these words as a postscript to a prayer he had begun to write during the crisis. Perhaps the whole psalm was written down after the crisis was over as a reflection on the whole experience and on David's feelings and prayers throughout the incident. At any rate, the psalm ends on a note of joy and peace with David victorious and his enemies defeated. It thus forms a fitting conclusion to the collection of Davidic psalms which is so concerned with David's troubles.

PSALM 72

Of Solomon.

The heading of this psalm is *Of Solomon*. This may also be translated "to or for Solomon." For this reason some commentators regard this as a psalm written by David to express his hope for Solomon. In 2 Samuel 7 God had promised David that he would have a great son, who would build God's house. God had promised that the kingdom of David's heir would last forever. Perhaps David had hopes for a while that this prophecy would be fulfilled by Solomon, just as Eve may have hoped that Cain would be the seed promised to her. However, even though Solomon built God's house when he built the temple in Jerusalem, he fell far short of building the kind of kingdom that God had promised to David.

None of the Davidic kings who followed Solomon matched either David or Solomon in glory and power. It would take one greater than Solomon to fulfill either 2 Samuel 7 or this psalm. Only Christ, great David's greater Son, fulfills this psalm. Only his kingdom establishes perfect justice. Only his kingdom lasts forever. Only his kingdom is universal.

We therefore understand this psalm, not as a prayer written for or about Solomon, but as a prayer written by Solomon, who recognized that he could not establish the true glory of the Davidic kingdom, but that God's people would have to wait for another king, the Messiah, to accomplish that.

A Prayer for the Messianic King
The King's Justice

1 **Endow the king with your justice, O God,**
the royal son with your righteousness.
²He will judge your people in righteousness,
your afflicted ones with justice.
³The mountains will bring prosperity to the people,
the hills the fruit of righteousness.
⁴He will defend the afflicted among the people
and save the children of the needy;
he will crush the oppressor.

The outstanding characteristic of the Messiah's kingdom is justice. His rule is not based on arbitrary power, but on genuine righteousness. The righteousness of Christ's rule is reflected in two ways. First, there is the justice of the gospel through which Christ gives his people forgiveness and eternal life. This decree of forgiveness is just, because Christ has paid for their sins in full.

There is also the justice of the law through which Christ crushes the enemies of his people and all who defy God. This decree of damnation will also be just, because the damned spurned God's forgiveness and by their sins merited God's damnation. On the last day, when Christ invites those at his right hand to inherit life and condemns those at his left to spend eternity in hell with the devil and his angels, perfect justice will be done.

In this psalm, as in many other prophetic passages, eternal things are described in earthly terms. In prophetic writing the mountains and hills often symbolize exaltation or being raised up from lowliness. Isaiah 2:2,3 is an example of the many passages which describe the Messiah's kingdom as a lofty mountain. "The mountain of the LORD's temple will be established as chief among the mountains; it will be raised above the hills, and all nations will stream to it."

The fulfillment of this prophecy begins when Gentiles stream into the church, but this exaltation of the mountain of the Lord is completed only when all of his saints are gathered into his heavenly Jerusalem (Revelation 21,22). The peace and prosperity enjoyed in the Messiah's kingdom are not merely earthly prosperity, but the peace and prosperity of eternity, which we begin to enjoy through faith already in this life.

Amos 9:11-15 is another passage that describes Messiah's kingdom in terms of earthly prosperity. The quotation of Amos 9 in Acts 15:16,17 shows that these blessings are not material blessings to be enjoyed in an earthly millennial kingdom, but the blessings of the gospel which we begin to enjoy already in this life and which we will enjoy fully in the new heavens and the new earth in which righteousness dwells.

Isaiah 2:1-5, Isaiah 11:1-9, and Isaiah 60-62 are other descriptions of the Messiah's kingdom in earthly terms.

The King's Eternal Reign

> **5He will endure as long as the sun,**
> **as long as the moon, through all generations.**
> **6He will be like rain falling on a mown field,**
> **like showers watering the earth.**
> **7In his days the righteous will flourish;**
> **prosperity will abound till the moon is no more.**

These words cannot be applied literally to any king of Israel. All the kings of Israel lived for a few years and died. Even their dynasty did not remain in power. They lost their dominion to foreign rulers of Assyria, Babylon, Persia, Greece and Rome. Only Christ rules until the end of this age and on into eternity. Though he died, he rose from the dead and now lives forever. His church will endure until he returns. Then his people will live with him forever, even though the present heaven and earth pass away.

The gentle showers that water the land are symbols of the spiritual blessings that refresh the soul. Another example of the prophetic use of showers as a symbol of Messianic blessings can be found in Ezekiel 34:26 and its context.

The King's Universal Reign

> **8He will rule from sea to sea**
> **and from the River to the ends of the earth.**

⁹**The desert tribes will bow before him**
and his enemies will lick the dust.
¹⁰**The kings of Tarshish and of distant shores**
will bring tribute to him;
the kings of Sheba and Seba will present him gifts.
¹¹**All kings will bow down to him**
and all nations will serve him.

The Messiah's kingdom is not only more enduring than the Israelite monarchy. It is also more widespread than the dominion of any king of Israel. At its greatest extent during the reigns of David and Solomon the kingdom of Israel extended over only a relatively small part of the Middle East — from the boundary of Egypt to the Euphrates River in Syria. Even during Old Testament times many empires were greater than Israel at its greatest.

However, the Messiah will rule the whole world. He will be King of kings and Lord of lords. Every knee will bow to him. We see the beginning of the fulfillment of this prophecy as people of every nation come to faith in Christ. We will see its completion on the last day, when every living being will acknowledge Christ's lordship, either willingly in heaven or unwillingly in hell.

The text again describes spiritual realities in terms which were familiar to Solomon's contemporaries. Tarshish was a Mediterranean port far to the west, perhaps in Spain. Sheba and Seba were places in southern Arabia and eastern Africa. For the Israelites these places were the extremities of the known world, and thus they represented the whole world. Isaac Watts caught the spirit of these verses well in his famous mission hymn, "Jesus shall reign where'er the sun doth his successive journeys run."

The Blessings of His Rule

> [12]For he will deliver the needy who cry out;
> the afflicted who have no one to help.
> [13]He will take pity on the weak and the needy
> and save the needy from death.
> [14]He will rescue them from oppression and violence,
> for precious is their blood in his sight.

If we think of one word to describe Jesus that word is "Savior." When he came to earth, he showed compassion for the poor and needy, for the weak and the oppressed. He often delivered them from bondage to physical ailments, and even from death. But most important is the fact that he delivered them and us from bondage to sin and Satan. He delivers us from spiritual and eternal death. No one else can help us against these enemies. Again, the psalm speaks of blessings only Christ can deliver.

A Prayer for His Blessings

> [15]Long may he live!
> May gold from Sheba be given him.
> May people ever pray for him
> and bless him all day long.
>
> [16]Let grain abound throughout the land;
> on the tops of the hills may it sway.
> Let its fruit flourish like Lebanon;
> let it thrive like the grass of the field.
>
> [17]May his name endure forever;
> may it continue as long as the sun.
> All nations will be blessed through him,
> and they will call him blessed.

This section beautifully summarizes the blessings of the Messiah and prays that we may experience them all. Everywhere in the world Christians bring offerings to Christ as expressions of their love and praise him with songs. Every day they pray eagerly for his return. Everywhere in the world Christians experience the blessings of faith — forgiveness, peace with God and spiritual contentment. All this will continue until Christ returns.

The words "All nations will be blessed through him" re-emphasize the Messianic character of this psalm, since they echo the Messianic promise God gave to Abraham (Genesis 12:3). May we be among those who are blessed by him and who call him blessed.

Closing Doxology

> [18] **Praise be to the LORD God, the God of Israel,**
>   **who alone does marvelous deeds.**
> [19] **Praise be to his glorious name forever;**
>   **may the whole earth be filled with his glory.**
>
> **Amen and Amen.**

This doxology is fitting praise to the glorious king described in this psalm, but it is also the closing doxology to Book II of Psalms. It honors the Lord for all the marvelous deeds and wonderful blessings described throughout this book.

Conclusion of Book II

> [20] **This concludes the prayers of David son of Jesse.**

This sentence concludes Book II and perhaps also the larger collection made up of Books I and II of Psalms. Both of these books contain many psalms of David. Both emphasize the welfare of the Davidic dynasty, which culminates in Jesus the Messiah. After Psalm 1, which serves as an introduction to the whole psalter, Book I begins with Psalm 2, one of the most important Messianic psalms, which describes the victory and reign of the Messianic King, the Son of God.

Book II ends with Psalm 72, which describes the glorious reign of the Messianic King as the Son of David. These two psalms serve as parentheses, bracketing the collection gathered into these two books and emphasizing their most important theme, the kingdom of the Messiah. With the exception of Psalm 110, the most important Messianic psalms are contained in the first two books of psalms.

The first two books, which form part of the larger book of Psalms, teach many important spiritual lessons. But most important is the portrait of Christ we have found here. We have seen him both as our suffering Savior and as our glorious King. We have learned, "Blessed are all who take refuge in him." If through our study of these psalms the Holy Spirit has encouraged us to take refuge in our Savior-king in every adversity, our time has been well spent, and God's blessings will continue to abound in our lives.

Commentary on Psalms 73-150, which make up Books III, IV and V of Psalms, will be provided in the next volume of this work.